CATHOLICISM: END OR BEGINNING?

Publication in 1968 of *The Church and the Second Sex* turned Mary Daly into a leading – arguably the first – Catholic feminist theologian. She then, in 1972, preached an incendiary sermon at Harvard Memorial Church, "left behind centuries of darkness," as she put it, and walked out of patriarchal religion. Daly next established herself, with *Beyond God the Father* (1973), as a post-Christian feminist philosopher. In between these trailblazing writings, she began to draft another book entitled *Catholicism: End or Beginning?* In the moment that she abandoned the text, she also seemingly renounced the institutional Roman Catholic Church. This volume comprises that lost, unfinished manuscript – remarkably rediscovered – augmented by complementary chapters from six preeminent feminist writers. Though partial, it completes the corpus of an iconic figure in radical liberationist and Catholic thought, delving deep into the mind of a woman who dared to leap into uncharted territories of faith and philosophical imagination.

In its obituary, the *Guardian* newspaper called MARY DALY (1928–2010) "one of the key feminist writers of the twentieth century." Challenging patriarchy in religion, society, and culture, Daly was a coruscating critic of the ways in which patriarchal institutions operate and discriminate. *The Church and the Second Sex* (1968), her best-known book, was an attempt to work within a Christian framework. Later works, such as *Pure Lust* (1984) and *Outercourse* (1992), emerged from a post-Christian mind-set. Written after *The Church and the Second Sex* and before the influential *Beyond God the Father* (1973), *Catholicism: End or Beginning?* explores a renewed and revitalized ecclesiology that transcends the perceived dichotomy between "Catholic substance" and the "Protestant principle." For Daly, resolving this polarity – by reclaiming a new freedom of spirit and intellectual power – would allow theologians to answer the central question: "Has Catholicism reached its end, or is there hope for a genuine new beginning?"

MEG STAPLETON SMITH is an adjunct professor of theology and ethics at Fordham University and a theological ethicist, educator, and ordained priest in the Episcopal Church. She uncovered Mary Daly's unpublished work in the archives of Smith College where Daly's writings and papers are deposited. Its discovery will be exciting for anyone interested in Mary Daly's work and her extensive and continuing influence. The editor has commissioned additional chapters by prominent writers working at the interface of feminism, women's studies, theology, and philosophy. These show how Daly's text remains a potent contribution by one of the twentieth century's most important thinkers.

Mary Daly, 1975, Woodstock Women's Center, New York.
Photo by Diana Davies (Smith College Special Collections).

CATHOLICISM: END OR BEGINNING?

Mary Daly

Sometime of Boston College

Edited by

Meg Stapleton Smith

Fordham University, New York

CAMBRIDGE
UNIVERSITY PRESS

Shaftesbury Road, Cambridge CB2 8EA, United Kingdom

One Liberty Plaza, 20th Floor, New York, NY 10006, USA

477 Williamstown Road, Port Melbourne, VIC 3207, Australia

314–321, 3rd Floor, Plot 3, Splendor Forum, Jasola District Centre, New Delhi – 110025, India

103 Penang Road, #05–06/07, Visioncrest Commercial, Singapore 238467

Cambridge University Press is part of Cambridge University Press & Assessment, a department of the University of Cambridge.

We share the University's mission to contribute to society through the pursuit of education, learning and research at the highest international levels of excellence.

www.cambridge.org
Information on this title: www.cambridge.org/9781009180634

DOI: 10.1017/9781009180641

When citing this work, please include a reference to the DOI 10.1017/9781009180641

First published 2026

Printed in the United Kingdom by CPI Group Ltd, Croydon CR0 4YY 2026

Cover image: Mary Daly, Boston, June 1999. Photo by Dana Smith, all rights reserved.

A catalogue record for this publication is available from the British Library

A Cataloging-in-Publication data record for this book is available from the Library of Congress

ISBN 978-1-009-18063-4 Hardback

Cambridge University Press & Assessment has no responsibility for the persistence or accuracy of URLs for external or third-party internet websites referred to in this publication and does not guarantee that any content on such websites is, or will remain, accurate or appropriate.

For EU product safety concerns, contact us at Calle de José Abascal, 56, 1°, 28003 Madrid, Spain, or email eugpsr@cambridge.org *for Mary Daly, and for all whom her legacy continues to inspire*

This is a time for pragmatic reconstruction, for new discoveries as we move ahead in our task. It may be that we can no longer imagine ourselves to have the sweeping vision of the great theological system-atizes of the past, but we can have the seminal and creative vision of explorers who have a heritage that drives them forward. This book will examine the most radical elements of that heritage in the hope of contributing to that forward movement.

—Mary Daly, *Catholicism: End or Beginning?*

"Mary Daly's unfinished *Catholicism: End or Beginning?* represents a brilliant example of a brilliant woman thinking, and indeed writing, out loud, as her explorations – and especially her burgeoning sense of the fundamental misogyny running through the institutions of Protestantism and Catholicism – led her to make an inevitable and inexorable break with those traditions that had no respect for what Luce Irigaray would call a dialectic between the sexes. It is an extraordinarily valuable record of a pioneering woman's struggle toward intellectual, theological, and personal integrity."

—Mary Teresa Condren, Centre for Gender and Women's Studies, Trinity College, University of Dublin, author of *The Serpent and the Goddess: Women, Religion and Power in Celtic Ireland* (1989)

"What a remarkable find! So here we see Mary Daly's struggle with traditional male theology come to a head. Perhaps encountering Paul Tillich was the last straw. She walks away and chooses another path that takes her Beyond God the Father. And onward she clears the path for the rest of us, for which we are most grateful."

—Marie M. Fortune, founder of FaithTrust Institute and author of *Sexual Violence: The Sin Revisited* (2005)

"Mary Daly fans will be delighted to encounter this newly discovered manuscript, written by Daly in the formative period between *The Church and the Second Sex* and *Beyond God the Father*. Its surprising contents are well contextualized by six very helpful contributions by leading feminist thinkers. The book makes clear the ideas that Daly rejected but also those that continued to shape her even as she led her famous walkout from Memorial Church."

—Judith Plaskow, Professor Emerita of Religious Studies, Manhattan College, author (with Carol P. Christ) of *Goddess and God in the World: Conversations in Embodied Theology* (2016)

"This is an astonishing find: an early 'lost' text of Daly's that fills an intellectual gap in her oeuvre. Students of Daly will appreciate her teaching voice in this text and see not only a foreshadowing of her later work in the existentialist content of the extant chapters but also clarity of their importance and helpful contextualization by preeminent Daly scholars. This volume constitutes a vital contribution to scholarship on one of the least cited but most influential intellectual luminaries of the last century."

—Laurel C. Schneider, Research Professor, School of Theology, Boston University, and 2026 President of the American Academy of Religion; author of *Beyond Monotheism: A Theology of Multiplicity* (2007) and co-author of *Queer Soul and Queer Theology: Ethics and Redemption in Real Life* (2021)

CONTENTS

Contents

Contents

FIGURES

CONTRIBUTORS

Xochitl Alvizo is an associate professor of religious studies in the area of women and religion and the philosophy of sex, gender, and sexuality at California State University, Northridge. She completed her PhD in practical theology at Boston University. Her dissertation, which contributes toward a feminist ecclesiology, drew upon the work of Mary Daly. Her work brings a feminist and queer focus to theology and to the study of religion, congregational studies, ecclesiology, and the emerging church.

Lisa Sowle Cahill is the J. Donald Monan, SJ, Professor of Theology at Boston College. She is a past president of the Catholic Theological Society of America and the Society of Christian Ethics. The recipient of eleven honorary degrees, Dr. Cahill has written over eight books and published dozens of articles. In 2020, a volume entitled *Reimaging the Moral Life* was published honoring the legacy of her work and teaching.

Siobhán Garrigan is Loyola Professor of Theology at Trinity College, Dublin and is Head of the university's School of Religion, Theology, and Peace Studies. Her most recent books are *The Real Peace Process: Worship, Politics, and the End of Sectarianism*, and *A Theology of Home in a Time of Homelessness*.

Mary E. Hunt is a feminist theologian who is co-founder and co-director of the Women's Alliance for Theology, Ethics, and Ritual (WATER) in Silver Spring, Maryland. A Catholic active in the women–church movement, she lectures and writes on theology and ethics with particular attention to social justice concerns.

Zahra Moballegh served as an assistant professor of philosophy and a researcher in Islamic studies in Iran. She has published several articles in *Zanan-e Emrooz* [Women of Today], the leading magazine for women's voices in Iran. Her book, *Faith as Reason: An Epistemological Approach to Feminist Theology*, a pioneer Persian work in feminist philosophy, sheds light on epistemological aspects of Daly's theology. As a visiting researcher in the Women's Studies in Religion Program at Harvard Divinity School, she explores feminist narrative theology within the Islamic tradition.

Jennifer Rycenga is Professor Emerita of Comparative Religious Studies at San José State University. Her areas of interest include American religious history, religion and music, feminist analyses of religion, lesbian history, religion and politics, and feminist analyses of music. Her co-edited volume, with Linda Barufaldi, *The Mary Daly Reader* (New York University Press, 2016), was first conceived in conversation with Daly. Her most recent book is *Schooling the Nation: The Success of the Canterbury Academy for Black Women* (University of Illinois Press, 2024).

Meg Stapleton Smith is an ordained priest in the Episcopal Church and an adjunct professor of theology and ethics at Fordham University. As a theological ethicist, her work focuses on virtue ethics and the ethical implications of queer theologies. Her doctoral dissertation, entitled, "Queer Virtue Ethics: Mary Daly's Challenge to Catholic Sexual Ethics," focuses on Mary Daly's understanding of courage as central for a reconstructed sexual ethic. In addition to her academic writing, teaching, and lecturing, Meg is a parish priest in the Episcopal Diocese of New York.

EDITOR'S ACKNOWLEDGMENTS

Thanks go, first, to all the contributors to this project. This volume was put together over the course of several years, all of which were marked by the ongoing Covid pandemic. Seeing this project to completion took a great deal of compassion and commitment. Thank you for Sparking and Spinning this book into *be-ing* with me.

I am particularly grateful for the insights and guidance of Mary E. Hunt – the first person I wrote to when I unearthed this unfinished manuscript. I have learned so much from you about what it means to be a scholar of Daly's work and legacy – a responsibility I take seriously.

I owe a great deal to my colleagues at Fordham University for the many conversations that offered wisdom and direction in the development of this volume. Thank you to Bryan Massingale, Christine Firer-Hinze, and Cristina Traina for challenging me to ask the deeper questions of Daly's vision, and to Brenna Moore, for igniting my interest in archival research. Thank you, most especially, to Christiana Zenner, whose mentorship and friendship have encouraged me every step along the way. I am also grateful to Women Shaping Theology – an online writing group of women theologians – who offered feedback on initial drafts of the introduction. I am indebted to the generosity and collegiality present in our Zoom room.

Thank you to the staff of the Sophia Smith Collection at Smith College for your enthusiasm over this project, and dedication to preserving Daly's work.

Thank you also to my editor Alex Wright, to Katie Idle for editorial support, to Nicola Chapman for her oversight of copyediting and production, and to all those other individuals at Cambridge University Press involved in getting the book into finished form. I am endlessly grateful for your commitment to and care for this volume.

My greatest thanks go to my family and especially my wife, Marcella. Your love sustained me in this project. None of this would have been possible without you. Thank you.

In Mary Daly's work, she makes many references to the ways that the women of today are the embodiment and realization of the dreams and hopes of women from the past. I never met Mary Daly, as many contributors to this volume have, but I am convinced that my vocational life would not be possible had it not been for her courage. I am a queer, married, Episcopal priest and theological ethicist, who is trained in Roman Catholic theology (and shaped by Thomas Aquinas's theology, as Daly was). Even though Mary Daly would have had many questions for me, as I would for her, the fact that I exist in all of the spaces is a testament to the path that she, and so many other feminist theologians and philosophers, paved. May we all continue to raise up new images of *be-ing*, as Mary Daly did for us. This volume is, of course, dedicated to her.

INTRODUCTION

~

Meg Stapleton Smith

During my last semester of doctoral coursework, I began
re-reading – or perhaps truly reading for the first time –
the work of Mary Daly. Like many who have pursued
graduate degrees in theology, and especially folks like me
who have attended Catholic universities in the United
States, I had read *The Church and the Second Sex* (1968)
and *Beyond God the Father* (1973). I had been handed the
conventional narrative of Mary Daly: although she
charted the way for feminist theology, her career ended
when she left the Roman Catholic Church. Though professors would mention that after 1973 Daly authored six
other books and dozens of published articles, I had been
taught that they were irrelevant.

Even though my exposure to the life and thought of
Mary Daly had been limited, my third time reading *The
Church and the Second Sex* during that last semester
brought forth new questions. I was struck by the difference between the Mary Daly who wrote the book in 1968,
and the Mary Daly who, in 1975 and 1985, wrote reintroductions to the text that ruthlessly scrutinized her own
previous writings. The dissonance sparked a curiosity
about the "later Daly" of whom I knew so little. And so,
I finally picked up *Gyn/Ecology*, *Pure Lust*, *Wickedary*,
Quintessence, and *Amazon Grace*. Through these readings,

I was brought to the following conclusion: of all the theologians and philosophers I have read, Mary Daly's intellectual journey is the most audacious. Mary Daly often wrote that she wanted to "throw her life as far as it would go."[1] And she did just that. The "early Daly" wanted to put new wine into old wineskins (Mark 2:22). The "later Daly" went in search of entirely different casings. The "early Daly" wanted her work to be intelligible to the academic standards of her day. The "later Daly" wanted her work to spark a deeper spiritual and moral revolution even though she didn't know where the embers would fall.

These differences between the "early Daly" and the "later Daly" encouraged me to delve deeper into her scholarship and philosophical vision. I was enthralled by her brilliance and her iconoclastic radicalism, drawn to the woman who dared to say what so many others of her time could not. To be sure, Daly was – and continues to be – a polemical figure. Still, I was captivated by her analysis of the intersecting forces of religion and sexism; her articulation and embodied demonstration of courage; her lasting indebtedness to Thomas Aquinas and the philosophical underpinnings of Catholic moral thought; her apt critique of ecological degradation, patriarchy, and capitalism; and her relentless hope to dream that a different world was possible. Above all, I was intrigued by the *person* of Mary Daly. I wondered about the woman who was trained as a Roman Catholic theologian and sought reform within the Church – and whether she abandoned

---

[1] Mary Daly, *Outercourse: The Be-Dazzling Voyage* (San Francisco: HarperSanFrancisco, 1992), 344.

this vision of transformation as vehemently as contemporary Catholic academics believe she had. My own interest in Daly was held in stark contrast to how easily dismissed she is in Catholic theology, as well as in feminist and queer philosophical spaces today.[2] I became convinced that there was a part of Mary Daly's story that was not being told.

With these questions in mind, I traveled to Smith College in Northampton, Massachusetts, to conduct research in Daly's archives. I went in search of an untold story, to try uncovering parts of Daly's story that might be worth returning to – facets of her life that could shine a new light on her writings. I began looking through boxes of materials from 1968–1973 – the time in between the writing of *The Church and the Second Sex* and *Beyond God the Father*. I figured that if there were to be any answers to my questions about Daly's relationship with Catholicism, they would be found around the time when Daly left the Catholic Church.

In my search, I came across a folder entitled, "Catholicism: End or Beginning?" Contained within the archival storage box were four chapters of an unfinished book that she wrote in between *The Church and the Second Sex* and *Beyond God the Father*. The four chapters, originally produced on a typewriter, had been edited by hand and marked up with several notes scribbled in the margins. Daly only drafted about half of the chapters she planned and outlined. Although Daly began writing

---

[2] Jessica Coblentz and Brianne Jacobs, "Mary Daly's *The Church and the Second Sex* after Fifty Years of US Catholic Feminist Theology," *Theological Studies* 79(3) (2018): 543–565.

the book, and had edited the first few chapters, she never finished it. It seems that the moment Daly abandoned the manuscript was the moment she left the Catholic Church and all institutional religion.

As I paged through the files, I recalled that Daly briefly mentions the book in her autobiography, *Outercourse*. She writes:

> During 1969–1970 I also worked hard on the manuscript of a book which had several titles. Among these was *Catholicism: Death or Rebirth?* Another was *Catholicism: End or Beginning?* One might say this was the beginning of the end of my concern over the fate of catholicism. Probably the question mark at the end of each title was the most significant part. At any rate, this project failed to sustain my interest. It fell apart in the middle. Or, one could say that it was an abortive effort. The publisher with whom I had signed a contract for this book (Lippincott) agreed with my sentiments.[3]

Given that Daly's metaphor for the end of this manuscript was that it was "aborted," I assumed she had destroyed the text. But there I was, holding the preserved manuscript in my hands. I came to the archives in search of answers to my questions about Mary Daly's relationship with faith and religion, and in search of an untold story that might continue to reignite an interest in her work. At that moment, I sensed that this manuscript had the potential to unlock new dimensions of Daly Studies. Far from being a mere footnote of feminist history, and a relic of Catholic theology in the academy today, Mary Daly must rightly

---

[3] Daly, *Outercourse*, 102.

take her place as one of the most important philosophical and theological minds of the late twentieth century.

The Formation of this Volume

After unearthing the manuscript, I began to wonder if anyone else knew of its existence. I could find no mention of it in any theology or philosophy text, and no journal article dedicated to its content. As noted above, the only footnote in which the manuscript is referenced is in Daly's own autobiography. I reached out to Mary E. Hunt and Jennifer Rycenga – two of Daly's friends who have been the most preeminent scholars of her work. Though they recalled Daly mentioning the manuscript, neither of them knew it had been preserved in her archives. Together, we decided that the manuscript ought to be published, though this decision was not made lightly. Daly is clear in her autobiography that even though she "suffered" from Lippincott's rejection of the book, it ended up being a "blessing in disguise." "It would have been embarrassing if the thing had been printed, especially since within a year or two of its demise I was thoroughly in disagreement with their frame of reference. I think I simply saw that I had been framed by that frame and wanted to break out of it."[4]

The reasons for posthumously publishing the unfinished manuscript before you are three-fold. First, even though Daly ended up disagreeing with what she wrote in the manuscript, she valued rereading and critiquing her previous writings. This is not only evident in the

---

[4] Ibid.

reintroductions to *The Church and the Second Sex*, but also in her continual references to her early career texts. In every book she wrote after *The Church and the Second Sex*, Daly engages her previous work and builds off it. Daly wanted people to read her books – even if she had moved beyond their frame of reference. At the very least, her early work demonstrated how many "spiraling galaxies" she had traveled since the original publication. As such, Daly offers a lesson about academic writing – namely that there is still value in the messy and chaotic, and in letting the process be known even (and especially) when it doesn't sustain our own energy.

The second reason for deciding to posthumously publish this manuscript is that it completes the corpus of one of the most important philosophical and theological thinkers of our day. For some, the manuscript might appear to be more of a theological artifact than a ground-breaking publication filled with new insights. Yet, the manuscript is a window into the "early Daly" that creates a new, deeper understanding of the "later Daly." In completing her corpus, this manuscript offers us a piece to the fullness of Daly's life and intellectual musings. In light of this, the third reason for deciding to publish the manuscript is in the hope that it will enrich the study of Daly's work. Daly wanted her work to spark "creative action in and toward transcendence," and to encourage the journey toward "Intellectual/E-motional/ Spiritual Integrity."[5] My hope is that this volume will

---

[5] Mary Daly, *Beyond God the Father: Toward a Philosophy of Women's Liberation* (Boston: Beacon Press, 1985), 6; Daly, *Outercourse*, 117.

serve as an invitation to engage Daly's work in new ways – ways that are life-giving and life-altering.

The first part of the volume is the unfinished and never-before-published manuscript, *Catholicism: End or Beginning?* The manuscript is followed by the reflections of six prominent feminist scholars – Mary E. Hunt (United States), Lisa Sowle Cahill (United States), Siobhán Garrigan (Republic of Ireland), Jennifer Rycenga (United States), Zahra Moballegh (Iran), and Xochitl Alvizo (United States) – who offer reflections on the content of the manuscript. Hunt, Cahill, Rycenga, and Alvizo all knew Daly personally. Although all of the contributors have a deep affection for Daly's work, they are not uncritical of her writing – a truth that is evident in the pages of this volume.

Mary E. Hunt's essay is the first in the volume because it situates the manuscript, and our collective work in the volume, within the broader landscape of Daly's work. In so doing, Hunt offers us a methodology for Daly Studies. Lisa Cahill locates the manuscript historically within the hopeful, reforming spirit of the Second Vatican Council, and argues that the manuscript is best understood as a remnant of that early theological feminism. Siobhán Garrigan engages the manuscript in its incompleteness – and analyzes its content through Daly's commitment to the life of the mind. Such a commitment demands constant self-reflection, Garrigan contends, but it is rare to encounter a work that so acutely embodies the tensions between who the writer is, and who they are becoming, as well as the tension between the scholarship they have been committed to, and the scholarship they dream of but have yet to fully realize.

Following Garrigan, Jennifer Rycenga sees *Catholicism: End or Beginning?* as representative of Daly's broader quest for intellectual autonomy – an autonomy, which, in the writing of the manuscript, Daly was aspiring for but had not yet attained. Still, according to Rycenga, *Catholicism: End or Beginning?* sets the stage for Daly's philosophical rigor and mystical intuitionism and ultimately offers a roadmap of key ideas found in Daly's later work.

Through a close read of the text, Zahra Moballegh explores the ways in which *Catholicism: End or Beginning?* creates a "theology of difference." Moballegh argues that Daly abandoned Catholicism, and all organized religions, because they restrict the infinite process of dialectical faith. The implicit announcement of the end of Catholicism within the pages of *Catholicism: End or Beginning?* (*CEB?*), Moballegh continues, paves the way for a "theology of difference" that establishes a humanist theology, a non-Christian vision of faith, and a process-oriented theological anthropology.

Xochitl Alvizo concludes the manuscript on a hopeful note. Daly's assessment of the crisis of faith, Alvizo writes, is sorely needed in the church today not only because Christianity continues to inhibit people's sense of *be-ing/becoming* toward the Divine, but also because such weaponization of faith continues to cause spiritual crisis.[6]

---

[6] Within this volume, the authors seek to use the terms "be-ing" and "Be-ing" as Mary Daly did later in her career. When Daly used the hyphenated present participle Be-ing, and the first letter was capitalized, she was referring "to what some might call God" (as she frequently said) (*Beyond God the Father*, 6, 38). When she used the same word, and the first letter was *not* capitalized, she was referring to our inner dynamism by which we participate in Ultimate Be-ing. Daly defines "be-ing" as

In turn, Alvizo constructs a "Dalyan ecclesiology," which offers a balm for the wounds inflicted by the current polarization and abuses in the church and reimagines the nature and practice of church as dependent on the inner, mystic life that Daly calls us to.

The Influence of Autobiography

Although each of the authors takes a distinct approach in their reflection on the manuscript, I see three common threads. First, each author weaves personal tales into their analysis of the manuscript. For some, this is merely anecdotal – like Siobhán Garrigan sharing that every class she has ever taught has, in one way or another, been "rocked" by Mary Daly. For others, these stories are more personally significant. Zahra Moballegh speaks of encountering *Beyond God the Father* for the first time – when no one knew of Mary Daly in Iran and there were no academic texts in feminist theology or philosophy of religion in Persian. *Beyond God the Father* has since been translated into Farsi and became a best seller the year it was published. For Mary E. Hunt, there is no separation between Mary Daly, the intellectual, and the Mary Daly who taught her daughter to howl.

"actual participation in the Ultimate/Intimate Reality – Be-ing, the Verb." She defined "Be-ing" as "1: Ultimate/Intimate Reality, the Constantly Unfolding Verb of Verbs which is intransitive, having no object that limits its dynamism 2: the Final Cause, the Good who is Self-communicating, who is the Verb from whom, in whom, and with whom all true movements move." Mary Daly, *Websters' First New Intergalactic Wickedary of the English Language* (Boston: Beacon Press, 1987), 64; see also Mary Daly, *Amazon Grace: Re-Calling the Courage to Sin Big* (New York: Palgrave Macmillan, 2006), 20; *Beyond God the Father*, xxix.

The authors of the volume not only incorporate their experiences and encounters with Daly but also reflect on how Daly's own life story shaped her writing. This comes to the forefront in *the* central theme of the manuscript – namely, Daly's relationship with institutional Christianity and, in particular, the Roman Catholic Church.

Daly and the Roman Catholic Church

Daly's relationship with religion is typically depicted in the dissonance between *The Church and the Second Sex* (where she establishes herself as a progressive Catholic feminist theologian, reforming the ways of sexism in the Church) and *Beyond God the Father* (where she emerges as a post-Christian feminist philosopher). In looking for a reason for this shift, most people point to Daly's sermon at Harvard Memorial Church in 1971 where she launched a scathing critique at Christianity for its complicity in the subordination of women. At the end of her sermon, aptly titled "The Death of God the Father," Daly implored the congregation – women in particular – to acknowledge that they "cannot really belong to institutional religion" for "[t]he crushing weight of this tradition, of this power structure, tells us that we do not even exist." With that, she urged her "sisters and other esteemed members of the congregation" to "leave behind centuries of silence and darkness," join her in a mass "exodus from centuries of darkness" and remove themselves from all patriarchal religion.[7]

---

[7] Mary Daly, "The Women's Movement: An Exodus Community," in *Women and Religion: A Feminist Sourcebook of Christian Thought*, ed. Elizabeth Clark and Herbert Richardson (New York: Harper & Row, 1977), 265–271.

Although Daly's sermon marked a public shift in her relationship with institutional Christianity, the personal undercurrents that led to that moment have been under-analyzed and have remained largely opaque. In her later writings, Daly casually remarks that leaving the Roman Catholic Church was simply the next logical step in her intellectual and personal journey.[8] Yet, in her autobiography, Daly writes that the years leading up the infamous "walkout of patriarchal religion" were filled with "drastic changes," and were a "trying time of transition."[9] Despite these admissions, Daly never reflected at length about her process of leaving the Roman Catholic Church – a decision which was likely painful for this person who had long hoped to bring about changes in the Church.

The ambiguity allows for each of our authors to offer their own perspective on what led Daly to abandon the manuscript, and to speculate why she formally left institutional religion. Lisa Cahill contends, for example, that the hope Daly had in reformist Catholicism had been lost. Cahill maintains that Daly left the Church in search of a deeper relationship with the Good, and in search of feminist community that was nowhere to be found within the Catholic Church at the time. Daly's call to revolution, she concludes, "met the fate of a biblical prophet: it fell largely on deaf ears."

For other authors in the volume – including Hunt, Garrigan, and Rycenga – the death of Daly's mother, her own sexual awakening, and the socio-historical

---

[8] Mary Daly, *Quintessence … Realizing the Archaic Future: A Radical Elemental Feminist Manifesto* (Boston: Beacon Press, 1998), 15.
[9] Daly, *Outercourse*, 101.

context of the Vietnam War, Civil Rights, and feminist movements all contributed to her moving on from the manuscript and the Catholic Church. These events, Jennifer Rycenga argues, were the actual mystical experiences she had been searching for in the pages of theologians and philosophers, but now were "urgent, alive, and achingly real." It's unsurprising, Garrigan observes, that the manuscript ends when Daly gets to the question of Christ – for it would have demanded Daly to engage with the practical, and required the book to become "fleshing, feeling, and individual" rather than "heady, abstract, and corporate." As Zahra Moballegh writes, in this manuscript we see Daly writing with trembling voice, in both fear and doubt, working to arouse courage within herself. Such courage, Alvizo concludes in the final chapter of the volume, ought to be the foundation of a renewed understanding of church for today.

As the working titles of the unfinished manuscript suggest, the central question Daly was facing both intellectually and spiritually during the writing of this book was whether Catholicism could generate new life and hope, or if it was destined to a dead end. Yet, the question of whether Catholicism will "end" or "begin" was deeply nuanced for Daly, as was her own relationship with this fate. In the unfinished manuscript, Daly writes that one must recognize the "complexity" of what it means to leave the Catholic Church. In fact, for one to claim that individuals are either "inside" or "outside" the church is a false dichotomy. Moving "outside" the church does not necessarily mean abandoning the church or "leaving it in every sense," she writes. One could describe themselves as an alumnus or alumna of the church, an expression which conveys the fact that a person is not severing all relationship to the church, but rather "establishing a free and adult relationship to it." To pursue the analogy, she continues, "alumni are in fact what an institution of learning is intended to produce, rather than perpetual undergraduates." The point of the church is "not to foster religious infantilism but spiritual adulthood." Daly maintains that there are some religious and non-religious thinkers who cannot "sustain" the idea of an individual having "an outside–inside relationship to institutional Catholicism." There are scholars who think that people living on the boundary of institutional Catholicism are "doomed to a kind of isolation and ineffectiveness." And yet, she concludes, "those who have been conditioned within the Catholic milieu" can bring a critical distance into "the tradition which is heritage, they may re-enliven this tradition both in their minds and hearts and in its outward manifestations" (1.8).

The manuscript helps us to see that the over-arching narrative on Daly that I was given during my theological training was false. Daly's career didn't end after her sermon at Harvard Memorial Church. That was only the beginning. Even the idea that she abandoned institutional religion is more complicated than many have previously thought. As Hunt writes in her essay, "In or out of the Church, whatever that means, is trivial. She did not go anyplace. She went everywhere." Importantly, even after she walked out of patriarchal religion, Daly continued to develop the tradition in which she was formed. She continued to participate in the process of changing the Christian theological tradition, radically transforming the institution from outside its walls.

A Mystic Ahead of Her Time, Yet Bound By It

Nearly every author in the volume suggests that Mary Daly was a mystic, and that the mystical intuitions in her writing often get overlooked. Throughout her career, Daly called for a fuller, mystical way of being beyond the confines of institutional religion. Though this idea is most evident in her later writings, the foundations for her mysticism are constructed within the pages of *Catholicism: End or Beginning?* Daly's own transcendent experiences and mystical intuitionism form a cornerstone of our contributors' reflections.

For our authors, Daly was a mystic ahead of her time, and yet also bound and conditioned by it. Within recent decades, accusations of transphobia and racism have come to the forefront in conversations on Daly's work. These charges have ignited suspicions of Daly's broader project, and these trepidations have caused many scholars to dismiss her work entirely.

Debates on Mary Daly's own racial bias surfaced after Audre Lorde wrote an "open letter" to Daly interrogating the racism present in *Gyn/Ecology*. Lorde critiqued Daly for presenting Black women only as "victims and preyers-upon each other," while white women are used as exemplars of power.[10] Much of the conversations that ensued in the years after Lorde's 1979 letter centered on Daly's silence and her apparent reluctance to engage in the charges of racism that Lorde launched against her work.[11]

[10] Audre Lorde, "An Open Letter to Mary Daly," in *Sister Outsider* (Trumansburg, NY: Crossing Press, 1984), 68.

[11] For some examples of authors who have addressed this conflict between Lorde and Daly, see Elizabeth Hedrick, "The Early Career of Mary

The content of these debates changed, however, when Lorde's biographer discovered Daly's response among Lorde's papers nearly a decade after her death.[12] This was a surprising revelation given that Lorde published her own letter stating that Daly never responded to the criticism.[13] Daly included her response to Lorde in her 2006 book, *Amazon Grace*, two years after Lorde's biographer found it. In her response, Daly admitted that Lorde "had a point." She writes, "You have helped me to be aware of different dimensions of my existence, and I thank you for this. Clearly there is no simple response possible to the matters you raised in your letter. I wrote *Gyn/Ecology* out of the insights and materials most accessible to me at the time."[14] Still, there is no substantive evidence that Daly thoroughly addressed in her subsequent projects the shortcomings that Lorde had identified.

The crux of Lorde's criticism is an important one – namely, that Daly's writing implies that "all women suffer the same oppression simply because [they] are women," which, Lorde writes, is a stance which "lose[s] sight of the many varied tools of the patriarchy."[15] Daly was unwilling, or perhaps unable, to compromise her belief that

Daly: A Retrospective," *Feminist Studies* 39(2) (2013): 457–483; Amber L. Katherine, "'A Too Early Morning': Audre Lorde's 'An Open Letter to Mary Daly' and Daly's Decision Not to Respond in Kind," in *Feminist Interpretations of Mary Daly*, ed. Sarah Hoagland (University Park: Pennsylvania State University Press, 2000); Traci C. West, "The Gift of Arguing with Mary Daly's White Feminism," *Journal of Feminist Studies in Religion* 28(2) (2012): 112–117.

[12] Alexis De Veaux, *Warrior Poet: A Biography of Audre Lorde* (New York: W. W. Norton, 2004), 252.

[13] Lorde, "'Open Letter,'" 66.   [14] Daly, *Amazon Grace*, 25.

[15] Lorde, "'Open Letter,'" 66.

"violence against women is the source and paradigm of all other manifestations of violence."[16] Throughout her intellectual journey, Daly maintained that racism, classism, ageism, and speciesism are all characteristics and symptoms of patriarchy. Yet, Daly also challenged racial stereotypes, admitted that privileged women can be "blind to the problems of their less privileged sisters," challenged women to speak out against racism, and articulated the interconnections among the structures of oppression in a patriarchal society.

As the title of Mary E. Hunt's essay implies, Mary Daly was often of many minds on issues. Throughout her writings, one can see Daly working out key ideas. In light of this, Daly's books are best understood when they are seen as a part of her broader intellectual and spiritual journey. This manuscript is but one instance of that reality. Even though Daly began to engage questions about racism in a deeper way towards the end of her career, one cannot help but wonder why there is no mention of racial injustice in this manuscript – especially because it was likely written the same year that Martin Luther King Jr. was assassinated. Perhaps this very omission is a sign of the bias she was unwilling to confront. Still, Daly's white feminism, as Traci West says, is indeed worth wrestling with.[17]

Similar paradoxes can be seen in Daly's ideas about sex and gender. To be sure, parts of Daly's writing are

---

[16] Mary Daly, *The Church and the Second Sex* (Boston: Beacon Press, 1985), 166–167; Daly, *Beyond God the Father*, xv, 174.

[17] Traci C. West, "The Gift of Arguing with Mary Daly's White Feminism," *Journal of Feminist Studies in Religion* 28(2) (2012): 112–117.

essentialist, and her approach to trans persons and realities are reductionistic. Yet, Daly was also deeply committed to deconstructing sex-role stereotypes, and to dismantling the theological and philosophical systems which define humanity by immutable essences. Daly rejected the fluidity of gender even as she seeks to deconstruct it in her own work.[18]

Even with a posture of intellectual charity, the authors of this volume wish neither to excuse nor make intelligible the shortcomings present in Daly's work – but to present the fullness of her vision as seen through this unfinished manuscript. One of the most inspiring facets of Daly's intellectual journey was her ability to critique her own work. In *Beyond God the Father*, Daly (drawing on Abraham Maslow) spoke of the need to "overcome the divided self [as well as] divisions from each other" so that we can become "developing, authentic" and "self-actualized" persons.[19] Daly was on this ever-unfolding journey herself, driven by an intense longing to continually "turn [her] soul around."[20] Throughout her life, Daly had a profound commitment to intellectual authenticity and wanted her work to reflect her radical personal and intellectual growth. Because of this, the authors of this volume maintain that taking Daly Studies seriously often means taking Daly to her most logical conclusion – even, and especially, when Daly did not come to those conclusions during her lifetime.

---

[18] I will explore this further in a forthcoming work.

[19] Daly, *Beyond God the Father*, 146.

[20] See Mary Daly, *Gyn/Ecology: The Metaethics of Radical Feminism* (Boston: Beacon Press, 1990), xxi.

Conclusion

Daly's own methodology was committed to the idea that in order to pave the way for the future, we must first understand the past. This insight is not particularly novel, but for Daly it was an important one. Her most central convictions stemmed from traditional theological sources – even as she sought to unshackle them from patriarchal misinterpretations. As I, and others in this volume have argued, the foundations of her own iconoclastic radicalism were grounded in her theological training in Thomas Aquinas (among other foundational figures in Christian theology). As she writes in her autobiography, "I needed to learn the rules extremely well in order to break them with precision."[21]

This manuscript situates us in 1969–1970, when Daly wrote, and subsequently abandoned, the manuscript. We travel back in time in order to understand the significance of Daly Studies for the future. The manuscript you have before you is complex: it is outdated, yet visionary; it is embedded in patriarchal assumptions, yet trying to dismantle them; parts are vague and abstract, while other sections are spiritually rich and profound. Daly's inconsistency is a mirror into the spiritual and personal struggles she was wrestling with during this time of transition. The manuscript is, as the title suggests, unfinished. Still, *Catholicism: End or Beginning?* helps us to discover Daly in refreshingly new ways – to see her struggles with faith and the church as apt for our time; to see her mystical intuitionism as hauntingly prescient; to see her

---

[21] Daly, *Outercourse*, 75.

righteous anger as calling for a bold, spiritual revolution; and to see her prophetic voice as offering a vision of hope for those still willing to work within, or on the boundary of, the religious institutions that have been forever changed by Daly's legacy.

Editor's Note

The text of *Catholicism: End or Beginning?* directly reflects the typed manuscript as it was composed. Mary Daly made some edits, and one can see on the original pages of the manuscript portions erased and whited out, as well as corrections marked with a pen. The text reflects those edits, with all the remaining errors and grammatical irregularities left as is. Importantly, the capitalization of church vs. Church remains inconsistent as it was in the manuscript itself. Such inconsistencies represent the broader questions of this volume. In the rest of the volume, Church is capitalized when referring to the institutional Roman Catholic Church and left uncapitalized when referring to broader Christian experiences of worship, spirituality, and ecclesiology.

Part I

Catholicism: End or Beginning?

~

Mary Daly

Introduction

This book will analyze the problem of the crisis in contemporary Catholic consciousness, which is often called a crisis of faith. In a sense, it would be more accurate to say that I will analyze the problem as it presents itself in contemporary Christian consciousness since this should not, and in fact cannot, be understood in a parochial and limited context. However, the main focal point of interest will be the Catholic consciousness. One reason for the choice of focus is that at this point in history, it appears to many that the attempt of Protestantism to become relevant to the modern world has failed. Indeed, one sociologist of religion has affirmed that Catholicism now stands as surrogate for Christianity as a whole, and that the future of Christianity depends upon the success of Catholicism's efforts to confront modernity. He sees a terrible dilemma in the Catholic situation, for in the unavoidable effort to catch up with contemporary consciousness, the church may destroy its symbols' power to sustain religious awareness. Moreover, "Is it not precisely those established expressions of Catholic faith, unchanged and defensively clung to, which rendered Catholicism increasingly irrelevant to the advancing Western world that preserved within its own ranks the interior intensity and authenticity of faith?"[1]

This dilemma is sometimes expressed with more poignancy by conservatives than by enthusiastic young revolutionaries, since the former feel keenly the sense of loss that accompanies the breakdown of traditional structures. One archconservative Catholic philosopher expressed this sense of loss and in moving terms, "It is the dying who suffer the cruelty of the new church. Their faith is stolen from them and this robbery of the only gift that ultimately means anything to man is something we shall never forgive the heresiarchs in our midst."[2] More objective thinkers would be less inclined to blame these "heresiarchs" for what appears to be an inevitable stage in the evolution of human consciousness beyond the literalism of the past – an evolution which has been occasioned by the convergence of profound cultural changes and social upheaval. Nevertheless, radicals often tend to be insensitive to the problems inherent in transition and to the extent that this is the case, their thinking lacks depth and complexity. For this reason, we probably should be grateful that there are some articulate traditionalists around who raise serious questions, even if their manner of articulating the questions is inadequate. They demonstrate, perhaps without realizing it, the need for serious

---

[1] Thomas O'Dea, *The Catholic Crisis* (Boston: Beacon Press, 1968), 155.
[2] Frederick Wilhelmsen, "Schism, Heresy, and a New Guard," in *American Catholic Exodus*, ed. John O'Connor (Washington, DC: Corpus Books, 1968), 181–182.

and sophisticated theological handling of the questions they raise.

The current situation of polarization can be viewed in different ways. It is enlightening to view it within the perspective of an ongoing dialectic between two complementary aspects of integral Christian faith, namely the Protestant principle and the Catholic substance.[3] These are two polarities within the faith. By the expression "Protestant principle," I do not mean Protestantism as an ideology, nor do I mean the Protestant churches. Rather, I use it to refer to an attitude which is self-critical, and which recognizes the relativity of all objectifications of faith. That is, it is an attitude which recognizes that all symbols, such as sacraments and creeds, and all structures, whether institutional, liturgical, or theological, are finite and not ultimate. I use the expression "Catholic substance" to mean the incarnation and the concretization of spiritual presence, that is, the whole body of objectifications, including symbols and structures.

These complementary aspects of faith are essential for all Christians, whether they identify institutionally as Protestants or Catholics. The question arises, then, of how they are related to the Protestant and Catholic churches. In recent centuries, these churches have functioned as separate and even hostile embodiments of the aforementioned principles – although the situation has never been simple and unambiguous. The characteristic perversions of the Catholic substance, such as idolatrous sacramentalism, "magic," and over-institutionalization,

---

[3] This terminology will be familiar to readers who are acquainted with the theology of Paul Tillich.

have been most visible in the Catholic Church. In Protestantism, on the other hand, we have witnessed the powerlessness of the Protestant principle when it is cut off from the substance that gives it life. This "amputation" has resulted in that emptiness, banality, fading of the symbols, and fatal acculturation which brought on the phenomenon of the "death of God." There have been ambiguous situations of course. For example, there has been over-institutionalization within Protestant churches as well as within the Catholic Church. However, these do not alter the general picture.

The distortions of faith from which we are suffering are in part the result of the separation of complementary elements of Christian faith which are meaningless without each other because they are essentially relational. Without the Catholic substance, the Protestant principle serves merely to relativize all knowledge and behavior; while without Protestant principle, the Catholic substance becomes a block to intellectuality and freedom of the spirit. The situation is more complex than this, however. For Protestantism, as soon as it became institutionalized, that is, even from the origins of the Reformation, it began to fail as an expression of a Protestant principle and became idolatrous not only in relation to the Bible, but also in relation to its own structures. The same problem of tyranny over the spirit, of over-institutionalization, can be seen in Geneva as well as in Rome.

Thus, the institutional division between the Catholic and Protestant churches has hardly worked out to anyone's satisfaction. It appears that many are looking for some form of reintegration of the dissociated principles. Thus, a leading Protestant, writing from the "the Protestant side," has supported Martin Marty's contention that Protestantism has arrived at a stasis, a frozen equilibrium. Wagoner sketches the signs of the stasis as filtered through the seminary milieu: theological exhaustion, ecumenical doldrums, parish bafflement, and devotional emptiness.[4] On the other side of the fence, a well-known Catholic author, witness to the inherent corruption of ecclesiastical power, has shuddered in print at the prospect of premature ecumenical reunions, given the state of present Catholic structures, notably the episcopacy.[5] In effect, then, concerned Protestants and Catholics alike are expressing malaise about their own situation. I've chosen the term "concerned" deliberately, for the writers referred to seem to represent that remnant of "born Christians" who have sustained a sense of belonging to the church and for whom the church is still of major importance. They still can hope, but the hope seems to be sustained more and more by looking at the other side. I do not wish to belabor this point, only to suggest that it indicates a general sense of incompleteness in the existing forms of Christianity.

Most of us are haunted by this sense of incompleteness. Yet, although there are signs of deterioration, there appear also to be indications of a reintegration of the Protestant principle within the Catholic consciousness. The spirit of iconoclasm has invaded this consciousness, which is becoming aware of its own idolatrous tendencies. This phenomenon is interpreted by some in terms of a

---

[4] Walter Wagoner, "Thoughts for Protestants to be Static By," *Christian Century* (February 19, 1969): 249–251.
[5] Doris Grumbach, "Never the Twain Shall Meet," *Commonweal* (February 1969): 616–618.

generation gap, but such an interpretation hardly seems adequate. The fact is that there's a tension within faith which is perpetual: between the Protestant principle and the Catholic substance, between eschatology and Incarnation, between transcendence and immanence. At this point in history, we are particularly aware of this tension. We are in a real sense living it out.

It would be a mistake to seek a premature or oversimplified form of integration. It would also be an error to seek some permanent integration. Indeed, when the tension or dialectic is not kept alive there are discernible tendencies in opposite directions – for example, toward demonic sacramentalism (perhaps realized in recent years in the traditionalist movement) and toward the other extreme of empty secularism. I[t i]s important to recognize however, that in order to foster the dialectic within faith must be authentic. There would be no point, for example, in attempting to preserve elements of the Catholic substance as mummified bodies. If some symbols no longer speak to our age, then they should be allowed to die.

The only hope for authentic integration would seem to lie in radical openness to transcendence. If the evolutionary process moves as Teilhard de Cardin would say, in the direction of ever greater self-awareness, then the assimilation of the reflective and self-critical Protestant principle into the Catholic consciousness can be seen as a stage of self-understanding as a kind of encounter with our past which is new in quality. That is, it can be seen as a way of moving forward.

This book will be an analysis of theological problems as they are confronting the Catholic consciousness and its current state of dramatic tension and transition. Its primary task will not be to describe symptoms of the current dilemma of Christianity. There have been numerous books in recent years which describe the critical state of the church, and which discuss the differences between the "new left" and radicals of an earlier generation.[6] Certainly, it is fascinating and worthwhile to watch the emergence of alternating signs of hope and signs of regression in the church. However, the basic theological task is deeper than the business of observation.

This book will deal in-depth with several theological problems. For the conceptual tools used in analyzing these problems, I am to some extent indebted to Tillich's theological synthesis and to the proponents of the theology of hope. There's something paradoxical in this since there are strong divergences between these approaches to theology. However, this is precisely the creative dialectic which I want to bring out into the open. A close examination of the differences between these radically different approaches to theology will bring to the surface problems which must be confronted in coming to grips with the present state of the Christian consciousness – and of the Catholic consciousness in particular. This book will confront some of the differences and will seek to discover the basic points of complementarity and of convergence between these conflicting theological perspectives.

Among the problems that trouble the contemporary Catholic consciousness, none is more deeply disturbing and none is more crucial than the problem of the nature

---

[6] Cf., for example, *The Underground Church*, ed. Malcolm Boyd (New York: Sheed & Ward, 1968); O'Connor, *American Catholic Exodus*.

of faith itself. This is the first issue with which I shall be concerned. This leads to the question of the transcendent reality which is sought by faith – a question which is discussed in the second chapter. Since man experiences alienation which hampers him in his quest for transcendent reality – this problem of estrangement, as expressed in the myth of the Fall, comes next under consideration in chapter 3. Moreover, man's inability to extricate himself from his alienated condition by his own unaided efforts leads to the search for New Being – the search for Christ – which is the subject of the fourth chapter. The last three chapters deal with the problems which are involved in the perpetuation of the community and of the movements sparked by the revelatory encounter with Christ. Chapter 5 deals with the problem of communication and community, Chapter 6 with theology as eschatology, and Chapter 7 revolution in the church today.

Has Catholicism reached its end, or is there hope for a genuine new beginning? It is not possible infallibly to know. Nor is it possible to unfold an infallible plan for the future. This is a time for pragmatic reconstruction, for new discoveries as we move ahead in our task. It may be that we can no longer imagine ourselves to have the sweeping vision of the great theological systematizes of the past, but we can have the seminal and creative vision of explorers who have a heritage that drives them forward. This book will examine the most radical elements of that heritage in the hope of contributing to that forward movement.

Chapter 1

Faith as Ultimate Concern

⁓

The Catholic newspaper columnist a few years ago recounted the story of a parochial schoolteacher who made her pupils repeat over and over again each day, "There is a God, there is a God, there is a God." The astonishing thing about the column was the fact that its author took a highly favorable view of this procedure, maintaining that although some might call this "brainwashing," there can be no objection to brainwashing someone with the truth. In fact, he argued, "If this is brainwashing, then let's have more of it!" While the procedure this journalist was describing, as well as his approval of it, may at first seem extraordinary, the fact is that the behavior and the attitudes exemplified are not essentially different from the cluster of behavior and attitudes often associated with the idea of "faith" in textbooks and in popular preaching and teaching. Although it can be presented in varying degrees of sophistication, this idea of faith basically comes to an uncritical assent to propositions proposed by ecclesiastical authority for acceptance by believers. The assumption is that when one makes such an act of ascent, one has true faith. This conception of faith is not new, but it has been particularly prevalent in recent centuries within Roman Catholicism. This is connected with the fact that the Catholic Church has come increasingly to experience itself as a severely threatened institution. There is a semblance of security in clinging to fixed formulae by which "heretics" can be separated from true believers. This false security must be abandoned if the Catholic substance is to be reborn.

1.1 Historical Background

We should recognize the fact that prevalent distortions, such as those centering around the idea of faith, did not simply pop out of nowhere. It is helpful to try to gain some historical perspective, and to recognize the fact that ideas, such as that of faith, have had a long and torturous history and that their development has been intertwined with the development of their concepts.

The history of the idea of faith is intimately intermingled with the history of the ideas of hope and love. In fact, all three are so closely interrelated that they are not always clearly distinguishable. This can be seen in the Epistles of Paul where, as some scholars have noted, man's attitude of response to God is usually expressed by the word "faith" since the idea of faith includes love. In order to probe into the history of the idea of faith, therefore, it is necessary to see it in the context of its complex relationship with these other concepts.

The historical connections among the concepts of faith, hope, and love are problematic to many scholars. The problem can be seen as rooted to some extent in the conflict between two distinct conceptions of love, that of love as eros and love as agape. These notions came eventually to be united in the Christian idea of caritas or charity. It is important to examine these conceptions briefly, since this will throw light upon the problem of faith itself.

The idea of eros was derived largely from the philosophy of Plato, for whom it meant a love of man for the Divine, a desire which reaches out for a contemplation which will be wholly satisfying.[1] This contemplation, according to Plato, really is a possession of the Good, and it is attained by a difficult ascent to the transient things of this world. Eros, then, is seen as an appetite for the Good. This appetite is not for the sake of the good (as if anything could be bestowed upon it). Rather, there is a reaching out, and attempt to satisfy spiritual desire. Since this yearning is basically for the extension of one's own being, it may in a sense be called egocentric.

In the New Testament, eros is largely overlooked in favor of agape. It should not be imagined that the latter term is simply a synonymous Greek term which also means love. In fact, a very distinct attitude from that of eros is being conveyed. In the highest sense of the term, agape refers to God's love. Whether in God or in man it is generous love. It is not appetitive in the sense of involving a need to satisfy some incompleteness in oneself, and it is not dependent upon the beloved. It is in a sense indifferent to value, seeking only to confer good upon another, rather than to obtain good. Agape is therefore spontaneous and creative and is rooted in abundance rather than in poverty. It is in this sense that God himself is called Love (1 John 4:8). It can really be seen, however, that the use of the agape idea to convey the Christians [*sic*] attitude toward God is extremely problematic. All the same, there are a few passages in the Pauline Epistles in which agape is used in the sense of love towards God (e.g. Romans 8:28;

---

[1] Plato, *Symposium*, 210a–e.

1 Corinthians 2:9; 1 Corinthians 8: 3; Ephesians 6:24).
Not surprisingly, though, the use of the term in this sense
is infrequent in Paul, although he does frequently use it to
denote the Christian attitude towards one's neighbor.

It is not astonishing, then, that Paul had to find another
word to refer to a man's attitude of response to God. This
attitude he usually calls faith, rather than love. One
scholar put it in this way, "Faith, for Paul, includes in
itself the whole devotion of love, while emphasizing that it
has the character of a response, that it is a reciprocated
love."[2] Although this interpretation of Paul can be
debated, it illustrates very well the inseparability of the
ideas of faith and love and the futility of divisions and
distinctions that are neat and simplified. It suggests that it
is by no means a clear "fact" that faith traditionally always
has been taken to mean a simple assent to a set of
propositions.

In the writings of the Church Fathers, however, we
can find conceptualizations of faith that do foreshadow
the attitude of the teacher who makes her pupils repeat:
"There is a God, there is a God, etc. ...." In the earliest
centuries of Christianity there were some who made a
distinction between "mere faith" and Christian gnosis.
Those who held this distinction generally considered the
"mere believer" to be someone with a superficial understanding of spiritual matters. The mere believer was
understood to possess that which is essentially necessary,
that is, to have been brought into some special relationship with God, while nevertheless remaining far removed

[2] Anders Nygren, *Agape and Eros*, trans. Philip S. Watson (Philadelphia:
Westminster Press, 1953), 127.

from the condition of those who have gnosis. This attitude was expressed by Clement of Alexandria, who wrote that faith points beyond itself to a higher and more perfect state, that is, gnosis. According to this viewpoint, then, there are two stages of development, and the true gnostic is the Christian who has reached a high level of vision. The Christian who is living on this level supposedly has true insight into the meaning of Scripture and thus does not depend upon external authority as does the mere believer. A similar pattern of thinking is to be found in Origen, who also divides the Christian life into the two levels of mere faith and gnosis. It is not farfetched, then, to see already in these early Church Father's anticipatory expressions of the distortions of faith with which we are familiar today, for there is a tendency in them to identify faith with mere blind belief. As I have pointed out, there is also a tendency to separate mere believers from those on a superior plane within a sort of caste system. Whether intentionally or not, this way of thinking prepares the ground for authoritarian structures.

In the Middle Ages the most cohesive and original synthesis of Christian thought on the virtues of faith, hope, and charity was that of Thomas Aquinas, who conceptualized these as three distinct but interdependent supernatural, infused, "theological" virtues which direct man to God. Moreover, it is particularly important to be aware of Thomas's doctrine because it later became officially accepted within Roman Catholicism. Like Bonaventure and the medieval Augustinians, Thomas considered himself to be a disciple of Augustine, but Thomas is too complex a thinker to be reduced to such a category or to be considered simply in this manner.

Indeed, there is something radically different about his thought, and this stems from a conscious choice to adopt Aristotelianism into his synthesis. This marriage of Aristotelian philosophy to Augustinian Platonism profoundly affected the course of Christian thought for centuries to come.

Thomas's concept of faith has to be understood in conjunction with his concept of charity. Since for him the basic thrust of the will toward God made possible by grace is charity, it is reasonable that faith is understood in his thought as a virtue in the intellect. This is expressed in a somewhat qualified way, however. Thomas thought that since there is a lack of evidence for that which is believed, since the object of faith is unseen, the act of faith requires also a will act. Thus he could write that "to believe is to think with assent."[3] Although Thomas's thought is subtle – indeed far more subtle and complex than that of most of his disciples and of the great body of Catholic theologians in recent centuries – it is undeniable that this notion of the act of faith invites deterioration into something which is actually a distortion of faith. Tillich has aptly described this distortion as "the will to believe":

> In classical Roman Catholic theology, the "will to believe" is not an act which originates in man's striving, but it is given by grace to him whose will is moved by God to accept the truth of what the Church teaches ... This kind of interpretation agrees with the authoritarian attitude of the Roman Church.[4]

---

[3] Aquinas, *Summa Theologiae*, II–II, Q.2, A.1.
[4] Paul Tillich, *Dynamics of Faith* (New York: Harper & Row, 1957), 36.

This tendency to deterioration from the idea of a profound and authentic inner commitment of the personality into a "will to believe" certain propositions on authority involves a surrender of personal autonomy. It involves a self-destructive descent into a heteronomous, other-directed situation. At its worst, this means that the capacity for intellectual honesty as well as for religious experience is profoundly damaged and psychic infantilism in religious matters is encouraged. It means also that the sense of relativity is lost and that religious symbols cannot be appreciated as much. Then it happens that dogmatic literalism or verbal fundamentalism becomes the believer's surrogate for deep religious awareness.

Closely related to the idea of the act of faith as thinking with assent is the distinction between explicit and implicit faith. It is not surprising that Thomas insists upon this distinction, maintaining that "men of higher degree, whose business is to teach others, are under obligation to have fuller knowledge of matters of faith, and to believe them more explicitly."[5] This distinction has been characteristic of Roman Catholic theology ever since, and it implies that for the masses of people subjection of personal judgement to religious authority is necessary. As Max Weber pointed out, implicit faith (*fides implicita*) really involves a placing of confidence in and dedication to a prophet or to the authority of a structured institution. The faith of Abraham, Jesus, and Paul had the central significance of reliance upon the promises of God and was no intellectual assertion of dogmas. When it became an assertion of dogmas and when the distinction between

---

[5] Aquinas, *Summa Theologiae*, II–II, Q.2, A.6.

35

explicit and implicit faith is made, it works out that the institutional church, with its hierarchy of priests and preachers, gains great power.[6]

Thomas's conception of the act of faith and his distinction between explicit and implicit faith has wide implications. It is interrelated, for example, with his treatment of the problem of man's knowledge of God. Thomas broke away from an idea prevalent in the Augustinian–Anselmian tradition, namely the idea that God's existence is self-evident. Having rejected the idea that God is self-evident to us, he proposed elaborate demonstrations for God's existence, based in large measure upon the Aristotelian philosophical principles. These arguments given by Thomas are very complex, and because of this complexity it was natural that he should come to the conclusion that "the truth about God such as reason could discover would only be known by a few, and after a long time, and with the admixture of many errors'.[7] This meant that for most men, efforts to demonstrate God's existence would prove fruitless. Something more is needed. That is, for most people, since they are incapable of such mediating discourse, ecclesiastical authority was judged to be necessary even for knowledge of God's existence.

In justice to Thomas Aquinas, it should be stressed that his own conception of faith was more profound and complex than any mere "will to believe." Thus, for example, he insisted that the object of faith is the First Truth

---

[6] Cf. Max Weber, *The Sociology of Religion*, trans. Ephraim Fischoff (Boston: Beacon Press, 1963), 194–195.

[7] Aquinas, *Summa Theologiae*, I, Q.11.

(God).[8] This in itself could have been a very liberating conception. Yet, at the same time, he held that faith involves assent to propositions, and this notion has had a strong influence upon the Christian tradition, particularly within Catholicism. The fact is that Thomas's impact upon the tradition in this matter both reflected and reinforced the conditioning process which by subjection to authority, in particular to ecclesiastical authority, was made to appear acceptable and right. It also reflected and reinforced the world view in which the universe and human society were seen as essentially hierarchical. According to this view each person, whether he was noble or peasant, cleric or layman, had his state of life assigned to him by divine providence. There was no reason to complain: everything would be explained satisfactorily at the Last Judgement. Given such a perspective on life, it seemed reasonable and appropriate that everyone should simply accept religious dogmas as handed down by duly constituted authority.

The contemporary situation is dramatically different. Mobility of every sort – spatial, social, ethical, and intellectual – characterize the climate in which we live. Thus, the idea of faith as assent becomes less and less acceptable, for this notion is essentially static. It leaves out of account the dynamics of personality. It ignores the fact that persons grow in interaction with a changing environment. Then, too, part of the reason for the unacceptability of this notion of faith is the exclusiveness which is inherent in it. In this age of mobility, a sense of community with others of different religious and educational backgrounds

---

[8] Ibid.

is common. Consequent upon this is a sense of relativity in regard to religious beliefs. Indeed, many today find the idea that only those who will accept a particular belief system have faith to be absurd.

1.2 Distortions of Faith in Protestantism

It would be a mistake to imagine that only the Catholic tradition offers to its adherent's conceptions of faith which many find damaging to their personal integrity and therefore inherently unacceptable. There are also Protestant notions of faith that appear to pose unsolvable dilemmas. According to Protestant theologian Karl Barth, for example, the only basis for the decision of faith is revelation itself. To this, one might pose the natural and predictable objection: How would one know that what he thinks is God's revelation is really God's revelation? Barth's answer to this is that the Spirit guarantees man his personal participation in revelation. He says that the act of the Holy Spirit in revelation is the "yes" to God's word, spoken through God himself on our behalf, not only to us but in us. This "yes" spoken by God is the ground of the confidence with which a man may regard the revelation as meant for him.[9] It is clear that such an approach to faith will not be satisfying to those who have had such an experience, and perhaps not intellectually satisfying even to some who would claim to have had it.

Another leading Protestant theologian of this century, Rudolf Bultmann, also presents perplexing problems as a

---

[9] Karl Barth, *Kirchliche Dogmatik*, 13 vols. (Zurich: Verlag der Evangelischen Buchhandlung, 1932–67), 1:475.

result of this notion of faith. His interpretation of justification by faith in the redemptive history received scathing criticism from existentialist philosopher Karl Jaspers, who described this as "frozen orthodoxy of redemption." Concerning Bultmann's theory Jaspers wrote, "For a philosopher this is the most alienating, the most outlandish of beliefs – this Lutheran dogma with its terrible consequences scarcely seems even denotative existentially."[10] The basic reason for Jaspers' objection to this idea of faith seems to be its lack of universality. That is, the doctrine as presented does not appear to correspond to universal human experience. To put it another way: it seems to exclude the possibility of faith or of revelation for those who have not received the Biblical message. Jaspers objects, "The reality of man is not a radical sinfulness which is overcome only by an alleged divine intervention that took place in a foreign country a long time ago."[11] Particularly strange is the Bultmannian idea that God without Christ is madness. For Jaspers – and many others – a major implication of this is that those who do not see it this way are "poor lost heathen."[12]

This kind of exclusiveness which is found in much Christian teaching on faith has been criticized by other thinkers as well. In fact, conceptualizations of Christian faith as somehow exclusive are so widespread that a historian of the stature of Arnold Toynbee, has seen intolerance as one of the outstanding characteristics of Christianity.

[10] Karl Jaspers and Rudolf Bultmann, *Myth and Christianity* (New York: Noonday Press, 1958), 58.
[11] Ibid., 50.   [12] Ibid., 79.

1.3 The Reaction of Modern Atheism

It is not surprising, therefore, that in modern times there have been violent reactions against Christian belief. These reactions, of course, are not all directly and obviously based upon the distortions of faith I have described. Indeed, often the dissenters have expressed their repugnance for and rejection of Christianity as due to its failures in the area of social reform, or as due to its irrelevance in modern life or to its tendency to support oppressive or alienating structures. However, serious reflection leads to the conclusion that these failures and deficiencies are connected in their deepest roots with distorted notions of faith. Conceptions of faith which reduce it to a stagnant will-act of assent to a body of propositions handed down by authority, conceptions of faith that reduce personal autonomy or that breed intolerance toward others who do not adhere to the same belief-system – these all lead to indifference and even resistance to social and political reform, since they hinder the possibility for profound personal insight and for original thought and action.

Modern atheism has in large measure been a revolt against the distortions of faith, as well as against inadequate ideas of hope and love that have accompanied these distortions in much of traditional Christian thought. Indeed, this was implied in Nietzsche's proclamation of the "death of God." That nineteenth century proclamation of God's death – reaffirmed constantly in our own time – was not merely an assertion that the term "God" had lost its force. It was a symbolic affirmation of the impending demise of an entire world view – of a static otherworldly vision of reality. Characteristic of that world view which Nietzsche so violently rejected was a hypocrisy which many came to identify with Christianity. At any rate, it cannot be denied that many and diverse thinkers of the nineteenth and [twentieth] centuries have felt compelled to reject Christianity. There are significant differences among such thinkers as Feuerbach, Marx, Freud, Camus, and Sartre, to be sure. Yet all share a fundamental antipathy to a world view which they have seen as basically at odds with man's deepest striving toward realization of authentic faith, hope, and love. However, many others, while retaining their identity as Christians, have shared to some extent this widespread disillusionment and have asked themselves why and in what sense they can continue to call themselves Christians.

1.4 The Dilemma of Institutionalized Religion

There is room for serious doubt, however, as to whether institutional religion as we now know it will be able to solve its own dilemmas and respond authentically to such criticism. A basic difficulty lies in the fact that institutional religion is subject to a process of routinization, by which structures, persons, places, and things become sacralized. In this process, the deep quest for transcendence is lost sight of. Indeed, faith itself comes to be envisaged as a thing or an object. This sort of image of faith is exemplified in many statements made about "losing the faith" (as if it could be lost in the manner one misplaces one's keys or wallet). Indeed, we are so accustomed to such images and to such language that we tend to lose sight of the peculiarity of the whole process. It has been pointed out that most Christians, indeed most persons in Europe and America are unaware that a strange prominence has been given to belief in Christian history. Characteristically, Christians will ask of a Buddhist or Hindu: "What does he believe?" The question may seem important and natural from the questioner's point of view, but it may not seem so to the person about whom it is asked.[13] In other words, belief systems have come to seem all important in the Christian milieu. Institutionalized Christianity has tended to lose sight of the original revelatory experience which brought it into being and which continues to sustain its authentic life. It has been inclined to focus upon transitory structures and belief systems as if these were ultimate. This being the case, it is problematic whether organized religion in its present condition will be able to meet the challenges posed by unbelief. The problem is that it has put a disproportionate emphasis upon orthodoxy and "beliefs."

1.5 Authentic Faith

An increasing number of Christians are coming to be aware of the dimensions of the problem. They are coming to recognize that the survival of Christianity may depend to a great extent upon our ability to attain and convey something approaching authentic understanding of faith. Although no formulation is without inadequacies, Tillich's description of faith as "a state of ultimate concern" suggests the significant dimensions of

---

[13] Cf. Wilfred Cantwell Smith, *The Meaning and End of Religion* (New York: Macmillan, 1963), 180.

the question of faith. The essential point is to lift the whole question out of the stultifying framework of belief-systems and will-acts in order to bring to light the awareness that engenders faith, that is, awareness that gives rise to a centered act of the personality tending toward transcendence.

When faith is seen in this perspective, it becomes evident that it cannot be viewed within the ordinary subject–object scheme of relationship, as if the divine reality were some "thing" or some finite person (no matter how superior) to which man relates. Rather, there is a movement toward that which is totally other and yet intimately present. The divine reality, to which one is related through faith, is not adequately described as "the supreme being." Rather it is the ground of all being.[14] Since this relationship – which is what I mean by faith – is not reducible to knowledge or to a will-act, since indeed it is the state of finite consciousness being grasped by the infinite, it defies simple categorization.

One of the consequences of envisaging faith in this way is a shift in one's attitude on the subject of doubt. If faith simply means adherence to a belief-system, then doubt must be seen as its opposite, as an evil to be eradicated. Indeed, doubt and faith would be related somewhat as disease and health. However, if faith is seen in depth, in the manner I have suggested, then doubt is not envisaged as precisely opposed to it, but rather as part of it. It must be so, for there is no "object" visible to cling to or to aim for directly. Faith, like hope, cannot be verified. Its

---

[14] This manner of speaking is repudiated, wrongly, I believe, by advocates of the theology of hope. I will discuss this problem in a later chapter.

certainty pertains to a different order from that of the scientist or even the philosopher. It is a certainty which must contain and encompass uncertainty. Thus doubt, existential doubt, is at the very core of faith.

1.6 Courage as a Part of Faith

In order to bear this doubt there must be an existential courage which is also a part of faith. This enables the one who has faith to affirm his being in the face of the threat of non-being. This metaphysical language should be understandable to non-philosophers because all do in fact experience the anxiety of non-being. It is anxiety and not fear that non-being evokes, precisely because there is no object upon which the emotion of fear could fixate itself. This does not mean, however, that non-being is not "real." It is as real as the experience of death, the experience of guilt, and the experience of meaninglessness.[15]

A large part of human behavior can be interpreted as a series of attempts to avoid facing the existential anxiety which is an unavoidable element of the human condition. We are always tempted to avoid the threat of non-being by limiting our own being, that is by settling for a shrunken form of self-affirmation, a stunted form of existence. By contrast, the tremendously difficult but only authentic response is to face the non-being in ourselves, in others, and in the world. This means taking existential anxiety into one's consciousness, reaching out always to

---

[15] Cf. Paul Tillich, *The Courage to Be* (New Haven, CT: Yale University Press, 1952), for an analysis of these problems.

fuller existence in self-transcending activity despite threatening non-being.

There is ample opportunity for pathological reactions to the threat of non-being. An extreme and obvious example of such a reaction would be the case of the neurotic who locks himself in his room because he is afraid that if he goes outside he will be struck down by a car or perhaps slip on a banana peel and be injured.

There are also less obvious but more common ways of shrinking one's own being because of the perpetual threat of non-being. Many of the pathological developments in society in general and in the church in particular reflect man's effort to limit his psychical, intellectual, and moral self. All concrete forms of church life can deteriorate into escape mechanisms warding off the darkness of threatening uncertainty. Indeed, because of the existential anxiety, there is a tendency built into religion to deteriorate into idolatry, giving an inordinate value to things and acts which in fact have value only as pointing beyond themselves.

The courage demanded by faith is the courage to look into the abyss of non-being. It drives us to transcend the subtle forms of idolatry to which we are inclined. The crisis of faith which is taking place in Christianity today is in fact in large measure a reaction to the excesses of idolatry to which the church has succumbed in recent centuries. Since the idols which were set up in the name of God and of religion have now been seen through, the total insecurity of the human situation and of faith has been laid bare. We seem, therefore, to be called to an awakening of the existential courage which is at the heart of authentic faith.

1.7 Polarization Resulting from Failure in Courage

It is not easy to be courageous, however. Many would prefer to live on the surface, to avoid looking into the abyss of faith. Others, perhaps in spite of themselves, have begun to accept the challenge of insecurity and change. Thus a tremendous polarization has been taking place, not only within Catholicism, but within Christianity and indeed within the whole of Western society. It is important that we look at this phenomenon, in order to understand ourselves.

It is evident to almost everyone that Christianity is in a state of polarization. I am not referring to the institutional separation which characterized the recent past, when we could conveniently divide Christians into Protestants and Catholics and feel reasonably sure that we knew what we were talking about. Rather, it is a division cutting across the old institutional lines. This polarization could be characterized in different ways. The description given by poet-prophet-scientist-theologian Pierre Teilhard de Chardin was probably one of the most adequate. Teilhard saw mankind as profoundly divided into two irrevocably opposed camps – "one looking to the horizon and proclaiming with all its new-found faith, 'We are moving,' and the other, without shifting its position, obstinately maintaining, 'Nothing changes. We are not moving at all.'"[16]

On all sides we witness the dichotomy described by Teilhard. Articulate intellectuals and activists on the side of revolution far outnumber those who could be

---

[16] Pierre Teilhard de Chardin, *The Future of Man*, trans. Norman Denny (New York: Harper & Row, 1964), 11.

considered their peers on the other side, the side of conservatism, of stasis. It would probably be a mistake, of course, to assume that this is indicative of proportions on each side within the general population. However, it is very significant in terms of "where things are going." That is, the fact that the emerging leadership is looking to the horizon is meaningful for the future of Christianity.

Typical in some ways of Christians who are looking to the horizon is Robert McAfee Brown, who continually has asked that the church in our day be willing to take immense risks in the arena of involvement in the secular order, that it err on the side of over-involvement rather than under-involvement, that it be specific rather than general, radical rather than conservative.[17] Another future-oriented Christian who almost typifies the radical Christian activist leader of the sixties and early seventies – Fr. James Groppi – wrote that the Church must become "the most radical civil rights group in this country."[18] On the other side of the fence, the beleaguered traditionalist group is represented by Frederick Wilhelmsen, the archconservative Catholic who proposes a new movement of Catholic power which could supply Rome with "troops" and "force a new sword at the service of the authority of Rome," and which would see Christ the King as the "Lord of Battles."[19] Another traditionalist author,

---

[17] Robert McAfee Brown, "The Church's Ecumenical Outreach," in *American Catholic Exodus*, ed. John O'Connor (Washington, DC: Corpus Books, 1968), 85.

[18] James Groppi, "The Church and Civil Rights," in *The Underground Church*, ed. Malcolm Boyd (New York: Sheed & Ward, 1968), 82.

[19] Frederick D. Wilhelmsen, "Schism, Heresy, and a New Guard," in O'Connor, *American Catholic Exodus*, 176–200.

Christopher Derrick, has portrayed the future as possibly holding two Catholic Churches – the true one "embattled and run strictly . . . and a much larger schematic body still claiming the Catholic name . . . but designed to disappear before long into a vague pan-Protestant fog, not nearly Christian, not clearly religious at all in any useful sense of those words."[20]

The differences between the two groups seemingly could not be more extreme. It is clear that more is involved than differences in logic or even in educational and social backgrounds. There appear to be sharply distinct manners of perceiving reality. Perhaps it would not be too far off the mark to describe the dichotomy in "McLuhanish" terms, as follows: Those Christians who have experienced a profound shift in consciousness in the direction of radicalization have come to recognize that their old perception of the church was distorted. What they have done in effect is to have changed their environment. Now, one does not really recognize his environment for what it is while he is in it (a fish does not discover water) but only after it has become his old environment. The complex phenomenon experienced by many Christians today is a kind of moving "outside" the institutional church, which they have more or less come to recognize as their old environment. As a result they have been forced to reassess these intuitions. In a real sense, their eyes have been opened.

---

[20] Christopher Derrick, *Trimming the Ark* (New York, P. J. Kenedy & Sons, 1967), 69–70.

1.8 The "Outside–Inside" Relationship to Institutional Christianity

One should recognize the complexity of the situation. Moving "outside" does not necessarily mean abandoning the church or "leaving it in every sense." Thus when James Pike, for example, described himself as an alumnus of his church, the expression conveyed the fact that he was not severing all relation to it, but rather that he was establishing a free and adult relationship to it. To pursue the analogy, alumni are in fact what an institution of learning is intended to produce, rather than perpetual undergraduates. So also the point of the church is not to foster religious infantilism but spiritual adulthood. For those who have graduated from their old religious environment, "going back" would be something analogous to the act of one who would refuse graduation from a university, preferring to retain his undergraduate status permanently.

The nature of this outside–inside relationship to Catholicism or to any institutional religion is obscure because faith itself involves unclarity. Obviously, I am not talking about faith understood as assent to a series of proposition on the authority of "God," the Scriptures, or the church. As we have seen, that idea – which has a delusive pseudo-clarity – has been used to separate true believers from heretics by the magic of identifying words with the reality they only dimly reflect. The faith I am talking about is that state of ultimate concern which does not exclude doubt but which contains doubt in its depths. Paradoxically, for this reason it carries with it a clear recognition that there is no sharp distinction between insiders and outsiders, Catholics and non-Catholics, Christians and non-Christians. This clarity about the fact of unclarity is a dizzying experience.

There are of course some religious thinkers (as well as non-religious thinkers) for whom the outside–inside relationship to institutional Christianity is an idea impossible to sustain. Such would appear to be the case with a theologian such as Charles Davis. However, these thinkers seem to be doomed to a kind of isolation and ineffectiveness. They have "left the church," and irrelevance often seems to be their fate. These somewhat rigid thinkers who opt out are not the ones I have in mind when I speak of the radicals at one end of the spectrum within the church. The radicals I have in mind are those who choose instead the difficult stance of outside–inside.

The acute polarization within Christianity, then, has many dimensions, and cannot adequately be described by such catchphrases as "generation gap." Those who have "left" the old environment while remaining Christians and staying in some way related to the institutional church tend to mythically and in depth to have a high tolerance of ambiguity and a high valuation of honesty. Their image of time is linear, projecting into the future. Their faith is strong but unclear. There is the other pole, who do not welcome change, tend to favor a rigid formal logic and literalism. Their thinking is rationalistic. Sincerity is understood in terms either of flat acceptance or of flat rejection of ideologies. Their notion of time is cyclic ("there is nothing new under the sun; history repeats itself.") Their idea of faith excludes doubt.

I have said that the phenomenon described here is not a division between institutional churches but rather that it cuts across such boundaries. How are we to approach and understand it, then? I think that we can find a clue in the language of those who see the split within Catholicism as a "Protestantizing" process – as well as in the talk of people who see some Protestant churches as desiring to become "Romanized." These judgements contain more than a grain of truth. I have already suggested, in the introduction, that in the current situation we are witnessing and participating in a lived experience of the dialectic between Protestant principle and Catholic substance, which are complementary aspects of an integral faith. Insofar as those who have been conditioned within the Catholic milieu can bring the Protestant principle explicitly into relationship with the substance, that is, with the tradition which is their heritage, they may re-enliven this tradition both in their minds and hearts and in its outward manifestations.

1.9 Theonomous Synthesis

What is the nature of the integration we are seeking? Basically, the common quest of Catholics and Protestants is for a wholeness that transcends institutional unification. This will not be the sort of wholeness intended by those who speak of "integration" as an end in itself. Indeed, a simple stasis or fixed union of poles within faith is neither desirable nor possible. The meeting of complementary opposites within faith is not an end but a new beginning. It initiates a process which is analogues to the process which Jung called individuation. That is, it brings into being a new center of equilibrium, a discovery of freedom and a surge of new life. The meeting of

Protestant principle and Catholic substance within the Christian consciousness sparks a qualitative leap beyond the security of fixed formulae and static structures to a higher synthesis which drives us onward. That is, it involves a theonomous synthesis.

In order to understand the nature of the theonomous synthesis it is necessary to recognize faith as a state of relatedness to the unconditioned. Since our mode of existence is one of immersion in the concrete, in conditioned forms of meaning and conduct, we are always confronted with a fundamental problem. This is the radial theological problem of the relation of the relative to the absolute. In other words, it is the problem of discovering transcendent meaning within limited and changing forms of thought and action, within our culture.

For the most part, we are unsuccessful in resolving this problem, attempting either to be completely autonomous, that is completely "rational" or else succumbing to external, heteronomous authority which does violence to our efforts toward self-realization. In either case, complete human stature is not attained. It is attained only by a qualitative surpassing both of one-sided autonomy and of self-destructive surrender to heteronomy. The kind of decision by which we move to a higher level of awareness and commitment involves abandonment of false security and facing the threat of meaninglessness. Yet it is the only choice which is not self-defeating. This should not be imagined as a kind of leap into the outer space of esoteric irrelevance. Transcendence is not realizable through flight from the concrete present. Quite the opposite; it is attainable only by a transforming confrontation with the concrete situation.

What all this suggests, then, is that the basic disillusionment of educated, concerned Christians on all sides points
to the need for qualitative change within the structures
which incarnate and at the same time distort revelation.
The disillusionment itself, which is combined with something like hope-against-hope, suggests that there is in fact
a qualitative change taking place within the Christian
consciousness. The problem lies in the transmission of
the new level of awareness into the objectifications of
revelation.

Many, of course, are sensitive to the problem of the
transformation of structures – such as structures of theological language, of church organization, of worship – so
that these may express and perpetuate the new or newer
awareness of the transcendent. There is a real danger,
however, of short-circuiting the energy within faith which
is always trying to push us towards a higher form of
integration.

Our situation is somewhat analogous to that of the
poet who has a genuine insight but who has not yet
acquired the skill to execute a work that is commensurate
to his creative vision. He may err in two directions: after
a few false starts he may simply stagnate, hoping that the
skill which can come only from practice will somehow
come in a flash; or else he may try to finish the end
product prematurely, producing a defective work which
merely caricatures his original insight. The first choice
will result in nothing but sterile passivity. The poet – as
well as the theologian – must create. But neither the poet
nor the theologian nor the Christian activist should
expect short-term results. Neither poetic intuition nor
revelation is total at its inception. Just as the poet does

not have a clear "idea" of his work before he begins toiling with the words which are his material, so the man of faith cannot have a clear idea at the outset of the theological, liturgical, or organizational forms which will most adequately incarnate his new plane of awareness. It should be obvious that the poet's inspiration is not clothed in words as if these were a costume not affecting his thought. Clearly, it is through the interaction of insight and material that the work of art comes into being. The process defies all naïve classifications such as "form" and "content." So it should also be clear that revelation is not an entity in itself, but is conditioned by the mind receiving it. We never have revelation "pure," and to imagine that we do is the basic error of all fundamentalists and traditionalists. Moreover, the mind receiving revelation cannot be imagined as a bowl receiving gelatin and giving it form. Human consciousness is active in the revelatory process, experimenting with its insights, interacting with them, remolding them in the context of new problems and situations.

The theonomous synthesis which is engendered by the encounter of Protestant principle and Catholic substance is form-creative in the sense I have just described, recognizing that its forms are always temporary and provisional. It implies a plane of insight which enables us to discover transcendent meaning in our concrete situation and to transform our situation so that it becomes more transparent to this transcendent meaning. We then participate in the revelatory process through our efforts to cope with the problems immediately before us in the concrete present, through our tentative efforts at rebuilding.

1.10 Toward Integration

The assimilation of the reflective and self-critical Protestant principle within the consciousness of "born Catholics," then, can be recognized as a movement toward a higher level of human development. So, too, the rediscovery by Protestants of the power of religious symbols is a mode of participation in the process of become [sic] self-aware. The catalyst moving us toward ever higher levels of self-confrontation is present in the manifold problems thrust upon us by our concrete situation. There is no clear guarantee, of course, that we will achieve synthesis and not simply further disintegration. We can be sure, however, that the preservation of an ancient monolithic institution – or the creation of a new one – is no guarantee against disintegration. On the contrary, our hope for higher integrity is rooted in our capacity for institutional and theological diversity. We need religious diversity – not based on "dogmas" but upon a variety of concerns, interests, and life-styles, and cutting across the institutions "Catholic" and "Protestant" [–] divisions which are almost meaningless. We need this because this is how we are in fact: complex, alienated, incomplete.

Although there is no simple solution to the problem of achieving authentic integration, we may find a sign of hope in the fact that in recent times faith has come to be experienced more and more as a driving force rather than as a doctrine. The theology of hope has reflected this new realization. Indeed, one of the proponents of the theology of hope has expressed this very explicitly, writing that faith is not primarily a doctrine, but rather "an initiative for the passionate innovating and changing of the world toward the Kingdom of God."[21] It may well be that this vision of faith as an initiative in the world will become an integrating force, and that it will help to heal the fractured body of Christianity.

It is important, then, that dialogue be carried on with the theologians of hope, for in being explicit and passionate about the eschatological dimension of faith they are driving the Christian consciousness to the level of a new integration. However, there is a bias in the theology of hope which suggests a lack of philosophical depth. I refer to a certain anti-metaphysical bias, which is reflected in the insistence that there can be no bridge between ontological thinking and history.[22] This poses serious problems which should be confronted, for it implied a rejection of what is most essential to our heritage of Greek thought and – more importantly – a rejection of what is essential in the religious experience of many. The following chapter will examine this problem of metaphysics vis-a-vis the theology of hope.

[21] Johannes Metz, *Theology of the World*, trans. William Glen-Doepel (New York: Herder & Herder, 1969), 93.
[22] Cf. ibid., 99.

Chapter 2

The Mystery of Being and The Catholic Substance

∼

The Catholic substance appears to many to be dying. The symbols which are the language of faith fail to speak to many, particularly to the young. Thus the sacraments, the creeds, liturgical ceremonies, and dogmas seem to reach out more and more to blind eyes and deaf ears. To many, the problem of the loss of the symbols' power appears to be far more profound than such problems as birth control, clerical celibacy, mixed marriages, or indeed than any questions centering upon authority, structures, and law. It is possible to disagree with the Pope about birth control and yet have faith. However, when the very substance of faith itself seems to be dissolving into meaninglessness, the anguish involved may be more acute.

The loss of the power of the religious symbols, or the apparent death of these symbols, accompanies another phenomenon which is less easily perceived by the majority of persons, although it is a preoccupation of some theologians. This other phenomenon is the loss of the sense of the mystery of being. It is the thesis of this chapter that this is a profound connection between these two events and that the rebirth of the symbols, of the Catholic substance, indeed of "Catholicism" in the deepest and most authentic sense will not take place without a rebirth of awareness of the mystery of being.

2.1 The Missing Dimension in Secular Thought

In their reaction against idolatry within the Christian churches, some theologians in the 1960s turned with relief to celebrating the process of secularization. The cover of Harvey Cox's best-selling theological work, *The Secular City*, proclaims that this book is a celebration of its [the secular city's] liberties and an invitation to its discipline. Although the distinction made by this theologian and others between secularism (an ideology) and secularization (a process) may be valid enough, many have since come around to taking a second and more critical look at optimistic portrayals of "the secular city." Some have come to believe that this is much to be feared in the possibility of capitulation to secularism, which lives upon the delusion of self-sufficiency and therefore bears within itself the seeds of disintegration.

It is remarkable that not only Christians but also some Marxists are growing in sensitivity regarding the problem of the missing dimension in the purely secular mode of envisioning reality. Some Marxists are beginning to seek a new openness toward transcendence. Indeed, a Marxist scholar has been quoted as saying, "Our Christian friends have awakened in us the courage for transcendence." Moreover, the leading French Marxist theoretician, Roger Garoudy, asked before an audience of Christians, "What would your faith be like if it bore not in itself the latent atheism which prevents you from serving a false God? What would our atheism be like if it would not learn from your faith the transcendence of a God of whom we have no living experience?"[1] What this suggests is that "relevance" to the exigencies of the present moment is coming to be recognized as insufficient by many thinkers, who bear different ideological labels, but who share a common quest for a deeper level of awareness.

2.2 The Rediscovery of Being

The rebirth of the Catholic substance will require a rediscovery of being. Although I have used the term "rediscovery" I do not mean by this that we should return to the past. This would be impossible, even if it were desirable. Our rediscovery will have to be within the context of the present situation and our manner of apprehending its implications will be shaped by the forms of contemporary consciousness.

In order to reacquire the sense of being we will have to experience wonder. For the Greeks, philosophy was born out of the sense of wonder. To be sure, we may wonder about many things without becoming philosophers. The wonder which is the source of philosophical thought is wonder about the secret mystery of being. The question which is implied is sometimes put this way: Why are there beings and not simply non-being? Certainly there are many who have considered this a meaningless question and there are many others who have judged it to be irrelevant. To the theologians who see one of their primary goals as the "dehellenizing" of theology to many

---

[1] Quoted by Jürgen Moltmann in *Religion, Revolution, and the Future*, trans. M. Douglas Meeks (New York: Charles Scribner's Sons, 1969), 64.

advocates of the theology of hope, anything like a mysticism of being is anathema. Yet, the wonder, the question, and the sort of mysticism which accompanies this remain permanent possibility in the human mind.

The sense of the mystery of being has been expressed by thinkers who seemingly are very diverse. Friedrich Schelling wrote of the question of being as "the final, desperate question: Why is there anything at all? Why not nothing?" Heidegger expressed it this way: "Why are there beings at all and not non-being? This is obviously the first of all questions, though not in the sense of a chronological order of questions."[2] Indeed, for Heidegger, authentic thought by its nature tends to being. In man's thought, "being" lights up, coming forth from its hiddenness. He is of course not speaking of "a being" but of the being that makes beings to be. For him, authentic thought is concerned with the unveiling of being.

Within Roman Catholicism the most ardent exponent of the mysticism of being within recent history was Jacques Maritain. He maintained that Heidegger's experience of "angst" could be a road to the experience that Maritain himself has called the intuition of being.[3] For Maritain, without the intuition of being all of one's philosophical knowledge is mere opinion, precarious and

[2] Martin Heidegger, *Introduction to Metaphysics*, trans. R. Manheim (New Haven, CT: Yale University Press, 1958), 1.

[3] Jacques Maritain, *Approaches to God*, trans. Peter O'Reilly (London: George Allen & Unwin, 1955), 3ff. For a complete bibliography of Maritain on this subject, see Mary Daly, *Natural Knowledge of God in the Philosophy of Jacques Maritain: A Critical Study* (Rome: Catholic Book Agency, 1966).

sterile. He becomes almost lyrical in his frequent descriptions of the intuition of being: When it occurs, I suddenly realize that a given entity – man, mountain or tree – exists and exercises this sovereign activity to be in its own way, in an independence of me which is total, totally self-assertive and totally implacable. This makes me realize my frailty and liability to nothingness. There is then a realization that the existence involved in anything at all implies some absolute existence, free from nothingness and death. There are thus three intellective leaps within the same unique intuition. Although no word can express the riches and virtualities of this intuition, it is described as a kind of "spiritual fire." Moreover, although this is an intellectual experience, it is associated with profound emotion. It may in some cases have the appearances of mystical grace.

For Maritain, then, there is a dynamism in this intuition, and its fruition is natural knowledge of God. This intuition is at the source of the analogy of being. That is, our natural ordination to the being of things which are on the same level as ourselves is like a bait or an enticement which compels us to rise to a higher level. Maritain asserts that the expansive energy of this intuition has to be understood in connection with the analogy of being. That is, being as being, which is the proper object of metaphysics, is not grasped in a pure and authentic intuition except when its polyvalence or its analogy is grasped at the same time. Being belongs intrinsically and properly to all the subjects to which it is attributable, because it is analogous from the very start. Since being is a consistent and differentiated object of thought, it is a vehicle which permits us to arrive at knowledge of God. Thus the analogy of being is seen as the philosopher's road to natural knowledge of God.

It is remarkable to find a thinker as different both from Heidegger and from Maritain as Mircea Eliade also speaking of special manifestations of being, although he does so in a very different context and language. Eliade maintains that at the origin of structured religions there have been hierophanies – experiences in which the sacred is manifested through the world. Writing of stones as manifestations of the sacred, he says that the hierophany of a stone is primarily an ontophany, that is, a manifestation of being. The stone is, and it strikes man by what it possesses of irreducibility and absoluteness, revealing to him the irreducibility of being.[4] Eliade's language bears a remarkable similarity to Maritain's description of the intuition of being. This suggests that the experience is not limited to philosophers of a particular school, nor, indeed, to philosophers. Yet, of course, philosophers and theologians have had the burden of describing, analyzing, and explicating the implications of this intuitive experience which they have shared with others, less learned and less articulate.

For the thought of Paul Tillich, the mysticism of being is a potent source. He speaks of a mystical a priori in which are rooted the conceptualizations of the religious philosopher and of the theologian. The mystical a priori is an awareness of that which transcends the cleavage between subject and object in the knowing process. If in the course of a "scientific" procedure this a priori is

---

[4] Mircea Eliade, *The Sacred and the Profane* (New York: Harper & Row, 1961), 155–156.

discovered, its discovery is possible only because it was present from the very beginning. This, Tillich concludes, is a circle from which no religious philosopher can escape.[5] According to Tillich, the circle within which the theologian works is even narrower than that of the philosopher of religion, for he adds to the mystical a priori the criterion of the Christian message. However true this may be, it is abundantly clear from Tillich's writings that for him the a priori is "the ground of being." The well-spring of Tillich's thought then, is the affirmation of being.

2.3 Opposition to the Mysticism of Being

There has been strong opposition in recent years on the part of some theologians to anything like an affirmation of the mysticism of being. The advocates of secularization claimed that modern man, that is "pragmatic man" does not ask ultimate or existential questions. It was argued that such questions are obviously not questions that occur to everyone, or to the vast majority of people, and that they do not trouble the newly emergent urban secular man very frequently.[6] Moreover, the theologians who have advocated "dehellenization" have protested all identification of God with being, claiming that what the religious experience of God discloses is a reality beyond being.[7] Furthermore, the proponents of a new theology

---

[5] Paul Tillich, *Systematic Theology*, 3 vols. (Chicago: University of Chicago Press, 1951–63), 1:190.

[6] See Harvey Cox, *The Secular City* (New York: Macmillan, 1965), 69.

[7] See Leslie Dewart, *The Future of Belief* (New York: Herder & Herder, 1966), 175.

of hope have been most explicit in their opposition to the mysticism of being. It has been claimed by one of them that the mysticism of being, "with its emphasis upon the living of the present moment, presupposes an immediacy to God which the faith that believes in God on the ground of Christ cannot adopt without putting an end to the historic mediation and reconciliation of God and man in the Christ event, and so also as a result of this, putting an end to the observation of history under the category of hope."[8] According to the theology of hope, then, an authentic and vital Christian theology precludes the mysticism of being.

2.4 Contrasting Experiences

If one were to judge by these theological movements of the past few years, it would appear that the sense of being is disappearing from the religious consciousness. However, before leaping to such a conclusion, it would be well to consider some other factors. First of all, it is important to recognize the fact that existential questions have never been expressed explicitly most of the time by most people. Indeed, most people seem to have spent most of their time in evading these questions. Urban secular man would appear to be no exception to this general lack of explicit questioning. The question of being and non-being, in all of its poignancy, probably arises usually in times of great distress or else on the occasion of certain peak experiences, such as that described by

---

[8] Jürgen Moltmann, *Theology of Hope*, trans. James W. Leitch (New York, Harper & Row, 1967).

Maritain. Second, some contemporary observers are pointing out that among the disaffected members of the younger generation there is now a resurgence of the sense of being and a nostalgia for the experience which the dehellenizing theologians were so anxious to dispense with.[9] In other words, it may be that there has been some loss of the sense of being in our culture, and that this is precisely what the alienated young are seeking to regain for themselves. Third, it should be asked whether there may not be diverse modes of religious experience. Thus those theologians who claim that we do not experience God as being or who maintain that such an experience is not authentically Christian should be asked to examine the implications of their prejudice, which would suggest that many deeply committed persons are simply deluded and lacking in genuine religious experience, because their experience and thinking is ontological and contemplative in nature.

2.5 Being and the Power of Religious Symbols

I would go further and suggest that the disparagement of the mysticism of being among theologians is not only indicative of a narrowness of vision, but more than this, that there is something deadly about it. I would suggest that without the sense of being-itself, there is every likelihood that the profoundly analogous power of the religious symbols will not be grasped, that the mind will think of them univocally and even literally and that the religious

---

9 See Michael Novak, *A Theology for Radical Politics* (New York: Herder & Herder, 1969), 99.

consciousness will be starved. At any rate, it is clear that the awareness of being has a certain liberating power, for it raises consciousness to the level of ultimate question, thereby giving a sense of relativity and a critical awareness of the finite. Thus it frees the mind to see symbols as symbols, to see them as pointing beyond themselves, yet as participating in that to which they point. The need to become liberated to see symbols as symbols can hardly be overestimated. Unless we achieve this inner freedom we remain in a state of childish literalism, blindly accepting or rejecting "doctrines" of which we have no real understanding.

2.6 The Problem of the Theology of Hope

I am not suggesting that in order to keep a living awareness of being we should regress to scholasticism. It is not a question of moving back but of living consciously now. Yet obviously there are problems. There has been a need for a "dehellenizing" of theology and there is also a need for a theology of hope in our time. The point is not to take an attitude of rejection toward what is valid in these movements, but rather to assume a critical attitude and to seek to discover whether the genuine insight that is there is indeed hopelessly irreconcilable with ontological thought.

The most evident difficulty lies in the rejection of the mysticism of being by the theologians of hope. We have seen the reason for this, namely that it would seem to put an end to the historic mediation of the Christ event. Briefly, it appears to be non-historical and to prevent men from taking history seriously. Thus it is claimed that the God of the exodus and the resurrection "is" not eternal presence, but promises his presence to him who follows the path on which he is sent into the future.[10] It is maintained that the present of the coming Parousia of God and of Christ does not translate us out of time, nor does it bring time to a standstill, but it opens the way for time and sets history in motion.[11]

Indeed, it is true that the church and its theologians have been guilty of creating an attitude of "otherworldliness," that is, of inauthentically translating us out of time. Indeed, the objection of modern atheists to a large extent center around this problem of unrealistic detachment from the political and social problems of the world. They rightly point out that the church has been so detached from these problems that it has tended not only to lag behind in the task of social reform, but even to be a serious obstacle to progress. Its theologians and preachers have promoted a privatized religion, according to which the individual prays, listens to sermons, receives the sacraments, and tries to "save his soul." Of course, alleviating the sufferings of individuals rather than in the sense of removing or transforming the powers that oppress them. The theology of hope has been in part a healthy reaction against this kind of inauthentic "timelessness" and this one-sided individualism which encourages "saving my soul" while remaining insensitive to social injustice. It stresses instead an ideal of Christian hope which is creative, realistic, political, and revolutionary. From the theology of hope we have received badly needed encouragement to rejoice in movement and in history, reaching

---

[10] Moltmann, *Theology of Hope*, 30.   [11] Ibid., 31.

out toward a "new creation" while bearing "the cross the present."

However, it is important to reflect upon the fact that in order to be truly aware of social, economic, and political realities we must rediscover a true inwardness. Pragmatism and politics are not enough. We must become aware of the mystery of the self as well as of the mystery of the community, which is to say, we must become aware of the mystery of being. Whereas the theologians of hope speak frequently of the cross and resurrection, we should recognize the possibility that awareness of their powerful symbolic meaning can hardly be sustained without an awareness of being. Should the theology of hope, then, as it has been developed thus far, be considered an unmixed blessing? I think that the answer to this question will have to be negative. The hope-ers have rejected not merely the idea of a "supreme being," which is indeed a caricature. They would also have us turn away from the experience of the ground of being, preferring rather to speak of a "God of the future" or a "God of promise." We should ask what meaning content there is in such an expression and to what human experience it can possibly correspond.

We should ask how we are to conceive of a "God before us" unless there is a present disclosure upon which such intimations of the future can be based. It is not enough to speak of God's promises without raising the question of the God who promises. It would seem reasonable, then, to think that the basis for even the most modest leap of faith in a "God before us" would be divine reality which is now, and which is somehow manifested to us now. It is helpful to stress that Christianity is an eschatological religion, but we are left with the nagging question of what may be the criterion for our hope. Moreover, if we do not wish to settle for some anthropomorphic image of "the divine promiser" it seems reasonable at least to consider the possibility that it would be appropriate to speak of this reality as the ground of being. The fact that this possibility is so easily dismissed lends support to the suspicion that there is a bias which simply blots it out.

The presence of such a bias in the theology of hope is linked with the desire to de-hellenize Christianity and to pursue instead a future-oriented, biblical outlook. It is, of course, a commonly accepted thesis that the hellenization of Christianity has had paralyzing consequences. I do not think that there is any reason to dispute this. Moreover, it is a relief, perhaps a source of exhilaration, to speak of a God of the future after centuries of stagnation under the image of the supreme being. However, it is important to ask whether perhaps we are being dazzled by future-talk which may be combined with a sort of "bibliolatry" – dazzled to such an extent that we no longer recognize the living values that have come to us from the Greeks. Some thinkers have suggested that we need more religion and less Christianity. That is, there is a very real possibility of a kind of fixation upon the bible, which can be accompanied by narrowness of vision and lack of openness to a more universal form of religious experience.

It would appear that the theology of hope as it is usually formulated tends to neglect a dimension of religious experience which is at the core not only of Christianity, but perhaps also of other religions. I refer to the immediate experience of something ultimate in value and meaning. While the scholastics spoke of "being-itself," Spinoza called his a prior "universal substance." For James it was "beyond subjectivity and objectivity." Jaspers called it "the Encompassing." In all of these cases, although the forms of the intuitive awareness may have varied, there has been some sense of presence and immediacy. Indeed, it would seem to be by reason of such intuitions that authentic faith and theology come into existence. As Jaspers remarks, in writing of the Encompassing, if awareness of the deep ground is missing, then we have nothing but the "random swirling of dead husks of words."

We have seen that the dimension of religious experience which the theology of hope generally tends not to recognize as valid is often expressed in ontological, Hellenic terms. It is an apparent conflict between ontological consciousness and historical consciousness. However, the use of terms which were employed by the Greeks need not be paralyzing. The fact that a theologian abundantly uses the term "being" reveals an ontological emphasis. However, must this mean that he has a "static" notion of God or that to speak of divine reality as ground of being, power of being, or being-itself is to be closed to the future. In fact, might not quite the opposite be true? Might it not even be the case that this manner of conceptualizing enables one to be open to the future? These are questions which we should now begin to explore.

I would suggest that the apparent conflict between the ontological consciousness and the historical consciousness is indeed only apparent. Insofar as it sees no possible reconciliation, the theology of hope as it has been developed thus far, cannot be judged to be an unmixed blessing. The hope-ers have blocked off a dimension of religious experience which many consider to be essential.

The fact that openness to the future is possible for an ontological theology is suggested even by consideration of the problem of communication. As the "noospheric net" of this planet tightens, as communication between Christians and the increasing legion of non-Christians becomes more and more imperative, it becomes ever more evident that we must break out of the bonds of our exclusiveness, and that we must become able to speak a language that can be meaningful to those who are not attuned to "the biblical message." The experiences of man's threatened existence and of the anxieties that accompany finitude and the threat of non-being is universal. By contrast, belief in "the divine promise" or in the Resurrection of Jesus is by no means as universal. From the point of view, then, of one who would look to future modes of communication with those outside orthodox Christianity – which means increasing multitudes of the radical young – the ontological approach to religious experience and values would seem to have more immediate possibilities.

Moreover, in an ontologically oriented theology, openness to the future as well as to the present is implied in the awareness of the ground and power of being. All finite beings participate in this power; otherwise they would be swallowed by non-being. It is the power of being that infinitely resists non-being, sustaining everything that is, and making possible the courage we need to exist now and move into the future.

If, as is the case with the theology of hope as presently formulated, openness to the future is stressed without a corresponding emphasis upon the presence of divine power, is there a possibility of serious distortion is [sic] one's theological vision? I have already suggested that this may be the case. I do not mean to imply that the only conceivable solution will be a return to Greek conceptualizations of this presence, although I do not see the necessity to reject a particular terminology simply because it was also used by the Greeks. Indeed, a philosophical basis for the theology of hope might well be developed along a variety of lines, such as those suggested in the writings of Teilhard de Chardin or in the process philosophy of Whitehead. In any case the problem is to reach for a more truly ecumenical (or post-ecumenical), universal, and authentic ground for hope. The "God before us" should be envisioned as the completion, not the rejection, of the God within us.

There is another and closely interrelated difficulty with the theology of hope as currently expressed. It has been suggested by one of its critics that its moving spring is not theology at all, but rather cultural pressure arising from a new stage of science, technology, and international politics.[12] Perhaps the criticism is an exaggeration. Nevertheless, it raises an important question: Might we not be tempted to settle for a theology which can too easily be made to serve technical ideologies? It would be well to listen to the warnings of those who remind us of the easy assimilation to which the major religious congregations have yielded in their growing desire to seem progressive.[13] We should also remember Marcus's warning that we live in a society in which, "Everything

---

[12] Cf. Novak, *Radical Politics*, 110n.
[13] For example, Theodore Roszak, *The Making of a Counter Culture* (New York, Doubleday and Co., 1969), 196.

can be co-opted, everything can be digested." Recognizing this situation, we should be wary of too facile discussions of political theology and theology of revolution. Indeed, mere social and political revolution, even if it is aimed against alienating structures and even if it is inspired by a theology of hope, could well result only in "more of the same" after the cards have been reshuffled. We should therefore turn our attention to the problems of the deepest meaning of revolution.

The deep dimensions of the revolution that are needed have been guessed by the most perceptive of the radical young, who see that theirs is not primarily a social but a psychic task. What these perceptive young – and others who share their vision – are working toward is not merely external change, nor ideological change, but a transformation of consciousness. They believe that they must give priority to the task of remodeling themselves, over and above the task of remodeling institutions.

If theology is to be of real help to those in quest of psychic revolution, or transformation of consciousness, it must return always to the deep intuitions out of which it receives its life. It must return to awareness of the divine presence in nature and in human life. Without this awareness, we are doomed to a kind of inauthenticity and may easily be exploited by a society which has generated false needs and a false consciousness.

2.7 Courage and Hope

We are driven back to our problem: Where can we find the key to reconciliation between the modern eschatological consciousness – the consciousness of moving into the future, while creating history, and the ontological awareness which is so essential to deep psychic revolution? Must those who are conscious of the values of both worlds live in a kind of schizoid situation, hoping that eventually someone will offer them conceptual tools for handling the problem of occupying two mental universes at the same time? Indeed, there is no easy solution. Some of us – and an increasing number of our contemporaries – are intensely caught up in the world of movement and of change. We seem to be hurled forward at a fantastic speed and we seem to be participating in the creation of this movement in history. At the same time, we can glimpse the greatness of Parmenides' vision of being. There is that which transcends history and yet which makes historic process possible.

I would not suggest that there is an infallible theological system which can solve this dilemma. However, there is a seminal idea which can speak very profoundly to our current dilemma – a key concept which can unlock the door between those two apparently sealed off rooms of the modern religious consciousness – the room labeled "being" and the room labeled "history." I refer to the idea of existential courage, an idea developed at length and with powerful persuasiveness by one of this century's great systematic theologians, Paul Tillich.

Existential courage, the courage to be, is essentially self-affirmation in the face of the threat of non-being. This should not be confused with the virtue of fortitude, the military virtue of courage praised by the Greeks. The latter – the soldier's courage – has as its task the overcoming of fear, which has a definite object. By contrast, the courage to be reaches out to conquer existential anxiety, which is particularly difficult to handle and to face because it has no definite object. Indeed, the only way in which one could possibly speak of an "object" of existential anxiety would be to say that it is non-being. The abyss of non-being is most threatening to all human beings, although there are different degrees of consciousness of this.

"Non-being" may at first seem a difficult concept to handle. Yet it signifies an experience – or rather experiences – with which we are all familiar. We may consider it as it manifests itself on different levels. There is, first of all, the non-being of fate and death, which means the inescapable cutting off of life's drive toward infinity. Secondly, there is the non-being of guilt and condemnation, which involves the awareness that I am not what I should be; it is moral non-being. In the third place, there is the non-being of meaninglessness – the absence of clear-cut, ultimate answers. All of these "forms" of non-being give rise to existential anxiety. This anxiety is not in itself abnormal. In fact, it belongs to the universal human condition of being finite and aware of this finitude.

What matters is the manner in which we cope with this anxiety. Basically, there are two directions in which we can move. One is pathological; that is, it is possible to shrink one's being in the face of the threat of non-being. The other direction is that of authentic courage; that is, we can struggle to affirm our being over against the threat of non-being.

I have already pointed out in chapter one that this existential courage is part of faith. What we now have to see is the complexity of this courage and what it reveals about being. For the courage to be is the key to the ground of our being and therefore also to the ground of our hope.

The problem of self-affirmation in the face of non-being is complex because there are of necessity two sides to this self-affirmation – individualization and participation. That is, it is necessary to affirm oneself as a self and as a part. It is essential to affirm oneself as a self, as an individual, in the face of the threat of absorption into a larger whole or into a process. The courage of individualization, then, is indispensable. On the other hand, it is equally important to participate consciously and actively in the universe. Although we normally think of this participation first of all on the level of communal action, it is important to analyze it more profoundly. Man is by his nature and situation a part of the universe and his interaction with wider and deeper reality is not only on the level of social activism. Thus the scholar who spends many lonely hours in his library may be participating in his wider environment more authentically than many an activist. So too the contemplative who strives for union with transcendent reality, even though he may appear isolated, is in fact living a life of deep communion and active participation.

There are, then, two sides to existential courage. Our need is for both modes of self-affirmation and there is a constant dialectic between these modes in human history. The dynamics of the living out of existential courage constitute human history and this process of self-affirmation, if it is fully lived out, reveals to the individual the fact that the ground of being is indeed power of being – that it is dynamic. All finite beings participate in this: otherwise they would be swallowed by non-being. It is the power of being that infinitely resists non-being, sustaining everything that is, and making possible ultimate courage which is based upon participation in the ultimate power of being.

2.8 Courage and the God-above-God

Recognition of the infinite of the power of being, which calls us forth into our future of self-actualization, both as a self and as a part, is a source of liberation from all tendencies to idolatry. When it is known experientially that God is unknown, that is, that he is not containable in any concept, such as that of the supreme being, and when it is recognized that he transcends all symbolization, then we are free to break the bonds that tied us to infantile images of God. This recognition of God's infinity is not achieved merely through intellectual games, but through the courage which enables us to progress in the direction of absolute faith. This absolute faith encompasses both the Protestant principle and the Catholic substance.

We have seen that existential courage involves, first of all, self-affirmation as a self. This implies that one must struggle for autonomy, that is, for authenticity and for fidelity to the rational principle within, even if this means painful clashes with external authorities, civil or ecclesiastical. Self-affirmation as a self implies fidelity to the Protestant principle. That is, courage demands that we be constantly ready to criticize established laws, doctrines, and practices and that we be ready for the emergence of new forms.

On the other hand, the courage to be also involves self-affirmation as a part. This means that we should be faithful to the values which are preserved – even though in a distorted fashion – in a heteronomous situation. Thus, the voice of tradition, the body of symbols, doctrines and structures we have inherited should be held in the esteem they deserve. This side of courage – self-affirmation as a part – demands some kind of fidelity to the Catholic substance (which is not equivalent to saying that it demands officially recognized membership in the Catholic church). The courage to be as a part demands that we continue to recognize whatever there is of value in the tradition which formed us and which formed the Christian community, while participating in the process of developing that tradition.

By our sustained efforts to affirm and grow in being as a self and as a part we can move toward a theonomous situation, in which autonomous reason will be united with its own depth. We can move in the direction of a situation in which external forms of government, doctrine, and worship correspond to the authentic needs of individuals. However, existential courage will also enable us to face the fact that a lasting situation of perfect harmony is not man's lot in this world. Struggle and growth are unceasing, and the power of being sustains us and propels us onward in this process.

The ontological approach to God, then, need not be static. If we grasp that the courage to be is the key to the power and ground of being, we are forced to take history seriously and to be creative participators in it. The idea of existential courage gives a philosophical basis for historical consciousness and for hope, for it implies the participation of finite being in the power of being, a power that is ever fresh and active and that always makes new demands for the fulfillment of meaning.

2.9 The Problem of Hypostasizing the Future

It is important to listen to Marxist criticism of the Christian God. Ernest Bloch, for example, rejects the common Christian propensity to hypostasize the future into an existent God. He is afraid of nihilism, but he wants to guard unconditional openness to the future by rejecting images and refusing to give it content. In order to resolve the dilemma of avoiding nihilism on the one hand and hypostatization or personification of the future on the other hand, he speaks of the future as a kind of "vacuum" which exerts a magnetic pull upon man and the cosmos.[14] This image for the future is interesting, but it is only dubiously successful. The question we should ask is whether this dilemma is necessary at all. For when God is understood as the ground and power of being, the reality pointed to by these expressions is precisely not a hypostatization of the future or of anything at all. We are not speaking of "a divine person" or of "the supreme being." These notions are indeed hypostatizations and should be rejected as such. They can point only to the God who is doomed to disappear when theism is transcended by existential courage. It is important to be

---

[14] Cf. Ernest Bloch, *Man on His Own*, trans. E. B. Ashton (New York: Herder & Herder, 1970).

critical of the various representations of the God of theism, including the God who seemingly is encountered in a person to person relationship, and therefore would be finite, and the God whose existence can be "proved," and who therefore also would be finite. These forms of theism are overcome in the experience of absolute faith, which contains existential courage. As we have seen, this courage has revealing power and is the key to being-itself.

It is when "God" has disappeared in the anxiety of doubt and when one has been grasped by the power of being-itself that the sort of dilemma expressed by Bloch is transcended. Transcending traditional theism also means transcending the dilemma of this troubled atheist. It is important to note, moreover, that Bloch is not the only puzzled Marxist to appear on the scene in recent years. The French Marxist theoretician, Roger Garoudy, has also expressed his rejection of the Christian God in similar terms.[15]

I am not suggesting, of course, that Marxist criticism should be taken as an absolute criterion for judging statements about God. Such criticism is often biased and short-sighted. Moreover, the adequate goal of the theological enterprise could hardly be adjustment or choice of language for the sake of pleasing Marxists, however desirable intellectual cooperation with them may be. The point is, however, that insofar as criticism has validity, whether its source be inside or outside the Christian community, it should be listened to, not merely in order to clear lines of communication but also as a means of purifying one's own

[15] Cf. Roger Garoudy, *From Anathema to Dialogue*, trans. Luke O'Neill (New York: Herder & Herder, 1966), 94–95.

knowledge and that of the community. Since conscious-ness never perfectly corresponds to being, there is always the possibility of learning from "the other," no matter how diverse the starting points may seem to be.

It would appear that one of the ironies in the present theological situation lies in the fact that in the writings of the theologians of hope, who are on the whole greatly concerned with the Christian–Marxist dialogue, there can be detected an unwitting vulnerability to the kind of criticism leveled by Bloch and Garoudy. Despite all the talk of the future, or rather in the course of it, the theology of hope is inclined to repeated use of expres-sions such as "God's promise," which call forth images of "a divine person." The frequent use of such an expres-sion as "God before us" also is suggestive of that hypos-tatization of the future which is dreaded and feared by humanists who look to a completely open and free future. This is not to say that anthropomorphic and hypostatization are intended by the advocates of the theology of hope. The fact is, however, that their lan-guage is strongly biblical and hence often comes through as anthropomorphic. Since there is no developed ontol-ogy to balance these tendencies in the theology of hope, it appears to fortify the dilemma of an Ernest Bloch – and of many intellectually sophisticated Christians – into an insuperable problem.

The problem of the tension between biblical religion and ontology is by no means new. What I am suggesting is that recent theological thought has, on the whole, failed to keep the tension alive, dismissing too easily the onto-logical dimension of human experience and reflection. There has been a tendency to forsake an essential dimension of the Christian heritage – to brand as "Hellenic" a mode of thinking about man and God which is authentically human because it is born out of man's existential situation.

An authentic theology should not be irreconcilably opposed to ontology. Perhaps, in order to realize this we shall have to free ourselves from the false consciousness and false desires imposed upon us by technological society. In order to give substance to our hope we need to turn inward again to the deep roots in consciousness, experience, and imagination from which the awareness of being secretly grows. In this awareness lies our ground for hope that what is authentic in the Catholic substance will be reborn in our time.

Chapter 3

The Fall: False Consciousness

∼

In order to find genuine inwardness, to find ourselves, and to find the deep source of the Catholic substance and of the Protestant principle, we have to fight off the false consciousness imposed upon us by our culture. Although the problem thrusts itself upon us in a particularly acute way in a technological society, in some sense it has been with us since the dawn of human consciousness, at last of human consciousness that would be recognizable as such. There are indeed specific aspects of alienation that face us in our own time. These I will discuss later. First let us consider the universal problem of the Fall.

3.1 The Problem of Original Sin

There is a great deal of resistance among modern thinkers to the idea of original sin. When Teilhard de Chardin wrote that original sin, as still imaginatively presented today, is the tight collar that strangles our minds and our hearts, he was reflecting the sentiments of thousands, perhaps millions, of Christians, and his criticism struck a responsive chord in the minds of many Marxists as well.[1] I do not believe that Teilhard was unaware of the problem

---

[1] Roger Garoudy discusses Teilhard's views on original sin. *From Anathema to Dialogue*, trans. Luke O'Neill (New York: Herder & Herder, 1966), 49–50.

of alienation, which is so poignantly represented in the myth of the Fall. Rather, his antagonism is toward the doctrine of original sin as traditionally presented because this keeps us from fully living out Christianity, intellectually and spiritually. It strangles history, making us past-oriented. The doctrine makes it seem that the best has already been: paradise is in the past. Moreover, theologically it throws us back into a world of reparation and of expiation. The traditional presentation comes through as an attempt to explain evil in a static universe, as though all the evil we experience now could be explained by one event in the past – by an initial sin. What thinkers such as Teilhard de Chardin oppose, then, are the life-defeating implications of the traditional doctrine of original sin.

Other critics of the tradition – particularly those who have totally divorced themselves from it – are even more severe. Some suggest that the very idea of original sin as implying some notion of a blemish in nature tends to develop a sense of guilt without responsibility. What this means is that people are conditioned to think that moral evil is the structure of the human situation as such, rather than to think of it as an alterable – at least partially alterable – quality of their living and acting in concrete circumstances and as a characteristic of the institutions they create.[2] This conditioning induces an attitude of negativity. That is, there is a pervasive guilt-feeling which is conceptualized or imagined as a stain which can only be disposed of by expiation, and there is induced an attitude

---

[2] For an interesting analysis of this position, see Jean Lacroix, *The Meaning of Modern Atheism* (Dublin: Gill & Son, 1965), 64–92.

which condemns life and its instinctive joys. The critics claim, moreover, that this refusal of life is experienced as frustration which becomes self-accusation and aggression against the self. Logically, this would appear to lead to self-annihilation. However, what usually happens is that it is projected in the form of aggression against others and thus becomes bearable. In this way, the self-hatred which has been encouraged by Christianity becomes a perversion of the basic desire and need to communicate with others. Ironically, the attempt at communication becomes destructive and self-degrading. It is clear, then, that when the doctrine of original sin is viewed in this perspective it can hardly be understood as anything but a source of animosity and alienation in society. The traditional doctrine thus appears to be a source of victimization of those regarded as "the others." It appears to be a cause of hatred, discrimination, and even of war.

The more tolerant of secular humanists, however, do not dismiss Christianity as worthless simply because of the inadequacy of some of its formulations. Roger Garoudy, for example, has insisted that religion cannot be considered solely in terms of alienation, as some Marxists would see it. Rather, alienation is in the answers but not in the questions.[3] That is, he recognizes that the questions religion raises such as the question of alienation itself, mythologically described as the Fall, are valid and universal human questions. Indeed, we should and must ask why we are as we are. The problem is that the religions, starting from a real need, transformed into answers that which really pertained to the order of questions.[4]

---

[3] Garoudy, *From Anathema to Dialogue*, 89.   [4] Ibid., 90.

In order to grasp the nature of this procedure of transforming valid and authentic questions into authentic "answers" it is helpful to look at a concrete example of the process in the writings of a traditional theologian. As an example, it is interesting to examine the presentation of the problem of the Fall in the writings of Thomas Aquinas, whose doctrine became officially recognized Catholic teaching. It may well be difficult for the modern reader to take his explanation seriously, but it is important to recognize that it has been taken with the utmost seriousness by the Catholic church for hundreds of years. Indeed, it has to a large extent shaped the religious climate in which we have lived – a climate which has been dominated by the themes of reparation and expiation.

Thomas's conception of the Fall, which he understood very literally and as historical fact, should be seen in relation to his understanding of man's original state. Of course, he quite literally believed that there was a first couple, Adam and Eve. He taught literally that the first woman came from the rib of the first man and that they lived together in paradise. The first couple supposedly had supernatural grace and all of the virtues, together with the preternatural gifts such as bodily immortality. Paradise was understood to be a corporeal place.[5]

Although it would seem incredible that such gifted creatures would want to sin, Thomas (and the whole tradition) taught, of course, that they did, and that in so doing they sinned for all of us. That is, the first sin of the first parent (it is Thomas's opinion that Adam alone was the transmitter) is, according to that theologian,

---

[5] Aquinas, *Summa Theologiae*, I, QQ.90–102.

contracted by all of us "by way of origin." Thomas had some difficulty explaining how this transmission comes about. He excludes such explanations as analogies with the transmission of physical defects – as a gouty father might produce a gouty son – and offers his own original elucidation which might be just as baffling to most contemporary minds. His argument runs as follows: The multitude of men born of Adam can be considered as members of one body. Now the action of any member of the body, of the hand, for instance, is voluntary not by the will of that one member but rather by the will of the soul, which is the first mover of the members. Thomas then concludes by way of analogy that the disorder which is in the man born of Adam is voluntary not by his own will, but by the will of his first parent who, by the movement of generation, moves all who originate from him, even as the soul's will moves all the members of the body of their actions.[6] As for the nature of original sin: it is construed as a habit, that is, as an inordinate disposition of the soul,[7] found equally in all men,[8] and infecting especially the generative power, the concupiscible faculty, and the sense of touch.[9]

However ingenious and reasonable all of this may have appeared to the medieval mind, and perhaps even to many theologians just a few decades ago, it hardly rings true to the contemporary consciousness. Regarding the explanation of the transmission of original sin, one is puzzled to know how Thomas could have thought he was solving anything at all. Most thinkers, of course, would be thrown

---

[6] Ibid., I–II, Q.81, A.1.   [7] Ibid.   [8] Ibid., I–II, Q.82, A.4.
[9] Ibid.

off by the idea that there was "one man" in the first place, and it seems absurd to think that – even if there were one first father – we could somehow be "moved" now by him. Moreover, the notion that some of our powers – particularly those associated with reproduction – which have been "infected" smacks of the antisexuality embedded in the Christian tradition which contemporary Christians are trying to overcome.

Most striking, perhaps, is simply the air of improbability and of unreality which is attached to such theological doctrines. We feel that we live in an entirely different intellectual universe, even if such religious beliefs, or at least watered down versions of them, may have colored the intellectual formation of our childhood. We feel curiously disoriented, and yet there is a haunting air of familiarity in the language.

I have suggested the reason for this disorientation, namely, that theology has attempted to transform a natural and authentic question into an "answer," which, of course, is inevitably inadequate and inauthentic. Thus the universal sense of alienation, which was expressed poignantly in the myth of the Fall, has been given a pseudo-historical "explanation" which in fact explains nothing but merely re-phrases the question. The mistake, then, lies in taking the myth as a solution to the problem rather than as an expression of the baffling mystery of human existence.

3.2 The Transition in Modern Consciousness

We may well ask why it is that we feel disoriented over this use of myth as explanation now, in this age, whereas our ancestors, even the learned among them, seemed not to be troubled by it. It seems reasonable to infer that there has occurred in recent times a remarkable transition in consciousness.

Some look upon this transition rather negatively. One scholar, for example, describes what has happened in the modern consciousness as a "new Fall of man" – meaning that "non-religious man" has lost the capacity to live religion consciously, and hence to understand and assume it. He believes that religion and mythology for modern man have become eclipsed in the darkness of the unconscious. The assumption is that for most moderns the religious sense has been forgotten.[10]

This interpretation of what is going on in the modern consciousness however, is open to challenge. Is it necessary to conclude that modern man, because he cannot accept myths as answers, should be labeled irreligious? It is certainly not the case that inability to accept traditional explanations means that the religious sense is dead. Of course, it may appear to be dead if no representation of explanation that is acceptable to the modern mind is at hand.

In the case of the story of the Fall, it may well be that the symbols contained therein really are not dead for large segments of humanity, even for highly intellectual and forward looking persons. It may be that these symbols simply are not acceptable as traditionally and popularly presented and "explained." It may be that it is the theology of original sin, that is, the cluster of conceptualizations that

---

[10]   Cf. Mircea Eliade, *The Sacred and the Profane* (New York: Harper & Row, 1961), 213.

89

have developed around the myth, more than the myth itself, (although the contents of the latter do present inherent difficulties) which have repelled so many of our contemporaries. For this reason, it is important to be overly susceptible to the attempts of theologians such as Rudolf Bultmann who would demythologize Christianity. On the grounds that modern man's consciousness has been influenced and shaped by the development of science, Bultmann concluded that mythological thinking is obsolete. However, as his famous debate with the existentialist philosopher Karl Jaspers has revealed, not all radical thinkers agree. Indeed, it was not only the fundamentalists and traditionalists who opposed Bultmann. Thinkers far more radical than himself were quick to perceive the weakness of his conception of religion without myth. Jaspers protested that our life would be wretched and lacking in expressiveness if the language of myth were no longer valid, and that to fill mythical forms with banal content is to commit an unpardonable error. The splendor and wonder of the mythical vision is to be purified but must not be abolished.[11]

Some might think that the only alternative to Bultmann's demythologizing is a kind of hyper-orthodox fundamentalism. This is by no means the case. The real problem is that Bultmann's approach is not radical enough. "Demythologization," in the sense of doing away with religious myth while saving some hard core of literal truth, is alien to profound religious awareness and to the authentic theological and philosophical thought which

---

[11] Cf. Karl Jaspers and Rudolf Bultmann, *Myth and Christianity* (New York: Noonday Press, 1958), 16.

grows from this awareness. It loses sight of the fact that "objectivity" alone is insufficient for the human mind. Mythical thinking is not a thing of the past but characterizes man in every age. It is the language of a reality that is not empirical but existential. Indeed, the authentic task of theology is not to demythologize, but to recover mythical thought and to appropriate its contents, which bring us closer to the imageless transcendence which no myth can fully express.[12]

I would suggest, then, that the transition experienced in modern consciousness in regard to the myth of the Fall is not at all a need to do away with religious myth, but rather it is a felt need to overcome the sterile theologizing which has choked the myth's power to express man's situation in relation to transcendent reality. It may well be that contemporary man has been so tormented by the reduction of his psychic life to measurable, empirical contents that he is more open than his forefathers to the recovery of mythical thinking in depth. This has mistakenly – and ironically – been misinterpreted as a need for demythologizing, that is, for even more empiricism and banal interpretation. Instead of experiencing a "new Fall," we may well be at the brink of a new resurrection.

3.3 Breaking the Myth of the Fall

We are faced with the problem of how to approach mythical thought when, as is the case with the story of the Fall, which is a myth about man's alienation, modes of transmission and explication have distorted the myth into

---

[12] Ibid., 17

a means of further alienation. The conception of "myth-breaking" is most helpful here: The point of breaking myths is not to destroy them, but the recognize that they are myths.[13] This recognition may in some cases come about painfully and slowly and it may involve a great deal of anxiety, particularly if social pressures are conducive to remaining in a state of childish literalism. The process of myth breaking should by no means be imagined as a simple "realization" that the beliefs of one's past were merely "fairy tales." On the contrary, what is involved is a deepening of faith. Thus, rather than calling the story of the Fall "just a myth," it would be more accurate to think of it as nothing less than a myth. The recognition of myths as myths – and of symbols as symbols – should mean that we become liberated to accept their full power of meaning, which is on a different level from the perception of historic fact. If, on the other hand, a mature person represses his questions and forces himself to stay back in a childish stage of literalism he is not only missing the profound meaning of the myth, but he is hurting his own intellectual and emotional integrity. This conscious literalism leads to the same banality of experience as does the effort to do away with myth. In both cases – that of the fundamentalist-traditionalist and that of the seemingly avant-garde demythologizer – the religious consciousness is short-changed. An "answer" is given before the deep question is allowed to develop.

Myths and symbols can indeed sometimes die. That is, they can recede into the unconscious of a large segment of

---

[13] Cf. Paul Tillich, *Systematic Theology*, 3 vols. (Chicago: University of Chicago Press, 1951–63), 1:50–54.

humanity if the cultural situation changes so radically that they can no longer be experienced as meaningful by a large number of persons. One might well ask, in view of the vehement modern reaction against the traditional doctrine of original sin, then, whether the myth of the Fall is a dead or a dying cluster of symbols. There are indications in modern experience that such should not be the case, at least, not in an unqualified sense. Indeed awareness of the problem of human alienation and estrangement probably has never been more profound or more widespread. The myth of the Fall is an expression of this awareness. Yet there is obviously something wrong. There is at the very least a problem of communication; the myth does not seem to speak to modern man.

The problem derives in part from a rigid adherence to the texts of Genesis. To mention one major difficulty, it can hardly be acceptable to the increasing number of liberated and self-actualizing women to be presented with an image of themselves as tempters responsible for the moral breakdown of the male. The texts are clearly andro-centric and do not correspond to the experience of the male–female relationship as it is emerging in the modern consciousness. To affirm, then, that the myth of the Fall might still be meaningful is not equivalent to affirming that, as it is expressed in Genesis, it can speak authentic-ally to the modern consciousness. Yet the essential image of a Fall from "paradise" may still speak poignantly to alienated modern man, if it can be understood in his future oriented perspective.

This leads us to the problem of theological formula-tions. The recognition of the myth as myth does not do away with the need for abstract theological thought, despite the fact that theology is constantly betraying myth by lapsing into literalism or succumbing to cultural limitations of time and place. On the contrary, the recognition of myth as myth demands a constant theological effort, a strenuous striving toward purification of the mythical content, so that this will not be grasped in a narrow or rigid way, restricting man's intellectual horizons and perhaps reinforcing prejudice. The problem of the need for theological reconceptualization is blatantly obvious in the case of the story of the Fall, which has been used for centuries as a support for antifeminine prejudice and for antisexual bias, and which has served as a source of anti-evolutionary bias. Abstract theological formulations are not to be disposed of, then. Rather, they have their source in mythical thought and in on-going human experience. Thus, they should operate to conserve that which is of value in tradition while at the same time criticizing and transforming that which is alienating and dehumanizing in the mythical content and in theological formulations of the past. That is, authentic theology is struggling in tensions between two poles – the heritage of the past and the insights of the present. It does not fail to recognize that the deep source of revelation manifests itself in the contemporary situation and demands openness to the radically new.

Despite all the needed efforts of theology to criticize and reinterpret the myth of the Fall, however, we are left with the impression that it conveys a basically negative evaluation of the human condition. Fundamentally, the story is expressing the tragedy of human existence; it is expressing man's awareness of his existential estrangement. The Fall is unavoidable in all our lives. Moreover, it is cosmic in its dimension implying that all of nature is somehow involved in the tragedy. Indeed, it expressed a universal quality of finite being. In classical theology, of course, the situation is not seen as hopefulness, for the divine response to the Fall is redemption through Christ – I shall discuss this in the next chapter. However, taken in itself, the myth does indeed communicate a negative estimation of man's situation and of that of all finite beings. On this point it is quite in harmony with much of contemporary experience and reflection on the human condition, and it shares in the incompleteness of such experience and reflection.

3.4 The Problem of the Contemporary Sense of Tragedy

Modern thinkers, non-Christian as well as Christian, convey, often poignantly, a sense of universal tragedy. When Albert Camus proclaimed that there is but one truly serous philosophical problem, namely suicide, he was too concerned only or primarily with physical suicide but rather he was interested chiefly in philosophical suicide. For Camus, the latter implied failing to face up to the inescapable absurdity of life and making a "leap of faith." This leap, in Camus' estimation, is an illegitimate act. Lashing out at Jaspers, for example, he claimed that without justification that philosopher suddenly asserts all at once the transcendent, the essence of experience, and the superhuman significance of life.[14] Kierkegaard

---

[14] Albert Camus, *The Myth of Sisyphus and Other Essays* (New York: Vintage Books, 1955), 24.

received similarly harsh treatment. Indeed, Camus regarded the sort of mystical thought which issues from such men as an almost intentional mutilation of the soul.[15] As for himself, he preferred to face and accept what he called "the absurd equation" between man's questioning mind and the world which does not provide the answers to these questions. Believing that it is suicidal to pretend that the answers are there, he refused to opt for this suicide, claiming that his reasoning wants to be faithful to the evidence of the absurd. Camus' hero is the absurd man, who is asked to "leap": religions, prophets, and gods are offered to him. But this is a temptation, and all he can reply is that he does not fully understand, and he does not want to do anything but what he fully understands. In other words, he wants to find out if it is possible to live without appeal.[16] Religious experience then, is rejected as debilitating.

A thinker such as Camus dismisses mystical experience with an ease that arouses suspicion. It may be that there is an admirable integrity in his thought, but it also may well be that his dismissal of the leap of faith is the result of a lack of important dimensions of perception in his own experience. Thus what would be a dishonest act for him might not be dishonest for a Tillich or a Jaspers. More than this, there seems to be something inauthentic about Camus' requirements. He wants "to fully understand." There is, however, an unfathomable distance between the "full understanding" of empirical knowledge and the gift of understanding which characterizes authentic religious experience. In the first case, there is a split between

---

[15] Ibid., 29.   [16] Ibid., 39.

subject and object, between the thinker and what he has in mind. In the second case, there is awareness of the deep ground which encompasses both subject and object, and awareness which cannot be reduced to the clarity which accompanies the split. Without this sense of the deep ground there is indeed an overwhelming experience of absurdity – "a result of withered leaves."[17]

I would suggest that the clarity demanded by Camus and others like him is the clarity characteristic of knowledge derived from the separation of subject and object. He gives no evidence (at least certainly not in this work) of perception of the deep ground of being. Yet it is just such awareness – which he claims to lack and which others affirm they have – which makes a leap of faith and of hope justifiable and authentically human. The consciousness of the absurd hero of Camus is so cut off from this deep ground that he hears only the dead rustle of withered leaves. It is true that insofar as this is the state of his consciousness there can be no legitimate leap of faith for him. The point I would make is that such a state is one of alienation, shared by all men at some periods of their lives. Indeed, it is what the story of the Fall is all about. Yet, we should ask whether a stubborn affirmation of the absurd, and a rejection of the experience which makes possible a sincere leap of faith, will lead any closer to authentic humanization than will the opposite form of rigidity. Indeed, there is every reason to be wary of the inauthentic leap of the "will to believe" what authorities proclaim as dogma. However, the opposite form of dogmatism does not lead us very far toward humanization either.

---

[17] Karl Jaspers's expression is apt. *Myth and Christianity*, 13.

The experience of non-being does not preclude the possibility of an awareness of the mystery of being. In fact, it implies such a possibility. If finite beings were not propelled toward self-affirmation by the power of being, there would be no experience of anguish and anxiety over non-being. A problem with the modern sense of the tragedy of human existence, then, is that it often offers a kind of short-sightedness as the only viable alternative to utopian and unrealistic pseudo-faith.

3.5 A Contemporary Psychological Approach to Alienation

A famous young British psychiatrist has warned of the mental sickness built into our society. So powerfully has he demonstrated his thesis that some of his threatened colleagues, who would advocate "adjustment" to our insane society, have labeled him a madman. This psychiatrist–philosopher, R. D. Laing, warns of the danger of social adaptation to a dysfunctional society. He logically points out that the perfectly adjusted bomber pilot may be a greater threat to species survival than the hospitalized schizophrenic who is deluded that the bomb is inside him.[18] In order to grasp the implications of Laing's approach, we should be aware of his distinction between "inner" and "outer." "Inner" includes all those realities that have no so-called external or objective presence – imagination, dreams, fantasies, trances – the realities of contemplative and meditative states. It also

---

[18] R. D. Laing, *The Politics of Experience* (New York: Ballantine Books, 1967), 120.

means our way of seeing the external world.[19] The problem is that we are socially conditioned to think of total immersion in outer space and time as normal and healthy. On the contrary, immersion in inner space and time tends to be seen as anti-social withdrawal, a deviation, invalid, and pathological, and in a sense discreditable.[20] Yet modern society is in fact starving for the inner, although it wants this presence in a "safe" way. This timidity is related to the fact that sanity today appears to rest very largely on a capacity to adapt to the external world, that is, the interpersonal world and the realm of human collectivities. This is disastrous because this external human world is almost totally estranged from the inner.

Laing believes that some can and must make a real break – a voyage to inner space. Rather than being what we need to be cured of, this voyage is itself a natural way of healing our own appalling state of alienation called normality.[21] In other periods, people intentionally embarked on this voyage, whereas in our civilization every effort is made to prevent people from making it. The irony is that this prevention of persons from overcoming their alienation and regaining awareness of the inner is done with the best of intentions, by friends, loved ones, and social manipulators such as psychiatrists. The struggle against the madness which is considered normal, then, is against great odds and is a lonely battle.

We have, then, a powerful affirmation from a practicing psychiatrist that the alienation which we sense so strongly and desire somehow to overcome is not fully understood when it is seen as the totally inescapable fate

---

[19] Ibid., 140.   [20] Ibid., 125.   [21] Ibid., 167.

of man. Rather, it is a sickness imposed by our social institutions in the name of health, sanity, adjustment, and religion. The Fall is a universal and age-old problem, and it is with us in a particularly acute form today. Yet, there is a possibility of struggle against it. If we are to move in the direction of inner space we must be prepared to take great risks. Yet it would seem that in no other way will we find again the living power out of which the symbols which constitute the Catholic substance can arise. However, our efforts to move in this direction will require a continual struggle against institutions that would resolutely deflect us from our path, including, of course, the institutional church itself.

Laing is, of course, not the first to speak of this inward journey. Probably the greatest groundbreaker in regard to this problem was Carl Jung. The question of whether Jung was completely "accurate" is not the point. The main point is that he did leave us clues which are important for understanding the nature of the battle against alienation. The goal which Jung proposed, for those who have approached the stage of strength and maturity necessary to reach for it, is a journey called individuation. In the course of this journey the individual confronts his "shadow," that is, the contents of his personal unconscious. He also confronts the archetypes of the collective unconsciousness, that is, the hereditary memories of the race as codified into symbols and preserved in all of us. Jung believed that this journey is possible only in the second half of life, when a certain degree of security has been attained. However, it may be that because of the conditions of affluence in Western society in recent years, and perhaps also because of the influence of electronics, significant numbers of the young may now be seeking individuation. This confrontation with the unconscious is the Jungian conception of the religious experience. Although he does not dogmatically deny that there may be other methods of explanation, as a psychologist, this is what he perceives happening. Noting the ambivalence of organized religion in relation to religious experience, he asserts that the former may help in sustaining some contact with the unconscious, but it may also work to prevent an original religious experience from occurring. There is, then, a kind of ambivalence in organized religion itself in regard to religious experience, an ambivalence which is reflected in the religious creeds. These are codified and dogmatized forms of original religious experience. The contents of the experience may become sanctified and usually congealed in a rigid and elaborate structure.[22] Thus organized religion with its creeds and dogmas can work in diverse and even opposite ways. For those who are too feeble to achieve an original religious experience these at least provide some channel to the unconscious. For those who are stronger, however, they can be a roadblock, providing just enough encounters with inner reality to take the edge of desire, while preventing deep, personal individuation. For this reason, Jung – writing a few decades ago – believed that Protestants are often in a sense in a better situation than Catholics, for if a Protestant survives the complete loss of his church and still remains a Protestant, that is, a man who is

---

[22] C. G. Jung, *Psychology and Religion* (New Haven, CT: Yale University Press, 1938), 6.

defenseless God is no longer shielded by walls or by communities, he has the unique spiritual chance of immediate religious experience.[23]

It should be noted, however, that Jung made this last-mentioned observation some decades ago, before the present wave of the Catholic crisis had loomed large on the horizon. It is conceivable, in fact probably, that in the present radically different situation, he would see the position of the Catholic very differently. Indeed, the contemporary Catholic, that is, one who truly has a contemporary consciousness, is experiencing a shaking of foundations, a breaking down of walls and communities, which is particularly shattering because nothing in his background has prepared him for it. His sense of alienation can be devastating. Yet he may, precisely because of his heritage of Catholic substance, be particularly open to authentic religious experience, to a genuinely personal encounter with the religious archetypes.

3.6 Organized Religion and Alienation

Organized religion, then, may work either in the direction of healing or of further alienation. At times, by its very corruption, it may drive individuals to seek their own religious authenticity. Moreover, there can be an ambiguity in this process, since the values and symbols which are personally reappropriated may well be similar to or the same as those insincerely and unconvincingly preached by

---

[23] Ibid., 62.

the official church itself. A contemporary priest-activist has described the experience of alienation endured by many American Catholics in relation to their church. Writing of Vietnam, he describes the feeling which some Americans have of impotence and cowardice, of complicity in unimaginable insane injustice, coupled with recognition of the incredible role of the Church in moralizing the whole procedure.[24] For those who have almost unbearable lucidity to recognize this legitimized insanity, the strain of breaking infantile forms of relationship to the institutional church and of criticizing it is difficult to say the least. Yet, those who share in this lucidity can help to liberate with the human consciousness the values and symbols which the church has "preached" but at the same time stifled. In so doing they can open the way toward individuation for themselves and others who have ears to hear them.

The ambivalence of organized religion in relation to alienation is reflected not only in connection with social issues such as the Vietnam war, but also in the seemingly more obscure and murky realm of symbols such as the Trinity. It is most striking that the latter is expressed in exclusively masculine terms. According to Jungian psychology the unconscious mind attempts to cope with this by transforming it into a quaternity. The fourth element of the quaternity (mandala) seems to be a murky symbolic mingling of evil, matter, and the feminine, all of which

---

[24] Philip Berrigan, "Blood, War, and Witness," in *American Catholic Exodus*, ed. John O'Connor (Washington, DC: Corpus Books, 1968), 7, 22.

have been in some way suppressed in Christian doctrine. Indeed, it is highly significant that although the mandala is an age-old, presumably prehistoric symbol, always associated with a world-creating deity, Jung found that people in Western society took it to symbolize themselves or rather something in themselves.[25]

The problem implied here has bothered many theologians. That is, modern man seems to have lost the sense of God's presence and immanence. In often used popular terminology, God has come to be identified with something "up there" or at least "out there." Of course, most educated people do not literally believe in a God who is literally "up there," but they do incline to accept (or reject) a God who is spiritually or metaphysically "out there."[26] The point is that the awareness of the divine presence is so buried in the unconscious and the term "God" is so linked to the idea of an outside entity that a potential or perhaps a real religious experience cannot even be recognized as such. There is an almost [systemic] blindness, which is the effect of the prejudice that the deity is outside man.[27]

The existence of this prejudice suggests that there is something deeply distorted in the Christian heritage. Moreover, it testifies to the profound alienation of modern man, who is like someone sitting on top of a volcano. It is as if conscious reason, unnaturally separated from the unconscious, were balanced precariously on the

---

[25] Jung, *Psychology and Religion*, 71.

[26] The whole problematic was popularized acutely by John A. T. Robinson, *Honest to God* (Philadelphia: Westminster Press, 1963).

[27] Jung, *Psychology and Religion*, 72.

hardened surface of the latter, rather than receiving life from it. Or, to look at the situation from a slightly different perspective, technical reason is dominating over ontological reason, causing religion to deteriorate into superstition.[28] Technical reason, when it is in this unnaturally dominant role, can either reject religion or else it can foolishly support it, for example with "proofs" for God's existence or with portrayals of God as "out there." And then, logically, it might turn upon such a God, rejecting him as irrelevant or perhaps as dead.

At first, perhaps, there would seem to be no connection between the church's inauthentic role of moralizing political and economic injustice on the one hand, and its support of the falsely "separate" God on the other. However, if we examine the situation more closely, we may discover that there are profound connections indeed. For it is the loss of the sense of God's immanence that paves the way for shallow moral judgements and which hinders insight into the complexities of one's situation. Unable to "cut through" to the significance of the barrage of data presented by the media, persons often turn for guidance to an external "authority" such as the church. That is, they accept a situation of heteronomy. If the leaders and theologians of the church have lost their sense of God's presence they will be inclined to support the existing political situation and to be assimilated into the prevailing cultural milieu, for they will have no inner resources to resist this. Ironically, then, the church which should be acting as a counter-balance to an alienating environment, supports that environment not only by its

---

[28] Cf. Paul Tillich, *Systematic Theology*, 1:74.

political pronouncements but also and more subtly by theological formulations which distract attention from the essential task of psychic revolution.

In the last chapter I pointed out that an increasing proportion of the perceptive young – and a small but significant number of their elders – are coming to the conclusion that building a good society is primarily a psychic task. The goal then becomes not a merely external change, but a direct attempt to uproot the sources of alienation within. This will mean that these revolutionaries will not turn the whole of their attention to specific social problems such as peace, poverty, and discrimination, although they may be very much concerned with these issues. The point is that they will not be primarily political activists. This will require patience and understanding, but it may be that this form of revolution will generate the visionary power needed to cope with these social problems in the future. At the moment, an increasing number are beginning to see the greatest urgency in achieving a new awareness of the self, of the other, and of the environment.

It is fascinating to observe that a large segment of the vanguard of this movement to overcome alienation through psychic revolution comes from the ranks of the middle-class young, who are conducting a politics of consciousness and who are one of the few forces of real dissent. This poses a major problem, for there is a need of assistance from mature thinkers so that the youthful bearers of the counterculture can learn to distinguish between superstition and mysticism, between what is shallow and what is deep. Here is a field in which the advocates of a psychic revolution in the church can exercise their prophetic ministry, giving support to the counter-culture and helping its creators to discover where its deep roots can derive sustenance from religious tradition. Indeed, a profound form of participation is being sought, an opening to the ultimate ground of existence.[29] This deep mode of participation, reaching far beyond the political plane, has been the driving force of theological thought from the beginning.

This is not to say, of course, that all theologians are or ever have been revolutionaries. The majority, at least within the Christian tradition, have been eminently safe, "sane," and hyper-rational. That is, they have followed the Apollonian way. However, there is also another way in which some theologians (and prophets and charismatics) have approached the religious questions, and this is the Dionysian way.[30] Whereas the former method stresses prudence, the latter emphasizes existential daring and creativity. The Dionysian way dares the extreme and thus leads to a form of consciousness which is alien to the law-abiding and moderate quality of the Apollonian mentality. The Dionysian way exalts ecstasy, freedom, and feeling. It rejects the security of inherited social and psychological

---

[29] Cf. Theodore Roszak, *The Making of a Counter Culture* (New York, Doubleday and Co., 1969), 265: "It is, at least, reality itself that must be participated in, must be seen, touched, breathed with the conviction that here is the ultimate ground of our existence, available to all, capable of ennobling by its majesty the life of every man who opens himself. It is participation of this order – experiential and not merely political – that alone can guarantee the dignity and autonomy of the individual citizen."

[30] For a good descriptive analysis of the difference in approaches, see Sam Keen, "Manifesto for a Dionysia Theology," in *Transcendence*, ed. Herbert W. Richardson and Donald R. Cutlery (Boston: Beacon Press, 1969), 31–52.

patterns and hence implies a sort of "madness" by the standards of repressive and manipulative Western culture. By the same token it implies insight and participation in reality not ordinarily attained in that culture and not encouraged by Apollonian theology.

The need for theologians and ministers of the church who are attuned to the Dionysian way has never been more acute. The Fall to false consciousness is a fact of our existence perennially, but it is particularly a fact of life in Western technological culture. Since the young have assumed leadership in searching out ways toward creation of a culture which will oppose and transcend the prevailing one, the mature, theologically trained persons who are still spiritually alive owe them the help and support and, at times, the guidance they will need for the carrying out of their enormous task.

3.7 The Fall and Transcendence

The myth of a paradise lost irritates contemporary man who wants to experience himself as moving forward, or, in Teilhard's sense, upward-forward, that is, toward transcendence through commitment in this world. This is eminently understandable. Indeed, there is a sense in which the myth inevitably fails; it is impossible to grasp with satisfying logic. Man must actualize himself; this is his destiny. Yet he must do so by free acts. Moreover, this glorious destiny means the loss of dreaming innocence. The myth portrays paradise as existing in the past. Yet, it would seem to be closer to our self-understanding to envision that paradise is really a projection of the future. We feel betrayed; therefore, mythically we speak of a loss.

Yet, through our commitment we can move in the direction of overcoming that betrayal. The Fall has been conceptualized as "downward." Probably it should be visualized as a fall upward. That is, what we experience as a loss is also a dream for the future which propels us onward and upward. What seemed to be the end was in fact the beginning. The sense of alienation was and continues to be a source of growth toward integration and yet further integration.

It may well be true that modern man is experiencing a "new Fall." However, this may have a positive as well as negative meaning. A new awareness of the split from inner space is accompanied by a desire for a voyage deeper into inner space. The sense of the breakdown of the symbols of the Catholic substance may be a necessary prelude to the rediscovery of the world of myth and symbol. As the maya created by science becomes more intolerable, the search within becomes more imperative.

Having learned from our calamatrous idolatry, we must be ready for a new assimilation of the Protestant principle. Warned by our past excesses we may reach for a qualitatively new and more detached form of re-mythologizing. In a sense, it doesn't matter that we know we will fall again. In fact, this knowledge can even be an incentive: we know that we don't have to reach for perfection, that this is in fact impossible, and so we are liberated to do that which is within our grasp. Of course, the delusion that false consciousness is a thing of the past may well be a recurring temptation. It is essential to remember that having learned from past mistakes is no guarantee that we will not fall into new ones.

The specific forms of alienation that haunt us in technocracy are obvious. There is the pseudo-participation – in work, "social life," play, and politics – which substitutes for genuine participation in the depth of being and for authentic human encounter. This really amounts to isolation in a most deadly sense: the lonely crowd around us. The experience of living with the surface of our minds, imaginations, and senses is common. The experience of nothingness, of boredom, pervades our atmosphere. Yet when this becomes acute enough the question of being may be born again and our fall upward toward the plenitude of reality may receive new impetus.

Chapter 4

The Arrival of New Being

~

Many would say that the counter culture and the psychic revolution toward which it is working are not specifically Christian (let alone specifically "Catholic"). This would seem to be an accurate judgement. Yet a quest for religious experience – or something suspiciously resembling this – is involved. Hence it would seem reasonable to suppose that the major religious traditions of the West would have something to offer out of their treasury of tradition and experience. Certainly this is true of Christianity, despite all of its failures, despite the fact that it has manifested the unfortunate effects of routinization and overinstitutionalization, and despite the fact that has indulged in idolatry, in regard to its own structures and symbols when it should have been sustaining a sense of self-criticism and relativity.

4.1 The Problem of Exclusiveness of Christianity

We are confronted with a problem, however – one already touched upon briefly in this book – the problem of the apparent exclusiveness of Christianity. As I have pointed out, there has been a kind of exclusiveness characteristic of even the best of Christian thought. Often there has also been evidence of narrowness, intolerance, and even of brutality in the attitudes and behavior of Christians. Christians have at times inflicted torture – both mental, as in the cases of discriminatory practices and social ostracization, and physical – not only upon outsiders but also upon each other over petty differences of belief. Moreover, we should not fail to remind ourselves that the liquidation of the Jews in Nazi Germany took place in a Christian country. All of this would suggest that there is a profound inner contradiction which has not yet been eradicated from the church.

This inner contradiction has been discussed by historian Arnold Toynbee, who sees it in the common tradition of Christianity, Judaism, and Islam. On the one hand, there is in these traditions a vision of God as self-sacrificing love. One the other hand, he is also seen as a jealous God. The duality of vision is reflected in a duality of conduct. That is, the jealous God's chosen people easily become intolerant persecutors, while the worshipers of the God who is love attempt to behave as though their fellow creatures were their brothers.[1] This duality can be found in people who are at the same time professing brotherly love and perhaps even practicing it toward certain "others." This intolerant strain which has existed in Christianity, and more generally in the family of higher religions to which it belongs, may often be an unconscious attitude. Nevertheless, it has not escaped the attention of the radical young.

Moreover, together with the problems common to the group of higher religions to which Christianity belongs,

---

[1] Arnold Toynbee, *Christianity Among the Religions of the World* (New York: Charles Scribner's Sons, 1957), 19.

there are difficulties peculiar to Christianity itself. Many of the young – and their more mature counterparts – see the centrality of Christ, indeed the worship of Christ – as expressive of the very intolerance and narrowness which they abhor. More than this, they see it as perpetuating this intolerance and as strongly at odds with the universalism characteristic of the revolution they so ardently desire.

There is some truth in the assertion that Protestantism has contributed more to this particularism and idolatry than has Catholicism. This is reflected in Moltmann's rejection of the mysticism of being, which, as I have already pointed out, is based on the idea that this means "putting an end to the historic mediation and reconciliation of God and man on the ground of Christ." This comes close to saying that one cannot have religious experience unless there is some explicit faith in Christ. It reflects precisely that aspect of Christianity which the radical young, in their search for authenticity and for communion with the depth of reality, feel compelled to reject. Such rejection is expressed by the college student who asks: "But what about Buddhists and Hindus? Can't they have revelation of God?["] Perhaps "Christolatry" would be a word for the phenomenon the student is questioning.

4.2 The Problems of Docetism and the "Sweet Jesus" Syndrome

It may well be that one source of the problems which many of the radical left are having with Christianity, Christology, and Christ is a kind of docetism, or at least a "crypto-docetism."[2] That is, there has been an almost superstitious form of identification of Jesus with God. The formulae of Chalcedon may have been necessary and helpful for Christians of an earlier age, but it is questionable that it can be very meaningful for contemporary man to think of Christ as a God–man, having two natures, one divine and one human. Whereas theologians of another era found it enlightening to speak of a "hypostatic union" in Christ, the same terminology may be more of an obstacle than a help at present. Moreover, it would be well to remember John A. T. Robinson's remark that popular supranaturalistic Christology has always been dominantly docetic. That is to say, it has assumed that Christ only appeared to be a man or looked like a man: "underneath" he was God.[3] That is, the supranaturalistic tradition suggests that Jesus was really God dressed up as a man. It suggests that God took a space trip to this planet and took the form of a man. Whether in technical form or in popularized form, what we are confronted with in such thought patterns is an exaggeratedly high Christology, with a Christology which does not seem to take seriously the humanity of the man Jesus and which goes off into fundamentalist-style assertions about the "divinity of Christ" without adequate sensitivity to semantic problems. This docetic or quasi-docetic Christology leaves many with the feeling of inability to relate authentically to Christianity as it is presented to them.

[2] Cf. Leslie Dewart, *The Future of Belief* (New York: Herder & Herder, 1966), 149–152.

[3] Cf. John A. T. Robinson, *Honest to God* (Philadelphia: Westminster Press, 1963), 65.

Aside from the problem of our heritage of docetic Christianity, there is also another source of difficulties, namely the apparent unattractiveness of the picture of the man Jesus as it comes through to many people from the gospels and from popular teaching. His message has come through to many as ambivalent and, paradoxically, many horrors have been perpetrated in his name. There has been a curious combination of sentimentality and bigotry surrounding this figure. Moreover, a multitude of pictures and hymns have portrayed a "sweet Jesus" who is less attractive to radicals, young and old, than a Socrates or a Martin Luther King. For a number of reasons, then, many are unable to find this image more compelling than the images of a number of other great historical figures.

Paradoxically, then, these two distorted renditions of the Christ figure, like two sides of a distorted mirror, falsely complementing each other, both fail to satisfy man's drive to know what it is to be fully human. On the one hand, we see a hyper-divinized figure too unreal to be identified with man. On the other hand, we witness deterioration of the Christ image into a kind of meek and mild but not really imitable model. That which we seek, the full human manifestations of God, is betrayed by such conceptualizations and images. We must, therefore, turn to our experience of what it is to be human in order to test out the authenticity of such projections. It is in our progressively more sensitized and more genuinely humanizing encounters with others that we can hope to experience a rebirth of the Christ symbol.

4.3 The Problem of Christian Identity

We are left with the haunting question: What value is there in remaining a Christian? I take this as a more primordial question than the problem of why anyone should remain a Catholic, although the answer to the question will be seen to be implied in the resolution of the first. It can be argued that to be a Christian is to be member of a historical people. Many contemporary secularization theologians have taken the position that, although the traditions, language, and methods of classical Christianity are to a large extent too parochial to speak to contemporary culture, it is possible to speak in a new, secular fashion, about the traditional attitude, values, and beliefs. If one adopts this approach, he manages to live somehow in two worlds at once, benefitting from the tradition, liturgy, symbols, and comradeship of the Christian community, and yet "hanging loose" from its structures.

Although this approach may work for some, and indeed may appear to be the only viable way to cope with the problem of relation to Christianity presently structured, it seems to leave unanswered the most searching questions concerning Christian identity. One may well ask: Why remain within this historical people? If the evils perpetrated in the name of Christianity are obvious, it is perhaps less obvious that there is good reason to retain one's identity with it. Many Catholics feel this problem is especially acute because of the tightly knit power structure of their church and because they are aware of a long history of corruption within that structure.

This contemporary lack of ease about Christianity identity was foreshadowed by Nietzsche. It is worthwhile to consider his criticism of Christianity, since it may give insight into present attitudes, although few of the alienated would be as violent in their expressions of disaffection. Giving vent to his repugnance, Nietzsche described Christianity as the most fatal and seductive lie that has ever existed, and urged people to declare open war with it. The reason for this repugnance is not far to seek: "the morality of paltry people as the measure of all things: this is the most repugnant kind of degeneracy that civilization has ever yet brought into existence."[4] Possibly the reason is even more obvious in another passage, in which he contends that basically Christianity has worked for the deterioration of the European race.[5] Fundamentally, then, Nietzsche's complaint against Christianity is that it works against human evolution; it preserves the weak and cuts down the strong. In sum, it teaches the denial of life. We might put the objection in other terms and say that it appears to work against the future, rather than being the religion of the future.

These objections, echoed by our contemporaries, force us once again to face the question: Why identify with Christianity? One could, of course, list the values it has

[4] Friedrich Nietzsche, *The Will to Power*, trans. A. M. Ludovici, in *The Complete Works of Friedrich Nietzsche*, ed. Oscar Levy (New York: Macmillan, 1924), 200–201.

[5] Friedrich Nietzsche, *Beyond Good and Evil*, trans., with commentary by Walter Kaufmann (New York: Random House, 1966), #63, 75. "Stand all valuations on their head – that is what they had to do. And break the strong, sickly o'er great hopes, cast suspicion on the joy in beauty, bend everything haughty, manly, conquering, domineering, all the instincts characteristic of the highest and best-turned-out type of 'man,' into unsureness, agony of conscience, self-destruction – indeed invert all love of the earthly and of dominion over the earth into hatred of the earth and the earthly."

bestowed upon Western society – its emphasis upon charity, for example, and upon defense of the dignity of the individual person. Moreover, the Christian church has been a comforter of the poor and afflicted and a protector of the weak, as well as a custodian of learning and culture. It would hardly seem necessary to catalogue the benefits it has bestowed upon the Western world. Yet, one might well counter that for the most part this is over and done with, and that the task can now be carried on more effectively by secular humanists. The haunting question remains.

4.4 First Consideration: Communication

I would suggest that there are at least two major considerations to be taken into account in facing up to this question. The first consideration has to do with the complex matter of communication (which will be discussed at greater length in later chapters). It is a truism that human beings exist and function within a network of communications – which is one way of saying that we need to be a part of a community. For many of those whose deep roots are in the Christian church, the most adequate communications network is, in fact, the church. It may be that some people in this category are profoundly alienated from the institutional church. Indeed, in many cases they may unofficially or in some formal way have severed relations with it. At the same time, it is possible that these people have a profound fidelity to the tradition in which they were formed. There exist channels of communication among such persons and to a certain extent between themselves and others who remain more or less "orthodox." They may be said to constitute that entity which has been labeled – perhaps somewhat ineptly – the underground church. The fact is simply that there are multitudes of people whose psychic histories have been developed within the Christian tradition and who remain, in some profound sense, part of this historical people. There is nothing derogatory about describing the situation this way: it is simply a fact. Since one's personhood is expressed wherever one finds it possible to communicate, it has to be said that these people, alienated though they may be, should stand within the Christian community, since this is where they communicate best. Their ultimate concern is reflected in their concern for this community.

4.5 Second Consideration: The Specificity of Christianity

A second major consideration is perhaps more essential. When we ask why anyone should remain within this historic people called the Christian community, we are asking a question that has implications beyond the realm of sociology. We are in fact raising the question of the specificity of Christianity. That is to say, we are asking whether it has a unique quality not found in secular humanism and also whether it has a special role among the world religions. In effect, we are asking whether there is a revelatory experience which is specific to Christianity.

If we attempt comparisons between Christianity and the various forms of secular humanism, it appears impossible to find clear-cut ethical differences and value differences. This is particularly striking in some of the current dialogue between Marxists and Christians. All express concern for the brotherhood of man and for the development of authentic humanity. All desire to overcome the wounds of alienation. Yet in the language of the Christian tradition there are strong suggestions that there is a difference. The use of such terms as "revelation" and "salvation," problematic though these may be, suggests that Christians aspire to a form of transcendence which is beyond the aspirations of secular humanists.

This aspiration to transcendence has been expressed down through the centuries by peasants and prophets, priests and poets, in language both simple and complex. In recent times Teilhard de Chardin expressed it by claiming that only ecstasy to the Omega Point would satisfy consciousness. He envisioned the Omega as a personalizing center, already existing now outside of time and space and exercising a magnetic attraction for men. It implies immortality; that is, there is a point outside space and time where the value of the unique individual survives irreversibly. This notion of the Omega, or the Christ-Omega, says something about the specific difference between Christianity and secular humanism. Of course, many humanists would object that such imagery is a distraction from the fulfillment of the tasks presented by this world. For the Christian, on the other hand, it can make possible commitment to these tasks and bestow upon that commitment a new dimension and a new hope. Man is trapped in his alienation unless this new dimension is brought into his awareness.

It is true that we do not have adequate conceptual tools to deal with the meaning of Christ. The formulas which we have inherited, such as those from the councils of

Nicea and Chalcedon, are inadequate. I have already said that the pictures of the historical Jesus are not universally compelling. Yet on some deep level, beneath that of conceptualizations and pictures, an encounter with transcendent [reality] has been transmitted down through Christian history – originally sparked by the meeting of a small community living over nineteen hundred years ago with the historical person, Jesus of Nazareth. This reality has assumed many forms in the process of transmission. None of these forms were or could be adequate manifestations of the original revelatory experience. Yet genuine encounters do continue to take place, bringing about a regeneration and transformation of lives.

In connection with the original Christian revelation, a cluster of symbols emerged in the consciousness of the community which is the church. We find these expressed in the creeds of the Christian churches, and in their sacraments and doctrines. The question arises: Can we say that it is the impact of this cluster of symbols that differentiates the Christian consciousness from that of the humanist? I have already suggested that there are many persons who identify as Christians but for whom these symbols are not very "loaded." One might contend that in some cases this is because the identification is merely sociological. However, it may also be that in some cases, although the symbols as traditionally presented appear not to be effective, there is some latent potentiality to respond to them. It might be, for example, that the Mass, even as celebrated in very contemporary styles, would seem meaningless to a person, and yet that the same person would have an experience similar to that of attending Mass when participating in a peace march or perhaps when simply having a meal with a group of friends. Perhaps, then, on some level he recognizes that this is what the Mass should be, and that this recognition makes him refuse to give up hope in Christianity. In such a case, despite the ineptitude of institutionalized religion's presentation of its symbols, the person has managed to sustain a sense of transcendence which is qualitatively different from the experience of the humanist. Moreover, this sustaining of the consciousness of transcendence is related to the Christian symbols, although this relationship may only be ambiguously perceived in the experience.

4.6 Christianity's Specific Character Related to Hope

In order to establish with conviction and complete clarity the specific character of Christianity among the world religions a comparative study would be required, which would be outside the scope of this book. There is some consensus, however, that Christianity's uniqueness is related to the quality of the hope that it offers man. I have pointed out that, unlike secular humanism, Christianity does not settle for hope of a completely this-worldly character. However, it is important to see this in conjunction with the fact that the transcendence it seeks is not totally other-worldly. Authentic Christianity, as it is understood by theology today, does not favor escape from the problems of this world. The adequate goal is not understood to be some sort of Nirvana, although theology in Hellenic style would often seem to have given this impression, as would popular preaching and piety, and the life-style of countless believers. The case of the person who would never miss Mass on Sunday but who is indifferent to social problems illustrates this distorted emphasis.

In recent years, the hyper-otherworldly distortion of Christian transcendence has been under attack. Teilhard de Chardin, an early prophet of this dawning change of consciousness, pointed out that there was in his time no sign of a faith that is really expanding, and this despite the fact that the world is not growing colder. The problem is that the total unity of which we dream seems to beckon in two directions – toward the zenith and toward the horizon. Thus, Teilhard says the emergence of a whole race of spiritual expatriates – human beings torn in two directions. What these people are really seeking, he believed, is the possibility of believing at the same time and wholly in God and in the world, the one through the other.[6] This is genuine Christian hope.

The race of expatriates is expanding today. Teilhard's prophecy rings truer than ever. The intellectual challenge which the situation presents has given birth to the theology of hope, as we have seen. Thus Christian hope is now seen in relation to Christ and his future. This implies that the Christian consciousness of history is a consciousness of mission.[7] That is, the Christian consciousness is coming to be understood more explicitly as directed to the transformation of this world. Some see the possibility of

[6] Pierre Teilhard de Chardin, *The Future of Man*, trans. Norman Denny (New York: Harper & Row, 1964), 268–269.

[7] Jürgen Moltmann, in *Religion, Revolution, and the Future*, trans. M. Douglas Meeks (New York: Charles Scribner's Sons, 1969), 225.

this consciousness being embodied in a church which will be a "second order institution," that is, a socio-critical institutional capable of protesting against and transforming the alienating structures of society. In order that this transformation may be brought about, one advocate of the theology of hope has called for the "deprivation and de-existentialization, or to put it more positively, the 'new objectification' of the Christian message."[8]

At the same time, there is an interesting dialectic going on within the Christian consciousness, perhaps more intensely among Catholics than among others. In opposition to the mentality described above, which stresses the role of the church as an institution – albeit a socio-critical institution – there is a tendency among many to insist that the "good news" of Jesus has already been spread abroad. The assumption is that this "good news" of Jesus has already been appropriated in the world of science and politics and in men's personal lives. The assumption of this position is that it is not necessary to be self-consciously "Christian" or to interpret reality in Christian terms. This seems to be the position increasingly of the young, particularly of young people brought up within the Catholic tradition.

The conflict represented by these attitudes cannot be resolved simply. The parochialism of traditional Christian forms of expression and of institutionalization is evident. Yet, it does not seem realistic to assume that the "good news" has adequately been spread abroad in a world plagued by war, racism, and other forms of discrimination,

---

[8] Johannes Metz, *Faith in History and Society: Towards a Fundamental Practical Theology* (New York: Crossroad, 1977), 126.

and poverty. There is a need, then, for the continuance of institutionalized Christianity in some form. If it is to be the kind of force in society that it should be, however, the church must be radicalized. It must raise its own level of consciousness in order to be the bestower of hope for men.

4.7 Consciousness-Raising in Christianity

This consciousness-raising process will have to include re-examination of the meaning of the very word "Christian." If, then, we have lost sight of the fact that Jesus was a human being, it is essential to regain awareness of this. It is evident that the excessively "high Christology," which I have described, has been characteristic of Catholic theology and preaching. That is, Jesus has been identified with God in such a way that there has been a failure to recognize his humanness. This phenomenon often manifests itself through a kind of word-magic, in other words verbal realism. Thus, for example, the heresy-haunting Catholic authority-figure may intimidate a subordinate by such a question as: "Do you believe in the divinity of Christ – yes or no?" If the person being interrogated is a thinking person, he may realize that this is an unsatisfactory question, for there is no simple "yes or no" answer possible. The questioner implicitly assumes that the words he uses directly reflect reality, even that they contain reality. What he is really doing is drawing a magic circle, and the yes or no answer is supposed to place the person thus interrogated either inside or outside that circle. Such verbal devices are commonly used by representatives of severely threatened institutions. They do not appeal to thought but rather elicit emotive reactions, for example, of loyalty or of defiance in relation to the institution represented. Usually, the victim does not see through the word magic involved and finds himself blindly responding without thought.

Paradoxically, a phenomenon that has accompanied this high Christology and word magic, as I have noted, has been an excessive sentimentality surrounding the figure of Jesus, as manifested in such devotions as those to the Sacred Heart and to the Precious Blood. Accompanying the hidden docetism of Catholicism we also find preoccupation with the person, or rather with fantasies of the person of Mary. There is no way of guaranteeing that these fantasies correspond to historical fact, since there is so little historical data about Mary. Also part of the syndrome has been a strong emphasis upon passive virtues, such as humility, meekness, and obedience, and the encouragement of various forms of self-effacement. There is indeed much that can serve as a target for Nietzsche's criticisms – particularly for his observation that Christianity shatters the strong and breaks down everything autonomous and manly.

The confusion that is bred by this complex syndrome – the assimilation of Christ to God and the corresponding sentimentalization of the figures of Jesus and Mary, accompanied by glorification of the passive virtues – would be difficult to exaggerate. One of the forms in which this confusion manifests itself is the persistent tendency to identify sin with pride, will-to-power, and self-assertiveness. Correspondingly, redemption comes to mean restoring man to what he supposedly lacks, such as the potentiality for sacrificial love, I–thou relationship, and the primacy of the personal.[9] What is noteworthy here is that the stereotypic "masculine" characteristics are somehow cast outside the pale of Christian virtue and to some extent even identified with sin, whereas the culturally stereotypical "feminine" characteristics are identified with virtue and redemption. I am by no means implying, of course, that these characteristics are innately male or female, but am merely pointing to the identification which our culture has made of certain qualities into two polarized categories. Since nearly all theologians in the past have been men and since the vast majority still are, it may be that the "Christian ideal" which has been set forth is in large measure a reaction against the excesses and perversions of the masculine stereotype. This poses some problems.

First, it is clearly a problem for women to have this mystique imposed upon them as the Christian ideal and it is explicitly and especially a problem and a source of confusion in our time, since women are engaged actively in the struggle to liberate themselves from this mystique of the passive virtues. It does not help the process of women's liberation to have the passive ideal imposed in the image of Jesus and Mary which are offered as models. The liberation which countless women are seeking – some very consciously, others less so, is precisely from the stereotype implied in the virtues of humility, obedience, and self-effacing love. The point is not that these are unworthy qualities but rather that they have been imposed upon women by our culture to the exclusion of the active qualities such as courage and daring, ambition and

---

[9] Cf. Valerie Goldstein, "The Human Situation: A Feminine View," *Journal of Religion* 40 (1960): 100–111.

creativity – those virtues that embody self-actualization. Many therefore feel the need for Christianity to stress the active virtues and think that the last thing women need is to have preached to them humility and self-effacement.

Second, this sort of Christian model also poses problems for men, even though it may have emerged as an effort to resolve the masculine dilemma created by a culture which denies men the right to be tender, loving, and humane. The difficulty is that, whereas this model in a sense suggests a healthy reaction against an exploitative, objectifying, over-aggressive masculine ideal, it is an over-reaction, to such an extent that men cannot identify with such a counter-ideal, just as women cannot be authentic persons and identify with it. This may be the reason for the striking absence of men in the institutional church, especially in the Latin countries.

Indeed, there would be something unhealthy for both men and women in identification with passive models for the basic reason that they present only a partial picture of self-actualized human beings and therefore cannot be truly satisfactory for anyone seeking realization of his or her full potential. Neither the image of Jesus in popular piety nor that of Mary satisfies the need for wholeness. The usual presentations of Christian virtue do not satisfy this need; hence the unattractiveness that many claim to find in the ideal.

4.8 The Problem of the Rebirth of the Symbols of Christ and Mary

Symbols are born when the situation is ripe for them, and they die when the situation is radically altered. We seem to be living through a time of the death of the Christian symbols for a significant segment of humanity. We should ask, therefore, about the possibility of some kind of resurrection of the symbolic power of Christianity as conveyed in the images of Christ and of Mary. This possibility of resurrection should not be understood univocally, that is as if the symbols must recur in precisely the same form they had in the past. A purification process may be necessary. This will only happen if a change in situation takes place or more radically speaking, if a psychic revolution takes place. The question then is, can we actively work to change the situation? Christian hope suggests that we can and should – in a creative, political, and revolutionary way.

The situation in which we find ourselves is puzzling and challenging. The hope that drives us on is somehow Christian, and yet the sense in which it can be said to be specifically Christian is radically called into question. That is, we are struggling under the impetus of creative hope to discover a new Christian identity. The pale images of Jesus and the totally self-effacing Mary must be replaced by more adequate models. However, these models are not lying around for us to select, as if they were ready made. We have to discover them in living out our own aspirations and potentialities. Indeed, it might be said that we have to create them, not in the sense of creating something arbitrarily but insofar as, inspired by the incipient ideals we already have, we work out our potentialities which are already within us. We come to recognize these potentialities more and more in the process of actualizing them. To put it another way, we can live out the process of creating a new language of transcendence. As we become more authentic through creative effort in interaction with others we begin to create a presence to ourselves and to each other of that toward which we are striving. As Plato recognized, the wise man is one who knows that he is not wise. So too, the Christian knows that he is not yet a Christian. By the fact of this recognition, he opens up the possibility of the fullness of the reality to which he aspires.

Revelation is not over and done with. It is taking place wherever there is self-transforming activity in the direction of becoming an authentic man. While there is some direction to be found in the heritage of the Christian people. Yet the danger of distortion arises constantly, and one particular virulent form in which it arises is, as I have pointed out, compensation for the "hyper-masculine" aggressive model presented to males in Western culture. The reaction results in religious attempts to impose another inauthentic set of models, misleadingly labeled Jesus and Mary. This kind of distortion should be combated through action. That is, there should be a conscious effort toward the intercommunication and equal cooperation between members of both sexes in carrying out the mission of the church in the world. Indeed this demonstration and acting out of equality is the essential part of that mission.

The cooperation between men and women that I am talking about implies equal participation on all levels and in all forms of activity. Only in this way can the stereotypes often mislabeled as Jesus and Mary be overcome. This means that there should be no exclusion from any church office or function on the basis of sex and that the church should work to eliminate discrimination on the basis of sex within other cultural institutions. What is at stake is nothing less than the coming into being of authentic Christianity and of genuine human community.

4.9 The New Being and the Symbol of Christ

It was a considerable shock to some of Paul Tillich's contemporaries when he remarked that even if future historians should discover that Jesus of Nazareth never lived, Christianity would still have meaning. The idea still comes as a shock to many, certainly to many Catholics, today. What the systematic theologian was expressing was the most valid element in the old Protestant distinction between "Jesus of history" and "Christ of faith." He was not declaring that there is no relationship between the historical Jesus and the Christ symbol, but he was attempting to place that relationship in a true perspective. He was affirming that the Christ symbol, sparked in the minds of the early Christians through their encounter with the historical Jesus, has a validity of its own, which escapes the methods of historical research. The truth of faith, which is expressed through myths and symbols, moves on a different level from that of the truth of history.

Jesus had a certain transparency to the divine. He was perceived as the Christ. This view of the Christ is onto-logical in quality: Christ is seen as the New Being – the essential unity between God and man. The humanity of the New Being encountered in Jesus as the Christ realizes within the conditions of existence – the conditions sym-bolized by the story of the Fall – the external unity

between God and man. That is, the New Being transforms man's existence and makes it really new.[10]

It is important to realize that in the Christian tradition
man's anguish is understood as due not merely to the fact
that he is finite being speaking the infinite, but also as due to
the fact that he is "fallen," alienated, estranged. Therefore,
he needs a special event of salvation, for he cannot save
himself. This special event comes through as revelation of
the essential unity of God and man. But what does this
mean? Many orthodox theologians, of course, have accepted
the traditional description of Jesus Christ as the hypostatic
union of two natures, divine and human. Other and more
radical thinkers, such as Schleiermacher and Tillich, have
preferred to speak of a general divine–human relationship
which simply becomes most apparent in Jesus.

Man, then, by his very existence is estranged from God
and he cannot save himself, although he tries in many
ways to do so. Jesus received the office of the saving one,
the Christ. As the Christ he brings New Being, restoring
man to his essential unity with God. Indeed, it is possible
that this healing can take place in those who have never
heard of Jesus or even of Christianity. The fact is simply
that the event was extremely vivid in the event of Jesus as
the Christ, and that the message of this event became
widespread in the Western world, making possible in this
culture a special dream and aspiration of wholeness
for man.

I have pointed out that there is a schizoid division
within traditional Catholic theology between the doctrine

[10] Cf. Paul Tillich, *Systematic Theology*, vol. 2 (Chicago: University of
       Chicago Press, 1957).

of the divinity of Christ on the one hand, and sentimental notions about the humanity of Jesus on the other hand. This schizoid Christology misses the point and meaning of Jesus as the Christ, the New Being. An example of how devastating this lack of integration can be was reelected in the experience of a woman who asked her parish priest: "But do you really believe that God is male?" The answer she received was; "I should be deeply shocked to think that he was not."[11] The mentality expressed here reflects a profound confusion. A particular characteristic of Jesus, that is, his sex, is attributed to God. The priest was not free to see Jesus as a fallible human being through whom God was manifested to others, nor was he free to understand that God is spirit. Thus, the maleness of Jesus was projected in a confused way as an attribute of God. Of course, if pressed, the priest would no doubt have affirmed that God is spirit, since this is a teaching of orthodox theology. However, we would also try to relate this to the incarnational theory of his tradition, according to which God, that is, the second person of the Trinity, took on an individual (and male) human nature. Thus, the grotesque possible of the affirmation: God is male.

In contrast to such a blurred and dehumanizing Christological theology, it is liberating to see Jesus as a striking manifestation of God. The Christ symbol then can be seen to transcend the individual qualities of the

---

[11] For another example of this kind of confusion, see Edward Vanchak, OP, "More from St. Paul on a Female Priesthood," *National Catholic Reporter* (May 26, 1965), 4. Fr. Manchak wrote that a woman cannot be ordained because "to the gathering of the Church her feminine nature cannot represent 'male,' which is precisely the symbolic sacramental distinction Christ possesses in relation to his Church."

man Jesus. Unfortunately, however, Catholic theologians has been slow to come to this realization. Frequently they seem to have felt compelled to compensate for the blurring of the God–male identity by the development of a rather strained Mariology and Marian devotion. Yet, despite the excesses there may well be a valid aspiration and intuition involved in Catholic Mariology.

We are faced with difficulties, then, if we intend to see Christianity as truly humanizing and as truly liberating for women and for full development in the man–woman relationship. One possible approach is, of course, to stress the fact that the manifestation of God such as the disciples experienced through Jesus can indeed happen through other outstanding human beings, men and women. In another, perhaps future culture, the hierophany might happen most strikingly through a woman. According to this approach to the problem, then, the historical fact of Jesus is not denied but it is seen in a somewhat universalist perspective. The Christ symbol is not seen as sex-linked, but as capable of manifestation in different ways in different cultures and ages.

4.10 A Jungian Approach

Another avenue of approach is suggested by Jungian theory. In order to discuss this it will be necessary to consider the Jungian idea of the mandala symbol, of the Trinitarian symbol, and of the Assumption of Mary. From his study of the history of religions and from his experiences in psychoanalysis Jung became convinced that the mandala was in a sense the adequate symbol for God. A striking characteristic of the mandala seems to be its fourness, which suggests that there is a rounding out or completeness about it. The mandala is somewhat difficult to reconcile with the Trinitarian symbol for God. It would appear that there is something lacking in the latter. Indeed, the Christian Trinity seems to suppress something, a kind of fourth part, which would be symbolically expressive of matter, the earth, the immanent, the feminine. The study of the history of Christianity, its theories and practices, seems to support this theory for there has been present from the earliest centuries an anti-materialist, Manichean streak in Christianity, as expressed, for example, in some of the Church Fathers. Closely related to this has been a persistent and often virulent antifeminism. As Jung pointed out, the Trinity appears to be of an exclusively masculine character. The feminine has been blotted out from the symbol for the deity and also from the conception of fully developed personhood. Interestingly, the unconscious mind would seem to rebel against this, for, according to Jungian theory, it transforms the Trinity into a quaternity.

For these reasons, and to the astonishment of many, Jung expressed his delight when in 1950 Pope Pius XII proclaimed the doctrine of the Assumption of the Blessed Virgin Mary into heaven. The doctrine had been present, of course, for many centuries, but it had achieved increasing prominence to such an extent that the Pope felt compelled to make it more explicitly and emphatic. What this event of proclamation meant to Jung – although this was certainly not consciously intended on the part of the Pope – was that the feminine was being raised up to partake in the Godhead. Jung saw the "Mother of God" as the matrix of the quaternity.

It would be well to recall also that the Holy Spirit has always been in some sense a feminine symbol. Although referred to by the masculine pronouns, "he" has always been described in theology, ritual, and popular piety as having certain qualities which in our culture are considered to be typically feminine. "He" is portrayed as nurturing, healing, loving, and in a sense, passive. If Jung's analysis of the place of the dogma of the Assumption in the development of the Trinitarian symbol toward wholeness has some validity, it is interesting also to see a certain balance between the stereotypic "masculine" and "feminine" emerging so that there appear to be two "sides" of the Godhead: Father and Son on the one hand, Holy Spirit and Mary on the other side. Thus, the stereotypical masculine and feminine symbols are equalized in the religious consciousness.[12]

I wish to re-emphasize that I am not, of course, proposing that masculine and feminine stereotypes of our culture actually represent the way men and women innately are or should be. There is no suggestion here that there should be two distinct models for men and women (although perhaps some Jungians would see it this way). Rather, I am attempting to convey that the qualities which our culture has artificially divided and apportioned to the two sexes are necessary for wholeness of being. This would be true for every person, man or woman. Insofar as we use symbolism for God, it is an exclusively patriarchal image to be used. Since the Christ symbol in the whole of tradition is seen in relation to that of the

---

[12]   It is interesting to consider in this connection the Christian Scientists' idea of a "Father–Mother God."

Trinity, any new developments in thinking about the Christ, the New Being, should be seen together with possible development of the Trinitarian images. At the same time, it is essential, of course, to recognize that the ultimate ground of being is not captured by or identifiable with any symbol.

4.11 Substance and Principle in Relation to the Christ

If, in the process of the development of doctrine, one were to attempt to choose between a completely universalized concept of the Christ symbol, so that Christ is seen as visible in persons, men and women, equally, and on the other hand a Jungian "elevation" of Mary – as if one had to move in either one direction or the other, exclusively, is probably a mistake. It is probably better to let the symbolism develop in both directions at once since both are inadequate and since in a sense each is corrective of the other. The universalized Christ suggests the possibility of plentitude of personality in all persons, but there is a difficult and an inadequacy, seemingly, because this is an exclusively masculine image. On the other hand, the elevation of Mary, although it might conceivably do something for the progress of consciousness in the man–woman relationship, carries with it the danger of hardening the stereotype of the eternal feminine into a model for half the species, exclusively.

The way out of this dilemma is suggested by recognition of the fact that both of these approaches are on the level of symbolism. They are ways of looking at, and perhaps developing, the Catholic substance. In itself there is nothing wrong with this. Indeed, given the fact that we have human imaginations, it probably is impossible to avoid models that are based upon sexual duality in some way, and on the same level of imagination projecting these onto God. On the other hand, it would be disastrous to stay here, to use these as reinforcements of culturally induced stereotypes or settle for some projection instead of continually searching for the hidden God in faith and courage. Therefore, it is always essential that we call upon the Protestant principle as a corrective, realizing that God is beyond our symbols and that the God–man relationship transcends sex. Only the liberation which this principle engenders in our consciousness will make possible the rebirth – or the new development – of the Catholic substance of Christology and Mariology in such a way that we need no longer be frozen in an orthodoxy that nourishes neither our minds nor our hearts.

Moreover, only the integration of this principle and the Catholic substance will save us from the "Christian" exclusiveness which has kept us from being Christian and from becoming fully human. Only when we understand the symbolic nature of the Christ as the New Being, and of Trinitarian and Marian theology can we accept these freely and thus freely communicate with non-Christians. When we have thus penetrated beyond the surface of our own tradition we may not feel compelled to relinquish it but rather we may discover a profound similarity between Christianity and other world religions. We will, of course, also see the specificity of the Christian symbols but in such a way that dialogue and cooperation with non-Christians will not be hampered. Having broken through the particularity that had isolated us we can rise to an understanding of the spiritual presence in other expressions of the ultimate meaning of man's being.[13]

[13] Cf. Paul Tillich, *Christianity and the Encounter of the World Religions* (New York: Columbia University Press, 1963).

Part II

Engagements and Reflections

∼

I

The Many Minds of Mary Daly

~

Mary E. Hunt

Introduction

The newly discovered manuscript of *Catholicism: End or Beginning?* (1969–1970) adds another dimension to the already multivalent study of Mary Daly.[1] I read it as a bridge from the Early Daly (1965–1973) to the Later Daly (1973–2006). I understand why she stopped writing after four of seven planned chapters: she was bored and convinced that she had reached a dead end in her thinking about Christianity, which, she concluded, was as limited as any other religion. Only a fresh start, and it was considered quite "fresh" by many, would allow her to stretch her intellectual wings and reach her spiritual depths.

Putting aside this unpublished manuscript, Mary Daly began anew. She questioned the fatherhood of God and the primacy of man in a unique, enduring contribution that still exists as a feminist line in the theological sand. Many mistake her views as mainly anti-patriarchal, but a careful read reveals that she was really calling for a deeper, fuller, mystical way of being that made institutional

[1] Mary Daly also used the title *Catholicism: Death or Rebirth?* to refer to this manuscript. Cf. Mary Daly, *Outercourse: The Be-Dazzling Voyage* (San Francisco: HarperSanFrancisco, 1992), 146.

143

religions seem superficial. She believed that direct experiences of transcendence are a possibility for all.

Mary Daly transitioned from her cradle Catholicism and early adult Catholic life to her mature feminist rejection of most things Catholic. She found Catholicism fraught with rigidity, arid in its content, and utterly lacking the feminist sensibilities she was developing. No one could tell her the Truth about the Divine which she did not discern for herself.

Daly had what she later named "Elemental" encounters with a block of ice and a clover blossom which sparked the beginning of her sense of being.[2] Given these transformative encounters, I am unsurprised that she decided not to finish or publish *Catholicism: End or Beginning?* because of her commitment to forward motion, intellectually. She worried that she would no sooner publish it than she would have to critique her own words – like she did, for example, in *The Church and the Second Sex*.[3] By leaving this manuscript aside she avoided repeating the exercise.

Nonetheless, I think Mary Daly would have relished the publication of this manuscript in the present form because she was often of many minds on issues. She was more flexible and honest than many academics in changing her position as new circumstances and data warranted. Ideas accumulate. So her decision to abandon the project is not disrespected by the choice of others to publish it. To the contrary. Even in her physical absence,

---

[2] Daly, *Outercourse*, 23.
[3] Mary Daly, *The Church and the Second Sex* (Boston: Beacon Press, 1985). These various responses reflect the author's reactions to her own work at several intervals after publication.

the work sheds light on her thinking process, her writing goals, and method. Her work – all of it and especially her books – was what she wanted preserved; what she considered the most important reason for her being in the world.

Mary Daly wrote this manuscript on the heels of *The Church and the Second Sex* (*CSS*) (published in 1968 and out of print by 1971) and before *Beyond God the Father: Toward a Philosophy of Women's Liberation* (*BGF*) (published in 1973). As she describes them, "The earlier book [*CSS*] manifested some of the anger and ebullient hope that characterized the period immediately following the Second Vatican Council. . . . the same anger and the same hope are the wellsprings of this book [*BGF*], but . . . the focus has shifted and the perspective has been greatly radicalized."[4]

Daly wrote the present manuscript during the transition period when she went from "radical Catholic" to "postchristian feminist."[5] Neither "anger" nor "hope" would be words I would use in describing this text. It is rather bland, as if written to satisfy someone else's idea of what is important. It reads more like a term paper than a best-seller. In that regard, it fails to fulfill her own criterion of groundbreaking work, which is something she apparently realized and acted upon by stopping writing.

I think Mary Daly outgrew the manuscript as much as she abandoned it. She had done quite enough of that kind of academic writing for her three doctorates. She was

---

[4] Mary Daly, *Beyond God the Father: Toward A Philosophy of Women's Liberation* (Boston: Beacon Press, 1973), xi.

[5] Daly, *The Church and the Second Sex*, 5.

good at it, for better or for worse, but it excited few if any of her passions. She was moving into a new phase of life marked by joy, justice, autonomy, and interdependence. This manuscript was a remnant of the old, not a product of the new, at best a harbinger but not even fully that.

Mary Daly's famous walk out of Memorial Church at Harvard University in 1971, the Harvard Memorial Church Exodus, can be seen as the embodiment and performance of the unwritten chapters of this manuscript.[6] After being the first woman invited to preach at the Sunday morning service there, she finished her remarks with a rousing call to leave the institutional church. No wonder she wrote of the extant manuscript, "It would have been embarrassing if the thing had been printed, especially since within a year or two of its demise I was thoroughly in disagreement with its frame of reference. I think I simply saw that I had been framed by that frame and wanted to break out."[7] Break out she did, and with panache. Not only did she push the boundaries on that famous Sunday morning November 14, 1971, when "hundreds of women and some men began stampeding out of the church the Moment I finished."[8] Though let the record show that at least one woman who left down the center aisle with the group later admitted to going back in for the coffee hour. It is an apt metaphor for the ambivalence and complexity of many people's relationships to patriarchal Christianity, including Mary's. Many more people left Christianity in subsequent decades thanks to Daly's example. Her writing and teaching set a

---

[6] Daly, *Outercourse*, 137.   [7] Ibid., 102.   [8] Ibid., 138.

new standard for courage and creativity that inspires this writing.

Such "carbon dating" is tricky and open to a wide range of interpretations as to why she deep-sixed the project. The Vietnam War, the Civil Rights Movements, and the nascent feminist movements were beginning to permeate her consciousness in ways that being in Europe for the better part of the previous decade had delayed. The spiritual dissonance was more than she could bear. The death of her mother who had become a dear friend, and her sexual awakening to the wonders of women were truths, better, Truths, next to which the fine points of Docetic and Trinitarian wrangling paled. Her mystical experiences of Life in a clover blossom or a hedge were more in line with her spirit.

I detect that Mary Daly came to see the limits of what even the most "radical" religious and secular male thinkers – for example, Harvey Cox, R. D. Laing, Carl Jung, and company – could possibly contribute that would be adequate to the needs of newly conscious women. Instead, she took on the task herself, exploring religion, psychology, anthropology, mythology, and other fields, throwing her intellectual life "as far as it would go," as she often urged others.[9]

Mary Daly realized that the ambitious project she envisioned was nothing less than the rejection of a two-thousand-year-old religious tradition's hegemonic claims, and the proclamation of a New Time and a New Space that was Biophilic. She got the ball rolling but understood it as

---

[9] Ibid., 41, 344.

the task of many generations. It is in that spirit that I comment on this newly discovered piece of her work.

Methodology

In this analysis, I begin with an explanation of how I approach Daly Studies. There may be more such treasures unearthed as scholars work through her archives. There are certainly many people reading her in all of her complexity, though not all of them understand the context in which she wrote, which is essential for interpreting her views. This manuscript contributes to that.

Then, I focus on three central questions: (1) What were the straws that broke the Catholic camel's back for Mary Daly? (2) How did the strenuous rejection of the patriarchal Roman Catholic Church and all its trappings still reflect her rootedness in Catholicism? (3) Is this manuscript a game-changer with regard to how scholars might interpret Mary Daly in the twenty-first century?

I conclude with a brief reflection on the importance of leaving aside projects like this when they cease to make sense. I also consider her work as illustrative of avoiding the mistake of dismantling religion and simply remaking it with a twist. Mystery trumps it all. With no guarantees of definitive answers to any or all of these questions, I look forward to other scholars delving into the same materials and making discoveries of their own.

Daly Studies

"Daly Studies" is a rather clinical way of describing the work of someone I knew quite well as a person as well as a scholar. It is a far cry from the phone calls, and letters we exchanged by mail with stamps on them, just to contextualize things. One time, she requested that the WATER office (Women's Alliance for Theology, Ethics, and Ritual in Silver Spring, Maryland, where I work) send her "The WATER Muse" to aid in her writing. We sent it by return post, happy to enter her fantasy for a good cause. Personal visits, some complete with picnic suppers on the grass near the lake in back of her apartment, or meals and chats on my porch or deck were times of sisterly affection. Such encounters, though they were amazing and reveal a great deal about the *person* Mary Daly, fade with time. What remains, as Mary wanted, are her writings, and especially dear to her, her books.

My considerations of Mary Daly's work are influenced by the person I knew, the sister Catholic (we were never Catholic sisters) whose background and early religious upbringing I could understand. We both came from Upstate New York (Schenectady and Syracuse, respectively). She was more than two decades my senior, but Catholic culture before the Second Vatican Council was fairly uniform. I experienced some of what she described about her childhood and adolescence in a similarly ghettoized Irish Catholic world. I found it all as limiting and misogynistic as she did. I was much younger when things began to give way after Vatican II, which attended and I only read about.

Nonetheless, most Daly Studies, what may develop into an academic cottage industry, are carried out by people who never met her and were not even in the world when she did some of her most foundational work. The texts can and must speak for themselves. That was why she insisted that her books be kept in print. Contemporary translations in Italian and Spanish, for example, demonstrate that her audience continues to broaden. Still, context is determinative of so much that it is important to locate her squarely in the midst of a very traditional brand of Irish American Catholicism, where, in her day, a woman theologian was uncommon. She knew that both nostalgia and objectivity distort. Many of us who knew her found her to be such a life force and such a remarkably unique individual that even our lenses for reading her work are colored by who she was as a person. My copy of *The Church and the Second Sex* is inscribed, "To Someone who will remember the contents," and *Outercourse* is inscribed, "To WATER – Courage!" Even as I engage in critical analysis of her work, the person Mary Daly, the one who taught my daughter to howl, is still part of my consciousness. It cannot be otherwise.

By the same token, Mary Daly, before many of her generation in theology, rightly rejected the myth of academic objectivity. She had a sophisticated philosophical sense of how deeply subjective one's worldview really is. This approach was novel at the time because she engaged in theological and philosophical studies in the US and in Europe before the intersectionality of race, coloniality, class, gender, and sexuality became a key part of theological method.

She learned theology and philosophy when sweeping pronouncements in Catholicism were still intoned by clerics, even after Vatican II, with its much-touted liberalism. Some professors actually read textbooks *at* their students. They did not realize that women were entirely absent from their world, worldview, and world-wrecking work. Mary was on thick ice when she wrote in a detached way about the sources and texts that undergirded their academic droning. But the ice thinned once she found her own voice and began to name and claim the particularity of women's experiences. She was seen as a traitor to and by a tradition in which she would never be an insider.

The easiest way to misread Mary Daly is to read her outside of this context. That is why understanding this "aborted" manuscript as set between her world-opening years of graduate study in Fribourg, Switzerland, and her first, challenging years of teaching men at Boston College helps to explain (at least in part) the reason why she abandoned the manuscript mid project. My reading is that she came to the end of her intellectual and personal tether, fed up both intellectually and existentially with the simultaneous tokenism and erasure that she experienced at a Jesuit university. It was one thing to deal with texts that were exclusive, and quite another to have the experience of one's self being excluded from men's space. She had had enough, and she had the personal wherewithal, community support from friends, and cultural shifts to do something else. So she did.

Mary Daly was certainly more qualified and accomplished than many of her faculty colleagues, some Jesuits of whom might have been Jesuit legacy or affirmative action candidates. But the degree to which she was marginalized as a woman, as a non-cleric, and as a creative intellect who was in increasing demand outside of the small pond that was Boston College made her position difficult. She refused to add insult to injury by laying out, with all of the historical rigor and theological depth of which she was so clearly capable, the interplay of one male idea with another male source, one little heresy after another tiny Vatican tempest. She knew that religion *qua* religion (not as an institutional force) was about more, and that she was destined for bigger things. So she courageously cut the cord.

A word on the provenance of the physical manuscript *Catholicism: End or Beginning?* is in order before I delve into it. As Mary Daly aged, a group of friends formed "Team Mary" to assure her safety and dignity in her later years, as well as the conservation of her legacy after that.[10] Team members packed her possessions when she moved from her apartment first to an assisted living center and later to a nursing home where she died. In early 2009, the year before her death, Jennifer Rycenga and I packed boxes for her archives which were established at the Sophia Smith Collection at Smith College in Northampton, Massachusetts.[11]

It was a dusty job as we hauled files out of her metal cases and boxed them for use by researchers. It never occurred to me that day that perhaps we were handling a manuscript of such value, a truncated piece of her work that would provide insights into her ways of thinking about foundational, if to her mind outmoded, issues. I cannot be sure, of course, that we handled *this* manuscript. Nor can I say that there are no other such "finds" to be unearthed in the papers we and others packed. But I like to think that our labor of love was not in vain, since

[10] Emily Erwin Culpepper, "Introduction to Special Section in Memory of Mary Daly," *Journal of Feminist Studies in Religion* 28(2) (2012): 89–90.
[11] Mary Daly Archives, Sophia Smith Collection, Smith College, Northampton, Massachusetts. https://findingaids.smith.edu/repositories/2/resources/1163.

this text is a strong hinge linking two important phases of her work. I do have a vague memory of a dumpster into which we deposited things that did not go to Smith. Heaven forefend we got any of those decisions wrong!

Daly Studies may well become an academic subspeciality, not unlike the study of Paul Tillich or Dietrich Bonhoeffer. In whatever form it takes, we can be grateful for the good stewardship of the Sophia Smith Collection and the enterprising scholarship of Meg Stapleton Smith who found this text.

Three Central Questions about the Manuscript

My scholarly interest in Mary Daly's work revolves around three central questions which I will explore in turn as a way to assess this text. First, what were the straws that broke the Catholic camel's back for Mary Daly? Second, how did her strenuous rejection of the patriarchal Roman Catholic Church and all its trappings still reflect Mary's rootedness in Catholicism? Third, is this manuscript a game-changer with regard to how scholars might interpret Mary Daly in the twenty-first century?

What Were the Straws that Broke the Catholic Camel's Back for Mary Daly?

The abrupt end to this project does not look so abrupt in light of Mary's discussion in *Outercourse* and in light of the "New Archaic Afterwords" to *The Church and the Second Sex*.[12]

---

[12] Daly, *Outercourse*, 102.

In 1985, Mary wrote:

> The Courage to Leave springs from deep knowledge of
> the nucleus of nothingness which is at the core of the
> fallacious faith that freezes/fixes its victims. It is essential,
> then, to turn to the consideration of this faith that is used
> to frame women, together with its partners, false hope
> and dead love (charity). I will examine some of the ways in
> which this deadly trio of patriarchal virtues blocks
> women's potential for Living Faith, Hopping Hope, and
> Biophilic Bonding.[13]

She considered the issues under consideration in this
manuscript to be part of the "nothingness" and she simply
left them in her wake. Once she saw things anew, once she
was able to name the contours of the "old" in bold terms,
there was simply no choice but to move ahead putting her
former faith in the rearview mirror.

It was the "Courage to Leave" that led her to dissolve
her contract with her publisher and put aside months of
writing. Some of the issues took new form in *Beyond God
the Father*, so the work was not wasted. For example, her
work on the Fall morphed from the old Adam and Eve
tropes about female evil into the idea that Eve fell into
Freedom.[14] That kind of shift, and so many shifts similar
to it, show how her perspective and priorities changed
substantially, marking a new intellectual start.

There is a reason Mary Daly is known by most people
as a radical. She struck at the roots of everything, including the very things that had shaped her life in the deepest

---

[13] Daly, *The Church and the Second Sex*, XIII.
[14] Daly, *Outercourse*, 146.

and most pervasive ways. In retrospect, the intellectual and spiritual courage is stunning. A look at some of the specifics in the text show this movement.

The Nature of Faith

In an excruciatingly detailed wrestling with the basic nature of faith at the outset of this manuscript, Mary Daly describes a vapid faith being drilled into school children as if it had any meaning. She calls this rote approach the result of the institutional Roman Catholic Church's predicament as a "severely threatened institution" (*CEB?* 1), – one threatened from inside and out as it emerged from Vatican II. New practices were proposed and implemented, such as liturgical reforms, but the same old hierarchical structures remained, allowing a quick backslide in subsequent decades.

Daly goes on to parse the meaning of love as *eros* and *agape* giving way to *caritas* (1.1), using the Thomistic category of appetite and Pauline texts to draw out the yawn-inducing concepts. No wonder she tired quickly of this bloodless discourse! Daly writes that boredom results "when dogmatic literalism or verbal fundamentalism becomes the believer's surrogate for deep religious awareness" (1.1).

Her own religious awareness was steeped in nature and relationships, not in abstract concepts or laundry lists of required beliefs, even if one dissented from them. It is easy to read Daly writing herself out of synch with the theological dialogue of her day. She was turned on to the power of relating in new ways, especially with women, and turned off by dry discussion of dogmas. She recognized the power of mystical faith devoid of easy answers. And, she hoped that more people would find their own faith, not imbibe someone else's.

Symbols are Symbols and Myths are Myths

My insight is that Mary Daly was a Mystic.[15] She was quite familiar with symbols, "as pointing beyond themselves, yet as participating in that to which they point" (2.5). Likewise with myths, "The point of breaking myths is not to destroy them, but to recognize that they are myths" (3.3). Her insistence that a symbol is a symbol and a myth is a myth was quite literally iconoclastic. Many of her contemporaries were content to say that certain images were "just symbols," and that certain scriptural texts were "just myths." She drew out the deeper insight that they were symbols and myths, period.

She moved well beyond a check list of Christian beliefs that could be tweaked by individuals or councils, but finally never inclusive of or adequate to the depth of Mystery toward which she moved. "I refer to the immediate experience of something ultimate in value and meaning" (2.6) she wrote. Daly observed that "The truth of faith, which is expressed through myths and symbols, moves on a different level from that of the truth of history" (4.9). All of this makes clear that the Early Mary Daly was finished with the static categories and

---

[15] Mary E. Hunt, "Religious Resources for Survival: Ecofeminism and Earth Community," in *Living Cosmology: Christian Responses to Journey of the Universe*, ed. Mary Evelyn Tucker and John Grim (Maryknoll, NY: Orbis Books, 2016), 180–189.

intellectual timidity of many thinkers that she left behind as she moved into the next phase of her spiraling journey. Little has been made of this depth of Mystery in most Daly Studies. I think it is the most distinguishing dimension of her work. It explains why she studied religion in the first place – in order to chase down the illusive as others had, or hadn't, experienced it. She became disillusioned by many and varied approximations of spirituality. These were unsatisfying because they were not rooted in what can never be understood fully. Theology tried too hard to prove what it could not.

She realized that the "study" of something is not the same as the experience of it. The experience does not go away. As she wrote of her own awakening in love and sex, "From that Moment nothing was ever the same again. That relation ended after a few years but the transformation was permanent."[16] Symbols may be symbols and myths are myths, but they are feeble human efforts to explain what words cannot. Mary Daly knew that; most of her peers did not. This put her work on a par with physics and poetry more than with philosophy and cultural change.

Openness to other Religions

The Second Vatican Council (1962–1965) included extended discussions on other religions, including, somewhat paradoxically, Protestantism.[17] Protestantism,

---

[16] Daly, *Outercourse*, 144.
[17] The document on relations with other Christians is the "Decree on Ecumenism *Unitatis Redintegratio*," November 21, 1964; the document

finally, was so close to Catholicism that Mary recognized the fallacy of considering it Other. Once she realized that she had limited herself (and had been limited to) Catholic sources, she extended her analysis to point out how deeply intertwined the two strands were. She quickly extended her critical analysis of Catholicism to the whole of Christianity.

In the present document, Mary Daly wrote that Protestant eschatology and Catholic incarnational thinking were both necessary to an adequate approach to faith (Introduction). She favored, though with serious critique, both the theological synthesis of Lutheran Paul Tillich and the theology of hope of Reformed theologian Jürgen Moltmann. She offered only the faintest of nods to contemporary Catholic sources, citing Pierre Teilhard de Chardin, whose work, which had been condemned by Vatican officials before his death in 1955, was enjoying some new appreciation in Daly's time.

Her fundamental analysis, which eventually made this manuscript her swansong in the mainline Christian conversation, was that all religious traditions, especially the Catholic Christian one that she knew best, failed to let individual experiences and intuitions of believers percolate. She held that as the conversations deepen, the differences in flavors fade before the commonality of Mystery. Mystery, and not faith, was her concern. Catholic, Protestant, Buddhist, and others affiliated or unaffiliated in belief all had, in her view, the same potential to enter into Mystery unfettered by their organizational

on other people of faith is "Declaration on the Relations of the Church to Non-Christian Religions," *Nostra Aetate*, October 28, 1965.

connections. Their symbols and images pointed to the depth of Mystery about which no one could be sure. Anything less, she implied, was infantile faith. Unfortunately, there was a lot of that in the Catholicism she came to reject.

Adult Faith Requires Looking into the Abyss

Mary Daly lived and encouraged spiritual adulthood (1.8). She wrote, "The faith I am talking about is that state of ultimate concern which does not exclude doubt but which contains doubt in its depths. ... it carries with it a clear recognition that there is no sharp distinction between insiders and outsiders, Catholics and non-Catholics, Christians and non-Christians. This clarity about the fact of unclarity is a dizzying experience" (1.8). The challenge of being a spiritual adult was not for the faint of heart. Dizzying indeed.

Ecumenism was the raging theme of the day in the late 1960s and early 1970s. Christians were beginning to move tentatively from their comfort zones and walled off religious spaces. For example, Catholics who had been forbidden to enter a Protestant church in Mary Daly's mother's generation were starting to attend Protestant divinity schools. Daly recognized the futility of finding tiny points of intersection, polite ways of praying together apart, and the other exercises that missed the larger point that no one of these expressions can ever be paramount.

The Later Daly emerges here. It was unacceptable to Mary Daly that believers were not considered competent to rely on their own experiences and intuitions. She rejected institutions that were structured hierarchically. The assumption that top-down authorities would protect the "faithful" from "unbelievers" and "unbelievers" from themselves was anathema to her. In an exclusively male-led religion like Catholicism, women had no chance to think for themselves much less for anyone else; they could never be authorities. Mary Daly "put aside such childish things" (1 Corinthians 13:11), and with them Christianity as evidenced by her decision not to continue writing and publishing the manuscript that led her to these insights.

Mary as Part of the Core Christian Myth and Symbol

Catholic girls were taught a great deal about Mary, the mother of Jesus, whom they were to idolize and imitate. What they were taught is the subject of many feminist critiques: the passivity of Mary and her utter dependence on Jesus for her reason for being are counterproductive to feminist goals of women's agency and autonomy. That Mary, both virgin and biological mother, is what no other woman could imagine (in the days before *in vitro* fertilization, for example). Such religious notions would not attract men, Mary Daly pointed out, so why should they ground women's religious ideals? (4.7). She understood too much about the nature of symbols and myths to accept the imposition of a soft, receptive, compliant Mary on Catholic women. She knew its corrosive power.

Her critique of masculine exclusive gender comes relatively late in what became this foreshortened manuscript. Mary turned to the problems of "exclusively masculine terms" (3.6) in the context of a discussion on the Trinity. It is surprising that she did not notice it before, as her text is strewn with generic male words. But apparently she did not. When she did catch on, there was no turning back.

She wrote herself out of one phase of her work and right into another, learning from herself as she went.

Discussions of the Trinity in the history of theology frequently become occasions on which scholars twist themselves into theological pretzels. So many and slippery are the slopes, so stretched are some of the claims, that clarity about the Trinity remains elusive. The suggestion that emerged here in an effort to diversify language was that Father and Son get to be the masculine elements while Mary and the Holy Spirit are gendered female. The approach is understandable, if misguided, in one of Mary's first efforts to balance the gender scales. But the resulting 'Quaternity' is as intellectually awkward as the Trinity. More tellingly, it is a quantitative solution to a qualitative problem, an approach that never works.

I suspect that Mary understood quite quickly that the proposed four-part puzzle was no more than an arithmetic fix for something that needed a wholesale overhaul or a complete debunking. I am not aware that Mary Daly pursued this dead-end line of thinking even as her feminist theology emerged. I am glad about that!

Mary Daly maintained a robust interest in Marian shrines and Marian images for most of her career. This was not surprising for a Catholic college girl who wrote poetry about the Blessed Virgin Mary as an English major at the College of St. Rose in Albany, New York. To her credit, she did not try more vigorously to shoehorn Mary into a relational constellation that is so vexed and fraught, and finally too hard to explain without some assumptions and consequences that she eschewed.

That this issue of Mary (not Daly) arises quite late in the manuscript (4.7) leads me to speculate that this topic

might have been the final straw for her. She realized that
the most popular, promising, and salient aspect of the
Christian myth about a woman was impossible to reshape
without upsetting the whole patriarchal applecart, including the patriarchal institutional church. So, she cut to the
chase in *Beyond God the Father* by laying out succinctly the
problem of the "impossible ideal" named Mary, "It throws
all women back into the status of Eve and essentially
reinforces the universality of women's low caste status."[18]

These factors taken together, and with others that
Mary Daly mentioned, were the straws that broke the
Catholic camel's back. Such issues would have broken
the Protestant camel's back too because the deeper issue –
and with Mary Daly there is always a deeper issue – is that
all efforts to make change are limited at best.

Whether social justice activism or church reform, what
is necessary is:

> a plane of insight which enables us to discover transcend-
> ent meaning in our concrete situation and to transform
> our situation so that it becomes more transparent to this
> transcendent meaning. We then participate in the revela-
> tory process through our efforts to cope with the problem
> immediately before us in the concrete present, through
> our tentative efforts at rebuilding. (1.9)

Change was a desired option of course, but small
changes, however historically important, were not ultimate, according to Mary Daly.

Mary Daly saw the futility of parsing the many kinds of
love, of trying to rewrite symbols and myths instead of

---

[18] Daly, *Beyond God the Father*, 62.

finding the many meanings in them, of trying to rank order religions. She rejected allowing authorities to consign most people to spiritual infancy or (at best) adolescence by trying to name their Truth for them and banish their doubt. She rethought Mary in light of the plight of the world's women. Many of them paid the price for the institutional Church's contrived version of Mary because of laws and customs designed to keep women subservient. Still, there were ways in which her deep rootedness in one religious tradition, Catholicism, endured. In her worldview, religions are prototypes and not archetypes. They can and do change; they mean everything and nothing.

How Did Her Strenuous Rejection of the Patriarchal Roman Catholic Church and all its Trappings Still Reflect Mary's Rootedness in Catholicism?

Is Mary Daly Catholic?

The publication of *Beyond God the Father: Toward a Philosophy of Women's Liberation* (1973) was the centerpiece of the second of four "Spiral Galaxies" into which Mary Daly categorized her life. She describes 1970, the year she decided not to finish the manuscript under consideration in this volume but published other writing, as a moment of "Leaping into the Vortex of the Second Spiral Galaxy."[19] Her beloved mother had died, and she was dipping her toes into contemporary social issues. She had floated some trial balloon articles on her new insights about women and was energized by the responses.

---

[19] Daly, *Outercourse*, 107.

Daly wrote:

> The quality of my writing changed after that summer of
> 1970. It Leaped. By the end of that year, as I Moved
> within the interwoven context of the rising women's
> movement, of friendships charged with intellectual E-
> motional energy, and of the spiritual realms of awareness
> that were becoming accessible, my writing, teaching, and
> public speaking began to thrive in New ways.[20]

No one would dispute the marked change in approach
and content. The biggest difference in her approach from
The Church and the Second Sex to *Beyond God the Father* is
the change from a "Catholic" perspective to a "catholic"
perspective. It was not simply that Mary moved from
within the Roman Catholic Church context out of or
beyond the institutional Church. That is a superficial
reading, and an inadequate spatial way of describing the
radical, expansive nature of the text. It misses her wholesale shift in focus from things Catholic to a much broader
(catholic) set of concerns. In or out of the Church, whatever that means, is trivial. She did not go anyplace. She
went everywhere.

Of course, there was not a bright line separating those
spaces. Mary Daly was still at Boston College, still
immersed in a culturally Catholic milieu. For example,
she reported that her "pro-choice position on abortion
called down the wrath of 'colleagues.'"[21] Note the qualification of the word 'colleagues' as faculty support for her
at Boston College was scant. It waned over time, but she

---

[20] Ibid.   [21] Ibid., 108.

chose to stay knowing that in all probability she would face the same problems elsewhere (if there were another institution that would even hire her). The choice of stability on the job front coincided with multiple invitations to lecture and teach elsewhere, meaning Boston College was a convenient base from which to carry on conversations in many parts of the world.

Mary Daly was clearly a cultural Catholic given her early upbringing and theological formation. It was not as if she suddenly became Presbyterian or Buddhist in her thinking just because she moved "Beyond God the Father." Her religious experience tended toward the mystical and sacramental rather than the textual. That is markedly Catholic.

This tendency was on display when she described experiences of the Catholic Mass. She argued that even contemporary ways of celebrating the Eucharist might be experienced as inadequate. By contrast, some other social interactions, like protests or dinner parties, might be so meaningful as to prod the Mass-goer to imagine what liturgy or ritual could be like. She concluded that "despite the ineptitude of institutional religion's presentation of its symbols, the person has managed to sustain a sense of transcendence which is qualitatively different from the experience of the humanist" (4.5), and "this sustaining of the consciousness of transcendence is related to the Christian symbols although this relationship may only be ambiguously perceived in the experience" (4.5). Hers is hardly a ringing endorsement for eucharistic theology, but she is generous in her perception that transcendent experience can take many and varied, even unlikely, forms.

Mary Daly's Catholic Background as the Springboard for Her Religious Imagination

This leads me to speculate that Mary Daly perceived, and most probably valued, the grounding as well as the springboard that her own Catholic background was for her religious imagination. How could it be otherwise when she had twelve years of Catholic school, Catholic college and Master's programs, and three doctoral programs in Catholic institutions totaling close to thirty years of her life? It was in those settings that she learned foundational morality, which, when extended to women and others who are excluded in patriarchy, proved useful. The same foundation led her to reject the contradictions within both organized Christianity and the larger world.

Mary Daly's Catholic Contradictions

Jewish feminist theologian Judith Plaskow once famously quipped that she knew Mary Daly was still Catholic years after she had left the Church by the arguments about abortion that Mary dignified with a response. Judith meant that Mary was still taking the Catholic bait, as it were, even to refute it. For example, most Jews believe that human life begins when a baby is born. Hence, there simply is not the same attention in Jewish circles to the notions of life beginning at the moment of conception; scientists agree that no such "moment" exists in what is the process of conception. That does not deter many Catholics from debating it to this day. Most Jewish scholars do not focus on the finer points of implantation, quickening, and more that keep many Thomists hard at work in efforts to usurp women's moral agency. Mary was an early pro-choice identified Catholic who had to defend an unpopular position among her Catholic theological peers, including some women.

I playfully accused Mary more than once of being a "peeping Thomist." By that I meant that she was someone who was so deeply imbued with and indebted to the scholastic philosophy and theology of Thomas Aquinas, as she readily admitted, that it was hard for her to move beyond it. One of her many minds was Thomistic. Mary found it impossible, and probably not very useful, to jettison the *way* she learned to think critically just because *what* she was thinking changed. She could keep the skill without the content. In this manuscript, she very openly defended Thomas Aquinas's honor in his medieval context on the question of hierarchy and authority (1.1) while at the same time affirming how times have changed.

She respected Aquinas, and even had a certain love for his work. Jennifer Rycenga and I saw that when, toward the end of Mary's life, we took her a few books to enjoy as we cleaned out her apartment. One was her own copy of the *Summa Theologiae*. She caressed it with affection. It was among the few possessions Mary kept in her new room when she moved to an assisted living center. We felt the love.

Religions are in part, some may say at base, businesses that rely on market share for their success. Mary Daly's kind of thinking, both sketching ways in which believers of many stripes can find some common ground through Mystery, and assuming and encouraging adult behavior, threatened not only the content of religions but their economic foundations. Mary's theological claim that there is no "sharp distinction" between faith groups was implicitly bad for patriarchal business. She understood this very practical aspect of religions and how they had to change.

Mary Daly at Vatican II

During her time at Vatican II, Mary gravitated more to Catholic journalists who knew what was going on than to clerics who largely did not. During her month-long, life-changing visit to Rome, she sent a postcard to her mother announcing that she would be returning to Fribourg later than planned because she was hanging out with journalists. She was trading tidbits of ecclesial gossip and learning the ropes. Seeing up close and personal how the whole process worked was an eye-opener even for a Catholic theologian with three doctorates.

Had she been a male, and probably a cleric, Mary would have been in high demand as a *peritus*, an expert, who would have assisted the voting bishops to understand what on earth was going on around them in Latin. Many clerics, at least from the US, waited for the translations and summaries to be distributed nightly to figure out what went on all day. Mary, still in the Catholic conversation, was undoubtedly horrified by the low level of ability of those who were making high-level decisions that had global and historical consequences.

The experience in Rome changed Mary's life because she saw obvious and ostentatious contradictions. Robed men, most with far less education than she (and surely no one with three earned doctorates), had voice and vote at the Council. A few veiled women, mostly nuns including many who were well educated and in charge of running large corporate institutions, were consigned to listening-only mode as auditors. The preposterous juxtaposition made a deep impression on Mary Daly. That month in Rome, with the pageantry and historicity that surely appealed to her at one level, and the rank discrimination that functioned simultaneously, informed her later work as much as any other single event about which she writes. The very ambiguity of it is instructive on the question of her being Catholic.

There is something quite "off" about the question of Mary's Catholicism. Historical or speculative matters do not definitively answer the question of whether Mary was Catholic or not. She made clear on many occasions, and foreshadowed it in the manuscript under consideration, that she was certainly not Catholic in the sense in which the word was traditionally understood. Nor was she a "practicing" Catholic after seeing with her own eyes and hearing with her own ears how official global ecclesial business was conducted. Still, her sensibilities and sense of humor, her social justice commitments, and moral compass all reflect a certain Catholic sensibility that would have been hard for her to undo.

After all, she came from an Irish Catholic "ghetto" in Upstate New York. She was educated in a kind of Catholic cocoon where all but the most marginal people understood the common assumptions without explan-ation. Where else would the term "Church" mean the Roman Catholic Church without marking? Where but in such a closed circle would ideas like Trinity, Virgin Birth, Assumption, be debated seriously? The wonder is that she had the capacity to transcend all of that for bigger, wider horizons.

Mary Daly was What Catholic/catholic Should Be

While I understand completely and share the repugnance she felt toward most things Catholic, it is not necessary to let the institution nor its ways define the terms of any conversation. These are simply not trustworthy moral or intellectual sources. I prefer to think that she was what "Catholic" should be if it is to function as one of those gateways to transcendence. She was certainly catholic in her scope and breadth. Moreover, claiming her as Catholic, and not letting a patriarchal institution define her out of her own experience, strikes me as consistent with the methodology she encouraged in this work. After all, Mary took the power of Naming seriously.

"Elemental Encounters" direct one deeper and deeper into Mystery. That Catholics, especially those in institutional positions of power, would define her out is even more reason to make Mary Daly the gold standard, the norm. The rest are a deviation – better, many deviations – from the mean. It is she who enhances their identity not vice versa. I think she would chuckle in agreement with one more opportunity to make change.

Is This Manuscript a Game-Changer with Regard to How Scholars Might Interpret Mary Daly in the Twenty-First Century?

I admit to a certain agnosticism on this point. As Daly Studies have only begun to emerge, and because this manuscript has thus far been viewed by only a small number of colleagues, I think it is too early to make any judgment about this. However, *if* it were a game-changer, what would that mean?

At least until now, there is relatively little interest in Daly among "mainline" Catholic theologians. She is not taught outside of Women's Studies courses, if that, in US Catholic colleges and universities (as far as I know). I am not sure about other countries, though there are recent translations of her work in Italian and Spanish that make me think there may be a renaissance of interest in Europe. Diocesan seminaries would steer clear of her theology if some of their leaders even knew about it. The cancelling of Mary Daly in Catholic circles has been thorough and profound, save in a few places where she is included in introductory survey courses when there is an intellectual obligation to explain the roots of inclusive language for the Divine and women's critique of patriarchy.

Where one might expect to find a hub of thinking about her work, there is typically profound silence. Much of this is due to graduate students in Catholic institutions being discouraged from doing feminist work which they are told will make the already difficult job search harder. I have low expectations that any of that will change with the publication of this manuscript. Nonetheless, it is in Catholic circles where this manuscript is most readily understandable and where its importance is clearest. The same theological circles in which she was marginalized would benefit from understanding what they excluded. Alas, the mistake will probably be repeated.

Much of the general scholarly interest in Mary Daly is in courses on literature, gender studies, linguistics, and philosophy. For instance, one finds her correspondence with Audre Lorde highlighted often, usually faulting Mary for not answering a letter from Audre Lorde. In fact, Mary Daly's completed the public record with the publication of the response she had indeed sent to Audre Lorde.[22] The theological matters are incidental to any of that, but Mary's fundamental integrity, a reflection of her early upbring, was important to her and intact. She had decided not to contest the false accusation of ignoring Audre Lorde until she was told that text of Mary's letter had been unearthed in Lorde's archives. Similarly, in Queer Studies she is often portrayed as someone who was anti-trans. That is properly the subject for another essay, especially in light of her close friendship with Pauli Murray, lawyer, civil rights worker, Episcopal priest, and now thought to have been trans. What seems important to me is that Mary Daly was a signal thinker whose views, however dated and rooted in a context which has now changed tremendously, are part of a larger, longer conversation.

For many Daly scholars, the finer points of how she got to her mature positions are of little interest. This manuscript may change that. Some Women's Studies scholars have, understandably, taken Mary at her word that she was a philosopher and not primarily a theologian, and that she left Catholicism. They have absolved themselves of the responsibility to explore her theologically.

I understand their thinking which has resulted in their passing over the Catholic questions in favor of broader

---

[22] Mary Daly, *Amazon Grace: Re-Calling the Courage to Sin Big* (New York: Palgrave Macmillan, 2005), 22–26.

matters. But I think they miss a very significant aspect of Mary Daly, which, now with this publication, is clear. She emerged from a very specific and powerfully poisonous Catholic context which she helpfully named and warned (one might say, inveighed) against. This manuscript is a testament to and a map of that landscape. The irony is that even in such a contradictory context she was able to have a deeply spiritual experience of Mystery, proving anyone can, despite their circumstances. She was persistent in exploring that experience and committed to sharing ways for others to access it as well. By eliminating some of the religious detritus that gets in the way, her strategy was a gamechanger all its own.

Conclusion

Mary Daly was of many minds – and what a mind she was. She engaged in a multidimensional intellectual life that included the teaching that she loved as well as the scholarship and writing that compelled and defined her over a long and productive life. Much of that is on display, if in shadow form, in this manuscript which predates but connects to what I consider her most impactful work, namely *Beyond God the Father*. This manuscript adds welcome detail to what brought her along from mid twentieth-century Catholic ponderings to some of the most explosive ideas about women, gender, and religion that have shaken postmodernity to its fleeting core.

Among the most instructive things to me in this project is that Mary stopped cold – left this manuscript for dead. Many authors might do themselves the same favor when the projects they are pursuing are so obviously going off track or down into such a deep hole that the only exit is a last chapter, regardless.

I applaud Mary Daly's intellectual honesty. I cheer her sense of self-worth and self-care that she did not complete this work just because she had a publishing contract. I take courage from her ability to see beyond the book on her desk to what really needed to be written. Imagine if she had continued with this comparatively superficial or at least limited conversation and *Beyond God the Father* had never been written. Perish the thought.

Another learning I glean directly from this manuscript, read in the context of the Daly corpus, is the importance of avoiding the mistake of dismantling religions and simply remaking them with a twist. Her adamancy on this point is clear in this manuscript in ways that I do not find in either what came before it or what came after. In neither the *Church and the Second Sex* nor in *Beyond God the Father* does she actually make the point that religions are by their nature constructs that can be made and remade to no real avail. Religions can be impervious to and unchanged by the deep experiences of people seeking Mystery and perhaps Mystery seeking people. But not even the moral poverty of the Roman Catholic Church could dissuade or misdirect Mary Daly from her Truth. Nor, ironically, can she be written out of the very history and tradition that she came from and critiqued.

For example, the period immediately following the publication of *Beyond God the Father* saw a flurry of efforts, especially in Protestant churches, to include women and other marginalized people in ministry. There were shifts from exclusive to inclusive and expansive language, and other attempts to remake religious organizations, theologies, and polities, with attention to some of the issues that Mary Daly raised. But, fifty years later, the changes look increasingly cosmetic. The role of many clergy people remains static even as the number of women in the traditionally nurturing ministerial role increases. Inclusive language has gone the way of all flesh. Ecumenism is a historical but not necessarily contemporary concern. Still, there are many people, especially feminists, who hold their Truths with both hands, thanks in part to Mary Daly.

Mary Daly realized that as important as such structural and organizational changes might be, they were no substitute for an entirely new way of thinking about and finding one's way into "the spiritual presence in other expressions of the ultimate meaning of man's being" (4.11). That was the work she undertook moving forward, thus relativizing all other efforts by reformers who were not keyed into her revolution. With this manuscript illuminating the path, Mary Daly makes it easier "to turn inward again to the deep roots in consciousness, experience, and imagination from which the awareness of being secretly grows" (2.9).

2

Reformist Catholicism: The Road Not Taken for Mary Daly

∾

Lisa Sowle Cahill

Introduction

The poet Robert Frost concludes "The Road Not Taken" with the lines,

> Two roads diverged in a wood, and I –
> I took the one less traveled by,
> and that has made all the difference.[1]

Catholicism: End or Beginning? (*CEB?*) is Mary Daly's "road not taken." Aspects of her choice are captured in Frost's portrayal of the traveler's dilemma in the opening stanzas of the same poem:

> long I stood
> And looked down one as far as I could
> To where it bent in the undergrowth;
>
> Then took the other; as just as fair
> And having perhaps the better claim[2]

---

[1] Robert Frost, "The Road Not Taken" (1915). www.poetryfoundation.org/poems/44272/the-road-not-taken.
[2] Ibid.

The thesis of this chapter is that Daly began *CEB?* in the hopeful, reforming spirit of the Roman Catholic Church's twentieth-century mega-event, the Second Vatican Council (1962–1965). Momentum in the Church toward greater gender equality had been growing for decades, inspired by European and North American currents of social change regarding gender (first-wave feminism concerned with political rights; and the beginnings of second-wave feminism advocating equality in sex, marriage, and reproduction). As will be detailed below, Pope Paul VI belatedly brought women into Council meetings, and though this was far from a radical move, it augured to many further progress. Daly, more presciently than most, ultimately discerned, that with male clergy still in control, future ecclesial accommodation of women would not produce the radical transformation of consciousness and culture she foresaw. *CEB?* ends just as Daly is about to assess and suggest prospects for specific, substantive changes in Church culture and institutions. I would modify Frost's characterization of the traveler's choice to say that, while Daly looked down the road of post-Vatican II reformist Catholicism as far as she could, and saw it lost in the undergrowth, there was no "perhaps" in her final determination to take another route. She was convinced that the hope inspired and the reforms promised by the Council were destined to a dead end.

The Church and the Second Sex, Daly's first book, published three years after the Council's conclusion, had mounted a powerful critique of ecclesial patriarchy. In 1968, she was not yet persuaded that the patriarchal Roman Catholic Church was irredeemable, could not seed or carry the transformation of gender consciousness.

But in 1973, her next monograph, *Beyond God the Father*, no longer imagined Christianity as a vehicle of reform. Between the two books, Daly not only began and dropped *Catholicism: End or Beginning?*; she authored at least two important short essays suggesting that feminists must walk out of and away from the Catholic Church and Christianity to attain liberation and fullness of being. Yet even in these later works Daly conveys a quasi-mystical sense of transcendent reality and of the possibility of life-giving human connection with it. She was convinced that a community of women could realize and mediate that reality in ways that institutional Christianity had not, through solidaristic practices, a sustaining spirituality, and new world-creating languages and symbols. Yet, the spirituality, language, and symbols of *Beyond God the Father* (as well as *CEB?*) still resonate with the language and vision of Christian predecessors like Aquinas, Tillich, and Paul.

The remainder of this essay will develop the Vatican II context of Mary Daly's early work, including *CEB?*; discuss the argument of *CEB?* as representing an early version of Vatican II theological feminism, albeit one that is incipiently boundary-breaking; briefly compare *Beyond God the Father* as a contrast case; and, in conclusion, place Daly's mature work as a sort of *theopoiesis*, an attempt with community-embedded writing to engender and mediate through the text the relation to transcendent reality it describes.

Vatican II and Women

The major participants in the Council were 2,500 Roman Catholic bishops from around the world. There were in addition 500 secondary (non-voting) theological advisors (called *periti*), and twelve auditors, who, as the Council opened, were all male. Midway through the Council, Cardinal Leo Jozef Suenens of Belgium asked his fellow bishops: "Why are we even discussing the reality of the church when half of the church is not even represented here?"[3] As a result, Pope Paul VI invited nineteen women auditors to participate, but without the right of speaking in the assembly or voting. Four additional women, including Dorothy Day, attended parts of the sessions as well. As Carmel McEnroy succinctly puts it, these women were included as "guests in their own house."[4] Mary Luke Tobin, one of the invited Council auditors, saw Cardinal Suenens's intervention as a "breakthrough" in the all-male assembly; nevertheless, the result amounted merely to reluctant inclusion of "a few 'token' women."[5]

---

[3] Mary Luke Tobin, "Women in the Church Since Vatican II," *America* (November 1, 1986). www.americamagazine.org/issue/100/women-church-vatican-ii. Tobin, then president of the Conference of Women Religious, was one of the women auditors eventually invited to the Council. On the history of women at Vatican II, see also, Carmel McEnroy, *Guests in Their Own House: The Women of Vatican II* (Eugene OR: Wipf and Stock, 2011); Mary Ann Hinsdale, "Vatican II and Feminism: Recovered Memories and Refreshed Hopes," *Toronto Journal of Theology* 32 (2016), 251–258; Patricia Madigan, "Women During and After Vatican II," in *Catholicism Opening to the World and Other Confessions: Vatican II and Its Impact*, ed. Vladimir Latinovic, Gerard Mannion, and Jason Welle (London: Palgrave Macmillan, 2018), 79–96; and Gerard Mannion, "Women and the Art of Magisterium: Reflections on Vatican II and the Postconciliar Church," ibid., 119–147.

[4] This was the title of McEnroy's book, cited in the note above.

[5] Tobin, "Women in the Church." In *Beyond God the Father*, Mary Daly was to confirm that "tokenism does not change stereotypes or social systems but works to preserve them, since it dulls the revolutionary impulse." *Beyond God the Father: Toward a Philosophy of Women's Liberation* (Boston: Beacon Press, 1973), 14.

The women's restricted participation in the Council sessions did not mean that their influence on the Council's outcome was nil. Several bishops consulted with women, treating them as in effect *periti*. At the urging of Bernard Häring, a Council theologian, women were invited participants in subcommittees drafting Council documents, where they made substantial contributions. Some spoke at meetings of bishops outside the Council proceedings. The women met together weekly, commenting on drafts. They offered open houses for bishops and seminarians, thus expanding their informal access.[6] Some bishops spoke in favor of women's equality in the formal Council proceedings. Archbishop Paul Hallinan of Atlanta urged the Church to move past limiting women's vocations to "mother or nun," and to cease perpetuating "the secondary status accorded to women in the Church of the 20th century."[7]

A sentence crafted by one of the auditors, Rosemary Goldie from Australia, was included in the final version of the Decree on the Apostolate of the Laity.[8] "Since in our days women are taking an increasingly active share in the whole life of society, it is important that their participation in various fields of the Church's apostolate should likewise develop."[9] The Pastoral Constitution on the

---

[6] Madigan, "Women During and After Vatican II," 86.
[7] Placid Jordan, "U.S. Prelate Asks Women Be Given Roles in the Mass," *The Voice* 7 (October 15, 1965), 4 (Archdiocese of Miami, Florida), as cited in Madigan, "Women During and After Vatican II," 85.
[8] Madigan, "Women During and After Vatican II," 86.
[9] Decree on the Apostolate of the Laity (1965), no. 9. www.vatican.va/archive/hist_councils/ii_vatican_council/documents/vat-ii_decree_19651118_apostolicam-actuositatem_en.html.

Church in the Modern World declared similarly that "fundamental personal rights" should be "universally honored." The document asserted further that such rights are dishonored in the case of any woman "who is denied the right to choose a husband freely, to embrace a state of life, or to acquire an education or cultural benefits equal to those recognized for men."[10] The Decree on the Laity called (all) "the laity" to "helpful collaboration for every apostolic and missionary undertaking sponsored by their local parish."[11] And, since "women have an even more active share in the whole life of society, it is very important that they participate more widely also in the various fields of the Church's apostolate."[12] The invitation to collaborate was, however, left in the hands of the local priest or bishop. There were no formal ecclesial roles to which women were in principle entitled. This did not augur well for change, given the disincentive to women's inclusion or power-sharing – then, as now – for men (especially clergy and bishops) who benefitted from the status quo.

Yet, up to and including *The Church and the Second Sex* (*CSS*), Mary Daly was still hopeful that token change would lead to incremental change, and, in turn, to monumental change in church, culture, and society. Daly was theologically well-educated, highly committed to Catholic Church reform, and equipped with sharp intellectual tools for the project. In 1943, Sr. Madaleva Wolff,

---

[10] Pastoral Constitution on the Church in the Modern World (1965), no. 29. www.vatican.va/archive/hist_councils/ii_vatican_council/ documents/vat-ii_cons_19651207_gaudium-et-spes_en.html.

[11] Decree on the Apostolate of the Laity (1965), no. 10.

[12] Ibid., no. 9.

CSC, president of Saint Mary's College, Notre Dame, Indiana, had inaugurated the first US graduate program in Catholic theology open to women. Mary Daly received her first PhD from Sr. Madaleva's Graduate School of Sacred Theology.[13] At the time of the Council, she was adding to her St. Mary's doctorate two more from the University of Fribourg, one in philosophy and one in theology. Like other women of her era (and even much later), she was treated dismissively by some male faculty; excluded by fellow students and male seminarians; and marginalized intellectually. Yet her love for the classic philosophical and theological "greats" was strong, and for Thomas Aquinas in particular. Also compelling to Daly were creative insights of Paul Tillich (God as the "ground of being") and Jürgen Moltmann (the theology of hope), among other theological innovators of the time.

In 1965, Daly went to Rome and gained entrance to some Council sessions by scoring a press pass. At this point, she began to write *CSS*.[14] Jessica Coblentz and Brianne Jacobs outline contributions of *CSS* that shaped the feminist theological agenda for the next fifty years – as well as ways in which later Catholic feminism moved beyond what Mary Daly had accomplished. They name five continuities. Elaborating on Simone de Beauvoir's critique in *The Second Sex*, Daly accuses the Church of being oppressive to women (by institutionally prescribing and regulating their secondary status); luring them into

---

[13] Mary Ann Hinsdale, "Vatican II and Feminism: Recovered Memories and Refreshed Hopes," *Toronto Journal of Theology* 32 (2016): 258.

[14] Jessica Coblentz and Brianne A. B. Jacobs, "Mary Daly's *The Church and the Second Sex* after Fifty Years of US Catholic Feminist Theology," *Theological Studies* 79(3) (2018): 545.

passivity (especially by extolling the supposed characteristics of the Blessed Virgin Mary); promoting doctrine that is "violent" to women (especially the idea that women are "ontologically" [in their essential nature] different from men and inferior); inducing in women a sense of inferiority (through ecclesially ratified gender stereotyping); and most significantly for the works here under discussion, obstructing "women's transcendence" (by denying both theologically and practically the full personhood of women). Yet, as she makes most explicit toward the book's end, Daly is convinced that it is possible to "hope for and work toward Catholicism's feminist reform."[15]

Later feminist theologians were able to persist in the reform process by moving beyond Daly in at least two ways. In an environment informed by postmodern, liberationist, and postcolonial scholarship, as well as by critical biblical studies and other critical theories, Christian feminists came to appreciate that gender discrimination is interdependent with factors of social location and identity, such as "structures of racism, xenophobia, transphobia, classism, ableism, ageism, homophobia, sizeism, nationalism, and colonialism, among others."[16] And feminist theologians (paralleling the methodology of revisionist biblical critics) were to stake their own ground within Christianity by critiquing the accuracy of traditional sexist theologies and doctrines, and supplanting them with more adequate and liberatory versions. They were even able to show that key premises of their revisionist theologies had greater claim to tradition-based "authority" (e.g., the role of Mary Magdalene as "apostle

---

[15] Ibid., 546.   [16] Ibid., 558.

to the apostles" in John 20; and prominent women leaders in the Pauline churches, as in Romans 1). Thus, unlike Daly, these later feminists saw potential for reform of the Catholic worldview, Catholic spirituality, and Catholic practice.[17] To these two developments, an important third may be added. As more women globally gained access to theological education and a voice, and as churches and theologians in the global North belatedly grasped the power of more diverse theologies from within their own cultures, as well as the originality of voices from the global South, what had begun as white, academic, feminist theology was challenged, learned, and changed.[18]

Given that Mary Daly was a prophet and forerunner of Catholic feminist theology, neither these later developments specifically, nor a collaborative and supportive community of feminist theological scholars with whom to imagine and invent a radical feminist Christian worldview, was available during her formative decades as theologian.[19] In the Catholic theological academy and higher

---

[17] Ibid., 561.

[18] An exchange of letters between the African American poet Audre Lorde and Mary Daly has met a fraught history of interpretation and reception. See the *Feminism and Religion* exchange, beginning with a blog post by Gina Messina on October 5, 2011. https://feminismandreligion.com/2011/10/05/mary-dalys-letter-to-audre-lorde/. For the viewpoint of an African American feminist theological ethicist, see Traci C. West, "The Gift of Arguing with Mary Daly's White Feminism," *Journal of Feminist Studies in Religion* 28(2) (2012): 112–117.

[19] Mary Ann Hinsdale, "Vatican II and Feminism," outlines the work of several who emerged in the years shortly to follow, including Rosemary Ruether and Elisabeth Schüssler Fiorenza, with a much greater variety of race, ethnicity, social location, sex and gender identity, and continental origin quickly to flourish. See also Coblentz and Jacobs, "Mary Daly's *The Church and the Second Sex*."

education, at least, Mary Daly's call to revolution met the fate of a biblical prophet: it fell largely on deaf ears. The publication of *CSS* in 1968 occasioned the attempted termination of her contract as a professor in the theology department at Boston College (a Jesuit university), a position she had assumed in 1966.[20] With student protests (BC students were then all male), a public outcry, and the support of at least some of her theology department colleagues (a Franciscan priest, Theo Steeman, was an ally),[21] the termination was revoked. Yet her thirty-three-year relationship with the university remained under permanent strain. Mary Daly was denied promotion to full professor in 1975, ostensibly on the grounds that her theological approach was not "scholarly" enough.[22] In 1990, she left the theology faculty in the wake of another controversy, involving a lawsuit brought by a student against her policy of all-female classes.

Mary Daly was hardly alone in her early hope for ecclesial reform. Many feminist interpreters of the Council and its effects appreciated that it represented

---

[20] See Mary E. Hunt, "Biographical Sketch," in *The Mary Daly Reader*, ed. Jennifer Rycenga and Linda Barufaldi (New York: New York University Press, 2017), xv–xvi.

[21] Theodore M. Steeman, OFM, 1928–1985. After Theo Steeman's unexpected death, Mary Daly visited his wake, hosted by the local Franciscan community in the Jesuit residence (St. Mary's Hall) on the Boston College campus. Daly also had a relation of mutual respect with the longtime Theology Department Chairperson, Robert J. Daly, SJ. When Bob Daly stepped down from that role, tenured faculty were asked to contribute to a parting gift, associate professors half the amount of full professors. Mary Daly returned an envelope with no message, but containing a donation of twice the amount requested of full professors.

[22] Hunt, "Biographical Sketch," xvi.

an enlarged "understanding of women, their role in the family, and their rising social, political, and economic status"; and that the Church under popes John XXIII and Paul VI "began to genuinely struggle" with gender equality. Yet progress was "subverted" by John Paul II, who reverted to a gender ideology of bipolar male–female "complementarity," romanticizing women's subservience with praise of "feminine genius."[23] In 1976 and 1994, the ban on women's priestly ordination was reiterated, with the additional proviso in 1994 that the matter was no longer even to be discussed.[24] (Predictably enough, this mandate exacerbated debate.)

According to Phyllis Zagano, an advocate of women's ordination to the diaconate, the "bright hope" of the Vatican II years "now wears a [then] forty year tarnish." Ordination of women to the diaconate (a non-priestly role – one that historians have shown to have been open to women in past centuries) has been reintroduced for consideration by Pope Francis. Yet the initiative flounders under controversy and resistance.[25] Though women's contributions, genius, dignity, and rights are constantly proclaimed, women's actual social equality and rights, and gender parity of roles within the Church itself, are not

---

[23] Madigan, "Women During and After Vatican II," 80. Not all feminist women in all cultures have the same problems with the term "feminine genius," nor with gender differences that are to a degree reproductively sorted, that advocates of gender equality in North Atlantic cultures typically do (including myself). Cultural humility and mutual respect are universal virtues.

[24] Congregation for the Doctrine of the Faith, *Inter Insignores* (1976) and John Paul II, *Ordinatio Sacerdotalis* (1994).

[25] Phyllis Zagano, "Women and the Church: Unfinished Business of Vatican II," *Horizons* 34 (2007): 205.

priorities of ecclesial action, even when they are not directly proscribed. Meanwhile, most doors to authority, governance, and jurisdiction in the Catholic Church are closed to women, because those doors, at least until very recently, have been marked "priests only."[26]

In 2022, Pope Francis appointed three women to the review committee for candidates for episcopal ordination. In 2023, he announced that about 20 percent of the participants in the 2023 Synod of Bishops (on "synodality") would be women, and that they would have the right to vote.[27] Undoubtedly, Mary Daly would have seen such moves as too little and much too late. She would presumably agree with Zagano that the waves of change after the Second Vatican Council opened new possibilities but "raised false hopes as well."[28] Mary Daly saw the failure of genuine inclusion coming down "the road not taken," but not clearly so until after the false start to a reform program represented by *CEB?*

Catholicism: End or Beginning? The Unfinished Manuscript of Mary Daly

CEB? is undated, but the latest reference in the notes is to a work published in 1970; all but one are earlier, though

---

[26] Ibid., 221.
[27] Hannah Brockhaus, "Pope Francis Appoints Three Women to Dicastery for Bishops," *Catholic News Agency* (July 13, 2022). www.catholicnewsagency.com/news/251778/pope-francis-appoints-three-women-to-dicastery-forrgr-bishops; and "Vatican Announces Laypeople, Including Women, Will Vote in Synod on Synodality Assembly," *Catholic News Agency* (April 26, 2023). www.catholicnewsagency.com/news/254176/vatican-announces-laypeople-including-women-will-vote-in-synod-on-synodality-assembly.
[28] Zagano, "Unfinished Business," 221.

there are several from 1969. This suggests that Daly was working on this manuscript two or three years after the completion of *CSS*, perhaps even before its publication; and continued work to 1970, when she seems to have ceased adding to the draft originally intended to become her second book (around the same time as her first highly alienating conflict with Boston College).

This work unfolds in drafts of an introduction and four chapters, of seven projected. Daly begins by identifying the driving force behind her theological work, her vision of Christian community, and her eventual break into a "post-Christian" mode: her passion for an experience of and a relationship with the power within yet beyond all finite being, which she calls "transcendent reality" (Introduction). Daly uses the "ontological" category of "being" (from Aquinas, modified with help from Paul Tillich) to capture the immediacy, the ultimacy, and the transformative power of a direct, present, and reciprocal relation to what traditional theology named "God." For Daly, divine being or "Being" (or *"be-ing"/"Be-ing,"* the term that begins to appear in *God the Father*) is not a static essence, but a dynamic, creative, and sustaining power, immanent within all that is.

In the introduction to the work, Daly takes up the danger of losing touch with the transcendent ground of theology and religion amidst unsettling if necessary waves of change. To grasp the tension between the enduring and transcendent character of ultimate being and the need for the adaptability and reform of the symbols and structures that only ever partially mediate the experience of that being, Daly employs Paul Tillich's rubric of the interdependent "Protestant principle" (continual reform, the church as *semper reformanda*) and "Catholic substance" (the doctrines, symbols, sacraments, that, while finite, connect faith to the transcendent reality "that gives it life"). On the one hand, Daly sees that reform and change are precisely what is needed in the Catholic Church to maintain the authentic relation to God that inspires just and loving human relationships. On the other hand, Daly has some sympathy with those who fear that too much accommodation to contemporary culture will lead to religious emptiness and banality. In bringing Catholicism up to "the modern world" (to borrow from the title of one of the Council decrees), Daly hopes that Vatican II will be able to "reintegrate" change and reform through "radical openness to transcendence" (Introduction).

Daly previews the chapters to come in terms of this basic concern for transcendence. The first drafted chapter concerns the nature of faith; the second, the transcendent reality faith seeks; the third, the fact of existential estrangement from that reality; and the fourth, the search for Christ as the New Being that overcomes this separation. The last three chapters were to have dealt with "the problems" attendant upon "the perpetuation of the community" – with relation to "transcendent reality" (the church), and with the movements and new visions "sparked by the revelatory encounter with Christ." Specifically, Chapter 5 would have dealt "with the problem of communication and community"; Chapter 6 with theology; and Chapter 7 with "revolution in the church today" (Introduction).

In my assessment, the constructive theological interventions of this book are uneven. Mary Daly is at her best when she envisions divine reality as a power beyond all finite being that sustains, liberates, and empowers human existence. Yet she is less successful when trying to explain how Jesus Christ is the mediator of humanity's authentic relation to transcendent reality and transformer of human community. Daly turns to Jungian (rather than biblical or theological) categories; and these now seem dated, to lack profundity, and even to fall short of feminist goals. Partly at issue are the philosophical and theological resources available to Daly at the time, her expertise in certain sources that carried powerful insights, yet had limited applicability to her subject matter, and the inadequacy of those resources to carry her where she wanted to go in the later chapters of the book. The manuscript ends just as Daly has incorporated the thought of Carl Jung into Chapter 4 on New Being and is about to launch into recommendations for the church and theology going forward.

This chapter will assess *CEB?* primarily in terms of Daly's theologies of being and transcendent reality; the Fall as alienation from that reality; Christ as the New Being; the lack of fulfillment and hence ambiguity present in faith; the consequent demand for "the courage to be"; and the "theology of hope" as offering a way of existing within incompleteness while anticipating and living out of the future. The argument is ordered so that New Being is the last treated of these themes; whereas, in my view, a more effective presentation would have ordered them more or less in the way I have just presented (with ambiguity, courage, and hope following on New Being). The fundamental concern of the first chapter and of the book as a whole is to define genuine faith as "a state of relatedness to the unconditioned" (1.9). Faith consists in a profound inner commitment and condition of one's whole personality, not simply assent to a series of propositions, taken on faith (1.5). In the state of consciousness which is faith, the finite human is "grasped by the infinite," experiencing as initiated from beyond the self, "a movement toward that which is totally other and yet intimately present" (1.5). With the twentieth-century Lutheran theologian Paul Tillich, Daly sees "the divine reality, to which one is related through faith" as "the ground of all being" (1.5).[29] For Tillich, and as appropriated by Daly, the ground of religious experience and of theology is a sort of "mysticism of being" or "mystical a priori" in which the division between knower and known is transcended (1.5).[30]

The thought of Thomas Aquinas on God as infinite Being is at least as important for Daly's theology as that of Tillich, and arguably more so. The theology of Aquinas was a prevalent and formative source in Catholic theological education at the time of Daly's doctoral studies. Daly found in Aquinas a generative complexity, despite problematic aspects of many of his ideas (especially about gender), and despite the fact that her own thought changed over time (1.1). There are evident parallels between Aquinas's metaphysics and Daly's key conceptions of transcendent reality as sustaining being, and of the gratuitous character of humanity's relation to it.[31]

---

[29] Citing Paul Tillich, *The Courage to Be* (New Haven, CT: Yale University Press, 1952).

[30] Citing Paul Tillich, *Systematic Theology*, vol. 1 (Chicago: University of Chicago Press, 1951), 190.

[31] A useful source for Daly's reliance on Aquinas and her expressions of indebtedness to him is Sue Waslin, "The Theoretical Contexts of Mary

Daly's "ontologically oriented theology" has as its first principle "the awareness of the ground and power of being. All finite beings participate in this power, otherwise they would be swallowed by non-being" (2.6). As Aquinas also affirms, "God is in all things." Since "God is very being by His own essence, it belongs to the great power of God that He acts immediately in all things" to sustain their existence. "As long as a thing has being, God must be present to it . . . Hence it must be that God is in all things, and inner-mostly."[32] By portraying faith as enabled by divine grace in the gift of charity, Aquinas captures the comprehensively engaging effect of both of these "theological virtues" on the intellect and will, as well as their quality of being sustained by a power outside themselves (1.5).[33]

Daly's Thought," PhD thesis, 1990, University of St Andrews (directed by Daphne Hampson), chap. 3 ("Thomism"). Waslin detects a tension in Daly's thought between her feminist agenda and the "masculinist" assumptions and "static worldview" of Aquinas. She asks whether Daly is able successfully to "lift" aspects of Aquinas's ontology or metaphysics, along with key categories or concepts such as God as Being, without also bringing along objectionable parts of the framework underlying them. Despite what was no doubt Daly's fraught relation with medieval Catholic worldviews, even that of Aquinas, her love for his work endured. Mary Hunt shares that she and other friends helped Mary Daly settle into assisted living in her later years. One of the items they brought to her from her previous home was "a well-used copy of Thomas Aquinas's *Summa Theologica* [*Theologiae*]. Mary was delighted to have it with her. Of course, by that time some of her brightness had dimmed but it was evident that she still valued the work of Thomas Aquinas that had so shaped her own thinking." Mary E. Hunt, "Celebrating and Cerebrating Mary Daly," *Journal of Feminist Studies in Religion* 28 (2012), 92.

[32] Thomas Aquinas, *Summa Theologiae*, I, Q.8, "The Existence of God in All Things," New Advent. www.newadvent.org/summa/1008.htm.

[33] Cf. Aquinas, *Summa Theologiae*, II–II, Q.62, "The Theological Virtues."

Thomist scholar Fergus Kerr elucidates the generative power of Aquinas for Daly's early theology when he explains that for Aquinas access to the one God is not limited to Christianity: "God as source and goal of all that exists, the God of whose reality knowledge was attained by the pre-Christian philosophers – literally 'wisdom-lovers' and effectively themselves religious."[34] In fact, Aquinas fashions his conception of God by drawing on the Muslim thinker, Ibn Sina (Avicenna, 980–1037), and the Jewish Rabbi, Moses ben Maimon (Maimonides, 1135–1204).[35]

In Aquinas's theology and metaphysics, God is in all things, even sinners and demons, because, although evil, they exist. Nevertheless, the human condition is marred radically by estrangement from God. For Aquinas, sin is a "deformity" of the human's relation to infinite being.[36] Like Aquinas, Daly interprets sin as alienation from transcendent reality. But, unlike Aquinas, she does not hold that sin derives from "one event in the past" (the sin of Adam and Eve). Today, neither critical biblical scholarship, nor most modern theologians, nor the Roman Catholic Church, regard the narrative of Genesis 1–3 as literal history, a premise which necessitated that premodern thinkers explain how the sin of two humans in the past could infect all subsequent humanity universally. Daly rightly complains that the inheritance by generation

---

[34] Fergus Kerr, "Why Still Read Aquinas?" *Thinking Faith: The Online Journal of the British Jesuits* (January 27, 2014). www.thinkingfaith.org/articles/why-still-read-thomas-aquinas.

[35] Ibid., 2, citing David Burrell, *Freedom and Creation in Three Traditions* (Notre Dame, IN: University of Notre Dame Press, 1993).

[36] Aquinas, *Summa Theologiae*, I, Q.8, A.1, ad 4.

theory of Aquinas carries an "air of improbability and unreality" that "hardly rings true to the contemporary consciousness" (which is even more true of Augustine's idea that original sin is passed on through the sex act as necessary for biological reproduction) (see 3.1). Daly explains the dynamics of human sinfulness, with the help of R. D. Laing and Carl Jung, as a "false consciousness imposed by our culture" (3.0). Yet she concurs with Christian theological tradition that healing from sin cannot be accomplished by merely human efforts at social reform. It requires reconnection with an ultimate reality that already "grasps" the sinner. At the end of the day, Daly shares the judgment of many theologians that the origin of sin and evil is difficult if not impossible to explain. While the myth of the Fall "poignantly" expresses humanity's "universal sense of alienation," it is not a solution to "the baffling mystery of human existence," which is so tragically estranged from that which preserves it from non-being and gives it meaning and hope. A similar conclusion is reached by the Thomist Denys Turner, who finds allies in Brian Davies, David Burrell, and Herbert McCabe. These thinkers are representative but hardly alone in joining Mary Daly to give up "logical" explanations (such as the so-called "free will defense") of why any humans existing in the blessed condition of union with that which gives them life and happiness would willingly separate themselves from it (explanations called "theodicies").[37]

---

[37] Denys Turner, *God, Mystery & Mystification* (Notre Dame, IN: University of Notre Dame Press, 2019), 4, 165.

The biblical story of sin's origin is not about historical fact, but Daly is not prepared to sideline the Fall as "only a myth." The myth must be reconceptualized (appropriated theologically in different concepts than traditionally) because it has been weaponized for centuries to advance "antifeminine prejudice" and "antisexual bias" (3.3). It is no less a powerful symbol that speaks truthfully to the modern consciousness of existential alienation, as well as to the fact that sin, while structurally deep in the human situation, and universal (3.3: "The Fall is unavoidable in all of our lives"), is not unalterable (3.4–3.5). As the Lutheran biblical scholar Phyllis Trible cleverly argued, already in the 1970s (reappropriating many of the relatively iconoclastic views of Martin Luther on the equal creation of woman and man), the biblical texts narrating creation portray women neither as secondary to man (if the woman was created from the man's rib, he was created from dirt, so the progression goes from lower to higher), nor as alone responsible for human sin (the woman gave fruit to the man "who was with her" [Genesis 3:6; NRSV], not bothering to get involved with much less advise against the serpent's rationalizations).[38] As a protester of Christian patriarchy, and a constructive feminist theologian, Mary Daly uses this myth to diagnose sin, to indict it, and to demand reforms.

The institutional churches are (or at least were in the 1960s) of little help in this world-reconfiguring venture. For Daly, institutional religion contributes to alienation by purveying false consciousness and unjust if culturally

---

[38] Phyllis Trible, *God and the Rhetoric of Sexuality* (Philadelphia: Fortress Press, 1978).

dominant political agendas. Daly cites ecclesial complicity with the Vietnam War as a prime example. The mainstream churches and their versions of faith have not been able to sustain "the sense of God's presence and immanence." Their symbols and doctrines are culturally dated, stultified, and dead. They promote a supernaturalistic view of God as an "outside entity" separated from the depth level of human experience. Hence, and lamentably, "a potential or perhaps a real religious experience cannot even be recognized as such" (3.6). The loss of the power of religious symbols "is the loss of the sense of the mystery of being" (2.0). What was sought and needed by Christians in the Vatican II generation – especially among its younger members – was "an opening to the ultimate ground of existence" (3.6). This is why authentic faith for the brave, the few, and the faithful means moving in some ways outside traditional Christianity or at least changing the environment one occupies within it.

Here Daly comes back to the Protestant principle and Catholic substance, borrowing from Paul Tillich, from whom "theonomy" is the resolution of the unbalanced poles of "heteronomy" (government by an extrinsic law) and "autonomy" (independence of the human person from the ground of being, 3.6).[39] The relation to transcendent reality, which is humanity's ultimate concern, requires a "theonomous synthesis" of relation to the unconditioned openness to continual change (1.9).[40]

---

[39] Paul Tillich, *Dynamics of Faith* (New York: Harper & Row, 1957).

[40] For a treatment of Tillich's thought on this subject, as well as its appropriation by Catholic authors of the day, see Brennan Hill, "Paul Tillich's Protestant Principle," *Melita Theologica* 37 (1986): 60–72.

In the Christian context, reconciliation of human sin, overcoming of separation from the Divine, and repair of relation with other persons and with nonhuman creatures, occur through the life, death, and resurrection of Jesus Christ, as portrayed in the New Testament gospels. In the doctrinal traditions of the Christian churches (formulated primarily at the councils of Nicaea in 325 CE and of Chalcedon in 451 CE), the biblical narrative of salvation through Christ is re-expressed in philosophical terms as the incarnation of God in the man Jesus Christ, who as the Christ has both a human and a divine nature.

Mary Daly – perhaps owing to her philosophical training, to her perception that familiar interpretations of the biblical Christ did not hold promise for women's equality (4.7), to her view that the doctrine of the incarnation tended to docetism and supernaturalism (4.7), or to her expectation that contemporary psychological theories (e.g., of R. D. Laing and Carl Jung) would better persuade her intended audience than theological clichés – chose to reconceptualize the symbol "Jesus Christ," not as historical savior or as incarnate God, but as New Being. One major advantage of this choice, as she states, is to underwrite the possibility of authentic religious experience outside of "explicit faith in Jesus Christ."[41]

But, Daly asks, what is the specific character or contribution of Christianity? It is the hope of a transcendence that is yet world-connected, with a mission to heal the

---

[41] This possibility was explicitly endorsed by the Roman Catholic Church in the *Council's Declaration on the Relation of the Church to Non-Christian Religions* (better known as *Nostra Aetate*, 1965), and by *Dominus Iesus* (2001), issued during the pontificate of John Paul II.

world of injustice (4.6–4.8). Misleading mythologizations of Christ aside, Daly believes that "Jesus had a certain transparency to the divine. He was perceived as the Christ." Daly sees Christ as the New Being – "the essential unity between God and man," and in this sense calls her theology "ontological." The "New Being transforms man's existence and makes it really new," restoring humanity to "essential unity with God" (4.9). For women, the New Being and renewed relation to transcendent reality empower necessary self-affirmation against the threat of nonbeing (4.8–4.9). But, practically or existentially speaking, how does this transformation come about? Traditional theologies of salvation (soteriologies) propose variations on the themes of Jesus' historical ministry of the reign of God, death on a cross, and resurrection; and of the union of human nature with the divine through the incarnation. Daly develops a soteriology to resonate with other religions, consisting in a universalized Christ, a reborn Christology and Mariology, and openness to "a plenitude of personality in all persons" (4.11). If to some readers this proposal sounds vague, abstract, decontextualized, spiritually vacuous, and not ultimately up to the job Daly has set before us (including the challenge of writing the next three chapters), it may have seemed so to Daly as well, for here she ends the manuscript.

Speaking from the vantage point (with its limits, to be sure) of a twenty-first-century Catholic feminist theologian, I discern at least three barriers that kept Mary Daly from moving on to the final chapters of *CEB?* The first is evident from the foregoing discussion of the Roman Catholic Church in the Vatican II era, and of its patent failure to enact meaningful reforms. Daly was beginning to imagine a faith-grounded, theologically vital, and gender-equal Christian future, and she needed a theological vision to rise to its level and birth it. Yet, not only were Roman Catholic women barred from any roles and offices requiring priestly ordination (which was in the 1960s by far the majority of roles carrying significant authority), but there was a dearth of nonclerical outlets for women's gifts and vocations (in Catholic universities, nonprofits, NGOs, and socially active women's religious congregations) that would multiply in the decades ahead. The institutional unsuitability of her church to her vision was an imaginative and theological road block. The second barrier was her own and the Church's limited theological repertoire. The many forms of critical biblical studies and theological scholarship that were soon to emerge from the Council were not yet available to encourage, inspire, and structure the thought of the early-career Mary Daly, while offering her a springboard to new intra-ecclesial heights.

By contrast, I think in particular of Daly's slightly younger contemporary (b.1938), Elisabeth Schüssler Fiorenza, whose careful and ground-breaking scholarship on the New Testament deconstructed standing assumptions about who Jesus and his first disciples really were, what was the role of women in early Christianity, how quickly after the death of Jesus the marginalization of women began, and what kinds of radical theological interventions and new biblical–theological expressions would be necessary to convey the magnitude of change required. Terms like "discipleship of equals," "hermeneutics of suspicion," "kyriarchy," and "*ekklesia* of wo/men," would have resonated with Mary Daly and magnified her energy and ideas.[42]

The third and derivative barrier is the absence of a community of feminist Catholic women and men, and of women scholars, who could support mutual ground-breaking research, and contribute to momentum for change in the Church. The exploding post-Vatican II theological era was to foster and foreground political theologies (beginning before the Council, in the years after World War II), liberation theologies, varieties of feminist theology, theologies of women of color in majority white contexts, and theologies of women of diverse ethnicities and races across the globe. Mary Daly broke the ground for many later forms of Catholic feminism, but their fruits ripened too late for her to reap their benefits while still a Christian theologian.

The faltering of Daly's voice at the termination of Chapter 4 represents an even larger, in fact huge, problem for Christianity generally: the finitude and to some extent failure of all historical expressions of the gospel, theologically and ecclesially. This is a dilemma that Daly does examine in *Catholicism: End or Beginning?* but she does so relatively early in the work, threading it through the first three chapters in relation to the subject matter at hand. This includes the contemporary meaninglessness of archaic symbols, loss of connection with transcendent reality, and difficulty of discovering a theonomous

[42] Of Elisabeth Schüssler Fiorenza's many works, two of the more important and widely noted are *In Memory of Her: A Feminist Reconstruction of Christian Origins* (New York: Crossroad, 1983) and *Jesus: Miriam's Child, Sophia's Prophet, Critical Issues in Feminist Christology* (London: T&T Clark, 2015).

synthesis. At the beginning of the last chapter itself, Mary Daly states that the doctrinal tools and other manifestations of the "encounter with transcendent [reality]" in "the meeting of a small community … with … Jesus of Nazareth" could never be adequate to "the original revelatory experience" (4.5). Nevertheless, transformative encounters do still take place. New Being has arrived. The Christian church is the "communications" network of meaning and of relationships, where encounters with transcendent reality are engendered, shared, and sustained (4.4). Where does this then leave the theological response to silence, distorted communication, and breakdown?

In earlier chapters, Daly has taken up the reality that faith comes with ambiguity, depends on honesty, and requires courage because it inevitably harbors doubt at its depth. These are themes or realities that do not disappear with the advent of Jesus Christ. Limits and distortions are perennial facts of the human and of the Christian reality. Even more fundamentally, human historical existence never fully escapes the threat of non-being, death, and meaninglessness (1.5–1.6). Chapter 1 already warns, "The courage demanded by faith is the courage to look into the abyss of non-being" (1.6) This is why "the courage to be" – rather than to avoid facing existential anxiety – is the necessary counterpart of a living faith (1.6). Thus, Daly must assure readers in Chapter 2 that the power of ultimate being "infinitely resists non-being, sustaining everything that is, and making possible the courage we need to exist now and move into the future" – for courage will surely be needed (2.6).

The same essential problem of the ambiguity of historical redemption from evil, sin, and death motivates the

post-World War II political "theologians of hope,"
among whom Daly cites the Protestant Jürgen
Moltmann, and (less centrally) the Catholic Johann
Baptist Metz (quotations in 2.3, 2.6, 3.1).[43] These theologians were appalled by the silence and complicity of the
German Christian churches of the Third Reich. Both
Metz and Moltmann were conscripted as teenagers into
Hitler's army, only to be devastated later by the realization of what Hitler's regime signified. For them (as for
their feminist counterpart Dorothée Sölle), faith is no
stultified set of doctrines, but a "passionate" initiative of
change in the world for the sake of the Kingdom of God
and "the healing of the fractured body of Christianity"
(3.1). This political edge of theology has natural appeal
for Mary Daly, as does these theologians' "eschatological"
theological lens. Historical Christianity will be dogged by
sin and failure, but God's renewed future offers present
possibilities that are "creative, realistic, political and revolutionary." For Daly, the theologians of hope provide

---

[43] See Johann Baptist Metz, *Theology of the World* (New York: Herder &
Herder, 1969); Johann Baptist Metz, *Faith in History and Society:
Towards a Fundamental Practical Theology* (New York: Crossroad, 1977);
Jürgen Moltmann, *Theology of Hope* (New York: Harper & Row, 1967);
Jürgen Moltmann, *Way of Jesus Christ* (London: SCM Press, 1990).
Daly has a classically "Catholic" worry about the theology of hope,
however, and that is that, lacking an "ontological" grounding (in favor
of historical particularity), it is also missing the criterion of validity and
truth that should come from the "immediate experience" of "reality as
the ground of being." This certainty of religious experience she
believes to be the *sine qua non* of hope itself. Metz and Moltmann were
and are no relativists, as their later works were more clearly to attest.
They grounded their criterion in the historical Jesus of Nazareth and in
the Christ of faith as presently experienced in the church ...
albeit partially.

"badly needed encouragement" to reach out toward "a 'new creation' while bearing 'the cross in the present'" (2.6).

This assurance would have made a highly appropriate transition into the book's projected three closing chapters on the church, theology, and reform movements – and the pitfalls, problems, and general recalcitrance reforms would encounter, especially as regards the status of women. Instead, the last line of the manuscript celebrates – in an undeniably triumphalist mode – that the symbol of Christ as New Being enables Catholics to rise above, without relinquishing, the particularity of their own tradition, thus to encounter "the spiritual presence in other expressions of the ultimate meaning of man's being" (4.11).[44]

It seems to me that Daly's satisfaction with the progress of *Catholicism: End or Beginning?* was hampered at least in part by her organization of the material. She in effect positions Chapter 4 on New Being as the "solution" to all difficulties. (Daly's tendency to circle back to the same themes in different chapters does not help the progress of her argument.) When she then arrives at the point of assessing potential developments in the Catholic Church going forward, she seems thrown off track by the immensity of the resistance that self-evidently remains, despite the reality of New Being. Final (not midstream) treatments of ecclesial tension between the old and new, the importance of the courage to be in spite of doubt, and the political–eschatological theology of hope that exists

---

[44] Citing Paul Tillich, *Christianity and the Encounter of the World Religions* (New York: Columbia University Press, 1963).

alongside sin and "cross," might have eased Daly's transition to the book's final chapters. As it stands, however, she was not able to move on – at least not with this project. I think she was not able to do so, given the way she had set up the question, which goes back fundamentally to whether her theological environment gave her the tools and perspective necessary to do so.

Choosing a Different Road

Between the drafting of *Catholicism: End or Beginning?* and the publication of *Beyond God the Father*, Mary Daly published two "occasional" pieces indicative of a transitional phase in her thinking. In the first of these, "After the Death of God the Father," published in March 1971 in the lay-sponsored Catholic weekly periodical, *Commonweal*,[45] Daly announces that the phase of creative research on the destructive heritage of Catholic patriarchy is over. The time has arrived for a "women's revolution" that will "change our whole vision of reality." This revolution will include the "becoming of new symbols," and "a more authentic language of transcendence" than traditional Christian God-language. Even more importantly, the new and revolutionary reality of women will only come to life within a radically transformed "communal situation and experience" – it won't be "decided around a conference table."

Later that same year (November), Mary Daly preached at Harvard Memorial Church, an event that concluded

---

[45] Mary Daly, "After the Death of God the Father: Women's Liberation and the Transformation of Christian Consciousness," *Commonweal* 94 (1971). www.commonwealmagazine.org/after-death-god-father.

with a dramatic and unscheduled exodus of most women and some men from the church building ("the Harvard Exodus").[46] Offering her view of the Harvard Exodus in the local entertainment paper, *Boston After Dark* (the event had garnered public attention), Daly granted that some protesters might walk away from institutional religion entirely, while others instigate reform within it. Denying that she is leaving faith behind, Daly is convinced that, "whatever has been authentic 'in the church' seemed to be very much present, alive, and well among us" in the walk-out from Memorial Church. In a further reflection published in 1972, Daly insists that unless the flip side of feminist insight is "externalized action it will die." The *praxis* of feminist insight is "new community" and "the bonding of women in sisterhood."[47]

A common major thread in these two essays predicts the course of the Mary Daly who wrote *Beyond God the Father*: the practical embodiment of a new reality though community and its language – connected to transcendent reality, if not in a Christian mode.[48] Daly concludes *Beyond God the Father* (still shaped by Aquinas and Tillich) with a riff on Paul's speech to the Greeks on the Aereopagus (Acts 17: 27–28), combined with the Prologue to John's Gospel (John 1: 1–5): The "power of

---

[46] All the sources on the Harvard Exodus cited in this paragraph are from Mary Daly, "The Women's Movement: An Exodus Community," *Religious Education* 67 (1972), 327–335.

[47] Ibid., 331.

[48] Indeed, this thread (at least the call for boundary-breaking language) may be slightly visible in the tapestry of *Catholicism: Beginning or End?* Daly offers almost in passing that a "risky" "voyage" into the "inner space" of "Imagination, dreams, fantasies, and trances" may be necessary to overcome alienation (40).

sisterhood" works "by attraction," by "the creative drawing power of the Good Who is self-communicating Being, Who is the Verb from whom, in whom, and with
whom all true movements move."[49]

Conclusion

As she herself moved out from the partly drafted
Catholicism: End or Beginning? Mary Daly (I hypothesize)
was coming to recognize that her driving passion was not
academic scholarship, theological or otherwise, but a quest
for relationship with the Good, with dynamic "Be-ing" that
sustains her own being and that of all finite reality. The
Catholic Church was not to her a hospitable community in
and with which to connect with Be-ing authentically and in
a life-giving mode. The patriarchy subverting Christian
institutions was incompatible with the transcendent reality
of Be-ing, and in fact excluded women from Be-ing by
design. The revolutionary experience of faithful sisterhood
broke the bounds of Christianity's theological language.
In *Beyond God the Father* and later genre-exploding works,
Daly forged ahead on a voyage of discovery and connection
with a community of similarly questing women.

Around this same time, an approach to theology as
theopoetics was emerging in the work of the literary theorist Amos Wilder. Wilder's programmatic pronouncement
resonates with Daly's mission:

> It is at the level of the imagination that the fateful issues of
> our new world-experience must first be mastered. It is

---

[49] Daly, *Beyond God the Father*, 198.

here that culture and history are broken, and here that the church is polarized. Old words do not reach across the new gulfs, and it is only in vision and oracle that we can chart the unknown and new-name the creatures.[50]

Callid Keefe-Perry explains that *theopoetics* or *theopoiesis* is "the study and practice of making God known through the text."[51] This characterization certainly applies to Daly's work, with the important caveat that her approach, while strongly text-dependent, explicitly uses textual discourse as a way of creating, sustaining, and reinventing a human communicative community (a "sisterhood" or "ekklesia of wo/men") in which divine Be-ing is interrelationally encountered. Theopoetics is a major contemporary theological avenue, indebted to postmodern philosophy;[52] the literature of and about it is immense (involving Keefe-Perry, Catherine Keller, Richard Kearney, John Caputo, and others). Suffice it to say that, while Mary Daly was theologically, ecclesially, and philosophically far ahead of her time (at least in the Catholic world), her essential instincts and commitments are vindicated by theological directions of thought that were to

---

[50] Amos Wilder, *Theopoetic: Theology and the Religious Imagination* (Philadelphia: Fortress Press, 1976), as cited as the epigraph to L. B. C. Keefe-Perry, "Theopoetics: Process and Perspective," *Christianity and Literature* 58 (2009): 579. This article offers an introduction to theopoetics as a field of inquiry, developed in Keefe-Perry, *Way to Water: A Theopoetics Primer* (Eugene OR: Wipf and Stock, 2014).

[51] Keefe-Perry, "Theopoetics," 579.

[52] It should be noted that as "postmodern," theopoetics tends to be antiessentialist and anti-foundationalist – potentially running into the same problem (if one sees it as that) Daly considered to arise for the theologians of hope, that is, lack of a criterion to assess the truth or authenticity of particular textual mediations of God.

become "mainstream," including theologies of gender equality. Concerning the practical, sacramental, and institutional participation of women on an equal basis with men, however, the Roman Catholic Church as a whole still falls under Mary Luke Tobin's verdict: reluctant inclusion of "a few 'token' women."

3

Feminist Intrigues at the Limits of Schizoid Theology

≈

Siobhán Garrigan

The emergence of *Catholicism: End or Beginning?* gives rise to a suite of intrigues, consideration of which will be the topic of this chapter. Why is the manuscript incomplete? If Mary Daly abandoned the project, why? Why was this manuscript kept and not destroyed? Why is its theological frame so consonant with Roman Catholic orthodoxy by comparison to the just-published and highly critical *The Church and the Second Sex*? How could Daly hold these disparate projects in tension? And, to start with, perhaps the most significant matter of all, *CEB?* is an intriguing read because of what it does not cover, the feminism for which Mary Daly is today so well known.

Every class I have taught has been rocked in one way or another by reading Mary Daly's radical white feminist critique of misogyny and Christianity's role in perpetrating it. Notwithstanding the deserved criticisms of her racism, gender essentialism, imperialism, and transphobia, all those different students from all those different backgrounds were moved to object or cheer or shuffle awkwardly by Daly's direct and uncompromising challenge to patriarchy. Moreover, they were affected by the example she provided not merely to deconstruct patriarchy but also to imagine alternatives to it. These alternatives came from an awareness of her situation in the biosphere as well as her embrace of mystical experience, but also, and mostly, from her indefatigably *feminist* hermeneutic. It is therefore intriguing to find this unfinished manuscript exhibiting a near total lack of any trace of explicitly feminist motivation, language, theory, sources, or focus. For example, human beings are referred to throughout the text as "man," God as "himself," and the scholar as "he." There are few women mentioned at all, even in the footnotes, which is a shocking omission even by the standards of the day.

This lack of what we expect of Daly is all the more surprising given the editor's suggestion that the manuscript was written between *The Church and the Second Sex* (1968) and *Beyond God the Father* (1973), the high period of Daly's feminist theological articulation. If *CEB?* were dated as originating during her long period of doctoral studies in the 1950s or from the early 1960s when she observed the proceedings of the Second Vatican Council, its "unfeminism" might be less surprising, but it comes right after her first major critical assault on patriarchy in the Church and just before the first in the trilogy of searingly feminist books for which she is famous: *Beyond God the Father*, *Gyn/Ecology*, and *Pure Lust*. The discovery of this manuscript therefore reveals that right at the moment Daly was realizing she could not be post-patriarchy without being post-Christian, she set about writing a new book which launched a program for how the Christian faith can coexist with modernity, but which advocated for hardly anything that could be read as feminist. My focus in this chapter will be on this as a moment – a moment in the development both of a theologian and of theology itself.

The moment, as Daly identifies it in *Outercourse*, was 1969–1970.[1] Others in this volume treat this moment as pivotal for what comes next, especially in the trilogy. My focus is on what was going on during this moment and immediately before it because my interest is in the formation of theology through and in the life of this person. This moment is significant because Daly has not yet transitioned from Catholic theologian to post-Christian philosopher. Both are present in her writing in this manuscript and it is clearly not working, but she has not yet jumped ship. The journey from one to another both predates and postdates this moment, but *CEB?* is the point at which the tension of trying to hold both together became intolerable. The significance of such a moment lies not only in deepening our understanding of Mary Daly but also in understanding what is involved in a commitment to the life of the mind and, specifically, the mind of a critical Catholic woman. And there are surprisingly few accounts of women who have made this journey (although this is perhaps not surprising when one considers how few accounts there are even of women who remain within the Church).[2]

What people who "abandon" a site of profound belonging go through is not widely studied or well

---

[1] Mary Daly's autobiography: *Outercourse: The Be-Dazzling Voyage* (San Francisco: HarperSanFrancisco, 1993).

[2] For an exception, see Susan Ross, *Extravagant Affections: A Feminist Sacramental Theology* (New York: Continuum, 1998).

understood, and those who "leave the Church" are no exception.[3] The times before and after their breach are often portrayed as entirely discontinuous epochs and their choice to leave is often framed as "the easy way out." Instead of curiosity about their journey, or respect for their integrity, they are often met with contempt and condemnation.

Early on in *CEB?*, Daly sets out to correct this "polarization" between perceived belonging and not-belonging when it comes to faith. Daly argues that a mature faith "carries with it a clear recognition that there is no sharp distinction between insiders and outsiders" (1.8). Indeed, for Daly, a mature faith is made up of ambiguities and unknowns, so it cannot be all-in or all-out; it is rather "that state of ultimate concern which does not exclude doubt but which contains doubt in its depths" (1.8). She is asking that an ambivalent relationship to Christianity be recognized as a sign of honest grappling and the product of learning, rather than as evidence of failure to reach mature faith or even disloyalty.[4]

In contrast to contemporaries like Charles Davis, who described themselves as having "left the Church," Daly positions herself among the "radicals" who "choose instead the difficult stance of outside–inside" (1.8). Her sentences in the middle of Chapter 1

---

[3] "The reasons why more and more people are turning away from religion are still poorly understood." Phil Zuckerman, *Faith No More: Why People Reject Religion* (Oxford: Oxford University Press, 2012), note on book jacket.

[4] She uses the example of James Pike, who described himself as an "alumni," a graduate of the Church, which Daly sees as a positive sign of growth through learning. *Catholicism: End or Beginning?*.

discussing "those who have 'left' the old environment while remaining Christians and staying in some way related to the institutional church" (1.8) constitute the most visibly edited (over-typed) section in the entire hard-copy manuscript, perhaps indicating the extent to which she was at this moment wrestling with her own outsider–insider boundary and others' perception of it. In this, we gain a potential insight into how Daly was experiencing and navigating this moment in her intellectual development. Having issued an extensive critique of the Church's sexism and called for its reform in *The Church and the Second Sex* – and having been roundly criticized for it (including nearly losing her job) – she is here struggling to find the right words so as not to let her earlier critique determine for her some sort of outsider status. Before too long, she chose such a status for herself; but right now, in this moment, she wants to change how the Church views the whole matter of belonging.

CEB? does this by attempting to construct an ecclesiology for the Roman Catholic Church capable of holding together factions that were, at the time, pulling in very different directions. Taking conversation partners from Catholic theology (Thomas Aquinas, Teilhard de Chardin, and Jacques Maritain), contemporary Protestant thought (Paul Tillich), and psychology (Carl Jung and R. D. Laing), Daly systematically romps through the standard tenets of Catholic ecclesiology (the nature of faith, the reality of God, the problem of sin, the quest for Christ, the role of sacraments, eschatology, and ethics) to argue that the Church needs to, in a phrase, stop splitting. The premise of *CEB?* is that the Church's mid twentieth-century character is endemically polarized and that this is problematic. Daly's proposed solution lies in persuading the Church to realize its fundamental identity as both integral and integrating.

What demands integration on a practical level for Daly are the opposing poles of "activists on the side of revolution" or "heresiarchs" (such as Robert McAfee Brown and James Groppi) and "traditionalists" or "archconservatives" (such as Frederick Wilhelmsen and Christopher Derrick) (1.7). The greater problem she discerns as lying behind this polarization and which demands integration at a more profound level is the division between what, following Tillich, she terms the "Protestant principle" and the "Catholic substance," whose separation results in a "sense of incompleteness" for Christianity and which instead should be "complementary aspects of an integral faith" (1.8). The Protestant principle is awareness of all aspects of religion as a construct and the concomitant ability to query them. The Catholic substance is an ontological understanding of the incarnation. According to Daly, both have led to "distortions." The former can lead to "emptiness, banality, fading of the symbols, and fatal acculturation which brought on the phenomenon of the 'the death of God'" (Introduction). The latter can lead to "idolatrous sacramentalism, 'magic,' and over-institutionalization" (Introduction). The answer for both, argues Daly, is integration.

While few would disagree that for a theistic faith "the only hope for authentic integration would seem to lie in radical openness to transcendence," Daly's repeated ordering that the Protestant principle needs to be integrated *into* the Catholic substance should raise the hackles of even the most accommodating Protestant ecumenists.[5] On another occasion in *CEB?*, Daly writes: "the rediscovery by Protestants of the power of religious symbols is a mode of participation in the process of becom[ing] self-aware" (1.10). This adds a patronizing tone toward Protestants to the problematic notion that their ways are to be assimilated into the more substantial forms of Catholicism. Later still, her approach to Protestants is downright Catholic-supremacist. When contemplating how some young people reject Christ because of the exclusive claims of Christianity (i.e., the proposition that only in Christ is there salvation), she states with little qualification that, "There is some truth in the assertion that Protestantism has contributed more to this particularism and idolatry than has Catholicism" (4.1). This is not the reconciling work of reaching integration through mutual understanding.

For all its claims to be on the side of the radicals, *Catholicism: End or Beginning?* is offering a rewording of standard Catholic teaching: yes, we are now open to Protestants, so long as they become a part of the Roman Church.[6] And thus to the intrigue of why there is no feminism in this manuscript, we add the intrigue of why Daly is including such uncritically orthodox Catholic conceptualizations when we know that she was also at this time striving to argue for transformative reform of that same Church, not just against sexism in *The Church and*

---

[5] The quotation is from the Introduction; the argument regarding Protestants is found throughout the manuscript.

[6] This is, in summary, the teaching of Vatican II's document on ecumenism: *Unitatis redintegratio*, November 21, 1964.

the Second Sex but also regarding ecclesiology in this manuscript. The orthodox nature of some of her propositions in *CEB?* perhaps indicates that she was more conservative than has been realized. Certainly, her categorical thought structures are often as (or even more) dualistic than those of Catholic theology: men/women, good/bad, Protestant/Catholic, Background/Foreground. And compared to Karl Rahner's work on the outsider/insider problem from this same period, and his attention to "universal Christians," Daly's vision for would-be outsiders is not a risk-taking thesis.[7]

However, Daly's promulgation of the standard Catholic view of ecumenism is more likely a product of the particular type of theological formation she had adopted than it is a sign of latent conservatism. This theological formation was, to use the terms of the day, speculative rather than practical in its approach. Accordingly, and as seen in the above outline of the thesis of *CEB?*, practical problems (such as conflict between heresiarchs and traditionalists) were epi-phenomena; what mattered for "real" theologians, like Daly, were the structural elements of thought that gave rise to them. In Thomist circles it was understood that these fundamentals, by their very nature, could only be approached speculatively. Moreover, such speculative investigations were seen as "proper" theology, where the value of intellectual endeavor resided. Thus, in *CEB?*, Daly calls over and over again, as she had in *The Church and the Second Sex*, for a fulsome "theological" (meaning speculative) response to

---

[7] Karl Rahner, *Foundations of Christian Faith: An Introduction to the Idea of Christianity* (New York: Seabury Press, 1978).

the problems at hand (polarization here, sexism there), in contrast to what she perceives as other habitually "shallow" (meaning practical) approaches.

We see another example of how her speculative approach to theology tends toward the abstract at the expense of the pastoral in her treatment of the doctrine of original sin in Chapter 3. Daly seems to be positioning herself, as Aquinas did, translating "core" theological concepts into the language of the day. In doing so, she is not denying or criticizing the fundamental concepts (i.e., speculations), only how they have come to be portrayed by Church teachings that have failed to update how they are expressed for modern ears and eyes (i.e., practicalities). Thus, she begins by noting popular objections to the Church's teaching on baptism, which (although she does not state it) consisted of a practicality whereby babies were understood to be born tainted with original sin and therefore if they died before they were baptized they were not permitted Christian burial (because, according to Catholic teaching, only baptism removes original sin). Then, she reframes sin as "alienation" (a very current concept in the cultural landscape of the US in the 1960s) and speculates that the myth of the Fall (from which the Catholic doctrine of original sin flows) is fine in and of itself, but it needs to be properly interpreted. She contends that "the universal sense of alienation, which [is] expressed poignantly in the myth of the Fall, has been given a pseudo-historical 'explanation' ... The mistake, then, lies in taking the myth as a solution to the problem rather than as an expression of the baffling mystery of human existence" (3.1). Rather than acknowledging the profound problems with a theology that has caused acute pain, especially in people not able to bury their unbaptized children, she goes on to conclude that,

> Mythical thinking ... is the language of a reality that is not empirical but existential. Indeed, the authentic task of theology is not to demythologize, but to recover mythical thought and to appropriate its contents, which bring us closer to the imageless transcendence which no myth can fully express. (3.2)

Although Daly insists that people need to understand Church teaching by doing better at reinterpreting myths, she herself makes no attempt to reinterpret the myth of the Fall in such a way that unbaptized babies could be given a Christian burial.

While these examples demonstrate Daly's insistence on a speculative approach to addressing a problem theologically (in the above cases, a form of ecumenical integration in response to a split between Protestant and Catholic ways of thinking and a call for theology to do a better job of interpreting its myths), they do not necessarily account for her sticking so closely to the Church's teachings when it comes to both ecumenism and sin. Perhaps she felt compelled to write something that aligned with Church teachings on certain key issues she genuinely supported – such as ecumenism, as opposed to the widespread sexism she famously opposed – out of fear of losing her position as an assistant professor of theology at Boston College, a Jesuit university. Or perhaps she worried that she would soon need to get another job somewhere else and would need to show her Catholic theological credentials to do so. At this moment, she had good reason to fear these eventualities.

When Daly started writing *CEB?* in early 1969, she had just received from Boston College a one-year contract in the wake of publication of The Church and the Second Sex, which she took as being fired. This was followed by a student-led campaign to get her reinstated on a longer contract and resulted in her being given tenure, though she could not have known that was how things would turn out when she undertook this book-length writing project. Even if she had, the reality of having tenure and yet being attacked by the quotidian aggressions of academic patriarchy (too few or even no students enrolled in her classes; being addressed as "Miss" instead of "Professor," and concomitant nightmares in which she never finished her doctorates or even her BA)[8] might still have led, in this moment, for her to feel the need to prove herself as worthy of being retained at Boston College, or of being granted a tenured post in theology elsewhere.[9] Legitimating oneself is, unfortunately, a constant requirement in academia; doubly so for women, and exponentially so for women in ecclesially associated academia.

Daly later wrote that the hostility and harassment she received during the same year in which she was writing this book, especially *after* securing her position as a tenured university professor, led her to realize that "the

---

[8] Daly, *Outercourse*, 96–97.

[9] In her "New Intergalactic Introduction" to *GynEcology*, she says that being denied promotion to full professor was "unbelievable" because her work was "super-scholarly." This manuscript is the sort of thing you put out if you want to *prove* your chops as scholarly enough.
So often, if you are a woman or Black, or in any way non-White-male, it will be doubted that what you are doing is "real" scholarship at all. Mary Daly, *GynEcology* (Boston: Beacon Press, 1990), xv.

personal is political."[10] This idea is evident in everything she wrote after 1973. Yet, in this precise moment in which she is writing *CEB?*, the personal is largely missing. The political is too, at least in the sense of directly addressing the world outside the Church. And so a further intrigue is: why *this* topic? Something recognizably and acceptably "Catholic" might have been needed to offset her worries about employment, but why ecclesiology and why focus with such verve on the Catholic Church's need to integrate? Without the second half of the book, it is very hard to tell. What we can tell is, as the book's title suggests, Daly perceives there to be a great deal at stake in this particular topic: for the Church to refuse the measures she proposes will mean "End." Or, in the book's alternative title, "Death."[11]

It is salient to recall as contextualization that at this time the fear of complete ending and death was heightened for everyone, not just church members, due to the arms race and the threat of nuclear annihilation. Furthermore, in ecclesial circles, Vatican II had brought a great deal of tumult to the western Church, its innovations being understood by its many critics as auguring the Church's demise, and there was also an outpouring of reforming attention to many sorts of Christian thinking. This is perhaps typified by one of the best-selling religious books of this time – of all time – and the fuss surrounding its publication. The media framed *Honest to God* as the

[10] Daly, *Outercourse*, 97.

[11] "During 1969–70, I also worked hard on the manuscript of a book which had several tentative titles. Among these was *Catholicism: Death or Rebirth?* Another was *Catholicism: End or Beginning?*" Daly, *Outercourse*, 102.

fulfillment of the death of religion that had been predicted in the nineteenth century caused by the rise of secularism.[12] Numerous church authorities condemned it. In the book, an English Anglican bishop exposes the inaccuracies he perceives in ecclesial theologies and argues that we should stop thinking of the divine as "God out there," and instead see it as "the ground of all being." In *CEB?*, Daly makes a very similar move, using identical language. The problem, she says, is that "modern man seems to have lost the sense of God's presence and immanence. In often used popular terminology, God has come to be identified with something 'up there' or at least 'out there'" (3.6). Daly here builds on her earlier argument that, "The divine reality, to which one is related through faith, is not adequately described as 'the supreme being.' Rather it is the ground of all being" (1.5).

The solution-phrase for Robinson, as for Daly in *CEB?*, is derived from Tillich, and this is not surprising, given there is a certain amount in common between their projects. Indeed, these commonalities can be seen in many other thinkers of the day too: the call for "honesty" in theological reckoning, and for admitting the truth as one sees it and not as a Church requires one to propound it, and all in order to tackle the big underlying question of how to reconcile the Church with modernity. It was in the public reaction to *Honest to God* that the end of the whole enterprise was threatened: if bishops are giving up on

---

[12] John A. T. Robinson, *Honest to God* (Philadelphia: Westminster Press, 1963). In this book, the author, an Anglican bishop, criticized Christian doctrine and communications for failing to keep pace with "secular" concerns.

traditional tenets of belief, then what hope has the Church? But for Daly, the real possibility of the end of the Church is the very title of her manuscript as well as being repeatedly and explicitly countenanced within it. She is, in this manuscript, as in *The Church and the Second Sex*, setting out a program for reform – but the stakes have been raised and the title of this manuscript is meant to indicate the consequences of reforming or not: end or beginning, death or rebirth. We see then that the outsider–insider dynamic that characterized the Church of her day, and the pernicious ways it prevented integration at multiple levels, mattered so much to Daly because she understood it as threatening to destroy the Church itself.

Even still, "reform or die" is quite an extreme warning. Comparing the two working titles of this book, it is interesting that Daly plumped for "End or Beginning," because "Re-birth" would seem to have been the more accurate word choice than "Beginning" for her proposed alternative for the Church. The Church has (more than) begun, it has already been formed, so what a re-former typically wants is a re-birth. Hindsight allows us easily to see *Catholicism: End or Beginning?* as Daly tussling not so much with the imminent end of Roman Catholicism but the imminent end of Mary Daly's Catholicism. There are few (if any) explicit signs of that in the manuscript itself, but if we consider the proximity of writing *The Church and the Second Sex* to this moment, the tensions and polarities Daly describes seem irreconcilable.

The choice Daly presents as facing the Church as a whole is what she herself was facing in this moment: end or beginning. And this is why this title is the right one, because it could do double duty: "Death and Rebirth" was true for the project of Church reform, but not also for the choice facing Daly. The tension between the sort of theology in this manuscript and the sorts of thinking she expressed in *The Church and the Second Sex* and its aftermath (as described in *Outercourse*) is acute; they are radically different points of view, held by the same person at the same time. One cannot keep two conflicting identities going at the same time because the tension is too great. Tension of this sort can only be resolved by something decisive, or by a split. Daly inhabited the tensions until they reached breaking point because, I suggest, splitting is what she herself was doing, intellectually, and she projects it onto the Church.[13] Beyond this split, Daly grew and grew in post-Christian feminist mystical experience, expression, and theorization; she was never again trying to make the Church okay or make it okay to be in the Church. Even *The Church and the Second Sex* had to be recontextualized for it to stand, the second edition importantly distinguished by its augmented "Feminist Postchristian Introduction . . . by the Author."

Reading *CEB?*, one is given to wonder if the process of writing it led to Daly's decision shortly afterwards to

[13] It was not the first time. In a 1965 article, Daly wrote: "Some minds have always seen a fundamental opposition between 'life' and the pursuit of knowledge. In the history of Christian thought, the antipathy for speculation has sometimes been expressed in strong terms; one finds a classic example in *The Imitation of Christ*. At worst, there appears to be a conflict between opposed demands; at best, a tension. When the question of the nature of theology arises, it is not surprising to see that it becomes the focal point of dispute and tension." Mary Daly, "The Problem of Speculative Theology," *The Thomist: A Speculative Quarterly Review* 29(2) (1965): 177.

publicly exit the Christian Church. Did she start to write with confidence in her approach, only to find that she no longer believed in it? She sets out to answer the question, "Has Catholicism reached its end, or is there hope for a genuine new beginning?" (Introduction). Perhaps reforming the Church was revealed as futile, impossible, or undesirable *through* the grappling involved in writing this manuscript. Similarly, the fact that it drops off right before the anticipated gear change to three final chapters on how the Christian community struggles in experiencing Christ might be taken as evidence that Daly just could not base her ontology of faith, or of anything else, around a masculine divinity anymore. We do not know – but heavens how this manuscript provokes wonder! Such speculations are typical examples of how the whole manuscript evokes a strange and unusual reading experience: one's own questions about Daly constantly interrupt the normal flow of reading; one is, at each turn, reading a story over a story, a theory under a theory – because one is reading for understanding Mary Daly at her moment of splitting from the Church, and from theology – and not only for the actual ecclesiology she is evincing.

It is perhaps no accident that *CEB?* stops before it presents its promised three chapters on Christ. The question of Christ, the central symbol of the human being's place in the created order, is where the manuscript can no longer bear the tensions in the life of the mind of the author. And so this is the concept upon which the narrative finally splits. The personal did get political. To write the Christ-focused chapters would have meant Daly dealing with the practical, because the incarnation is practical and not speculative. It would have required the book to become fleshy, feeling, and individual rather than heady, abstract, and corporate (as the extant chapters are). In one sense, Daly's later books do this. One might even suggest that she became Christic: a cosmic traveler, calling out fear and hate and re-making the world anew for the purposes of love and justice. In such an interpretation, the eventual fulfillment of her (repressed in this manuscript) desires is actually the fulfillment of her baptismal identity, and her work would chime with later feminist philosophers of religion in the conceptualization of feminist spiritual growth as *becoming* divine.[14] However, it would be wrong to overwrite her own new beginning with a Christian identity that she refuted and, besides, it would be getting ahead of this specific moment.

Writing the Christ-focused chapters would have demanded a confrontation between Daly's feminism and her desire in this moment to stay within the Church, to reform it, and to defend aspects of it. We find strains of this emerging in the very last paragraphs of *CEB?* Daly identifies the potential for a theology of Christ universalized in all persons, but immediately articulates the problem posed by Christ's gender to an incarnational reimagining of the world: "this is an exclusively masculine image" (4.11). Moreover, Daly notes that turning to Mary as an alternative exemplar, as was Catholicism's wont, is not going to help because of "the danger of hardening the stereotype of the eternal feminine into a model for half

---

[14] See Grace Jantzen, *Becoming Divine: Towards a Feminist Philosophy of Religion* (Manchester: Manchester University Press, 1998) and Pamela Sue Anderson, *A Feminist Philosophy of Religion* (Oxford: Wiley-Blackwell, 1997).

the species, exclusively" (4.11).[15] Applying her proposed schema to this dilemma, Daly calls on the Protestant principle to remember that "God is beyond our symbols," and so to conclude that "the God–man relationship transcends sex" (4.11). This reads as a hugely unsatisfactory conclusion to the problem; one imagines it might not have read any differently to Daly. It is certainly a far cry from what she wrote just a couple of years later, and for which she has become so well remembered: "if God is male, then male is God."[16] And it is almost certainly no accident that the writing of *CEB?* ends on this very topic, suggesting that here is the point where the axe made it through the log and split it.

The intellectual process to which the life of the mind commits a person seldom accepts only one line of thinking at one time. Serious scholarship necessarily demands constant self-querying. But there is rarely such a profound difference in lines of thinking as we see in Mary Daly at this moment. Like a person heading for a psychotic break, tensions like these are acute, and not tolerable. In *The Church and the Second Sex*, Daly justifies her remaining a Catholic because she sees the church's trajectory as being toward enabling social transformation.[17] In *CEB?*, she mounts an argument based on the incarnation to attempt to re-integrate a split Church. Yet, she finds its

---

[15] Daly is here returning to a theme from *The Church and the Second Sex* (Boston: Beacon Press, 1985), where she criticized the objectification of Mary as a symbol.

[16] Mary Daly, *Beyond God the Father: Toward a Philosophy of Women's Liberation* (Boston: Beacon Press, 1985), 19.

[17] Mary Daly, *The Church and the Second Sex*, 1st ed. (New York: Harper & Row, 1968), 178–181.

fundamentally patriarchal language won't let her. It is quite possible that the challenge of writing the concluding chapters on Christ led to her becoming "disillusioned."[18] Perhaps in the process of returning to her notes, constructing them into an argument, tapping it all out on her typewriter's keys, re-reading and editing the manuscript, she failed to convince herself of her own argument. Or perhaps she lost faith in the power of this sort of argumentation to change anything in the Church.

However, if Daly did write her way out of Christianity by writing this manuscript, it bears remarkably few hints of it, and while the "full stop" of the final paragraph justifies speculation of the sort given above, there is little other evidence for it in the text. Moreover, we know from *Outercourse* that the publisher, Lippincott, with whom she had a contract for the book, declined to publish the manuscript. This is interesting because it implies that Daly had been satisfied enough with the work to send it over to them. Indeed, she tells us that, "I suffered from this rejection of my work."[19] She goes on to say that later in life she viewed the publisher's decision as "a case of the proverbial 'blessing in disguise,'" but in this moment, in 1970, it hurt.[20] In this moment, she *wanted* to be making this argument in the world.

When Lippincott rejected the manuscript, Daly could have sought another publisher. A further intrigue, therefore, is the unfinished status of *CEB?* The manuscript has

---

[18] Daly defines "disillusionment" as "the Courage to See – to see through male mysteries." *Websters' First New Intergalactic Wickedary of the English Language* (Boston: Beacon Press, 1987), 69.
[19] Daly, *Outercourse*, 102.　　[20] Ibid.

the feel of a project Daly had had in mind for some time. The thinking is developed, the argument is exquisitely structured, the rhetoric is polished, and the manuscript bears the marks of multiple edits. It was not something written in a hurry or, one imagines, tossed aside lightly. While the writing is dated to 1969–1970, the passion for and diligent working-through of the topic evidently far predates it. So, one reaches the end of the fourth chapter, having been promised seven, and it feels cut off in its prime, its strong rhythm stopped dead, leading one's mind scanning for clues to solve mysteries: where did the rest of this vital, flowing, incisive, mature prose go? Is there a further manuscript to be discovered somewhere? Has anyone looked? Is there evidence that the manuscript is unfinished, as claimed, or might the remainder, or earlier drafts of it, or notes for it, be sitting in an archive somewhere? If Daly was not done with its subject matter at the point at which the publisher rejected the manuscript, then why does it end? In *Outercourse*, Daly says, "It fell apart in the middle, or one could say it was an abortive effort ... I couldn't go on with it."[21]

I speculate that something happened, something big enough to throw her off course, or, more to the point, on course. What happened? Jennifer Rycenga, in this volume, suggests it was, "in a word, Women." The Women's Liberation Movement did indeed take hold at this time, and Daly was a key figure in it, not least with the famous walkout at Harvard Memorial Church. The sense of support, solidarity, new life, and alternative possibilities from her fellow Women's Libbers certainly must have

[21] Ibid.

been hugely empowering and encouraging. However, Daly had been part of flourishing women's groups in Europe as a younger woman, and it had not caused the tension/splitting that we see in this moment. Moreover, many other feminist Christian women who were also part of the women's movement did not conclude they had to become "post-Christian," so immersion in the women's movement alone might not offer a satisfactory explanation of why Daly felt she had to do so.[22]

The energy of so much actually changing in the world in 1969 and 1970 altered and diversified the previous ways in which people theorized the need for change. Change was now afoot seemingly everywhere. In the US at this exact moment, in addition to the extensive organizing of Women's Libbers, there was also the ongoing movement for Black civil rights, the first Pride parade/Stonewall protests, the Woodstock Festival, and intense protests against the Vietnam War. However, one might profitably speculate that even more than any of these changes, *Humanae Vitae* (July 25, 1968) would have had at least a contributory role in Daly losing heart in her project to reform the Catholic Church.

The disgust with which this encyclical was met by reform-minded Catholics was grounded not only in deep

[22] See, for example, Rosemary Radford Ruether, who goes further, saying it's not the post-Christian stance that's the problem in Daly's *Beyond God the Father* but its basis in inattention to class, socio-economic conditions, and the ways women can oppress: "The abstract analysis of the women's movement that separates rather than unites women with all other struggles against oppression is precisely what is likely to lead the women's movement to remain unconsciously upper-class, Western and racist in its operations." Rosemary Radford Ruether, "Theology by Sex," *New Republic* 169 (1973): 25.

disappointment at its content (it had been widely expected that it would permit the use of contraception). *Humanae Vitae* was also interpreted as a sign that Vatican II had been mere window dressing and not, as many Catholics previously imagined, as a movement that would carry on and effect ongoing progressive changes. One possible objection to the suggestion that Daly was affected by *Humanae Vitae* is that *The Church and the Second Sex* came out in 1968, so Daly cannot have been that perturbed by the encyclical or she would not have written that book. However, while *The Church and the Second Sex* was published in 1968, it was submitted to the publisher on the feast of the Assumption, August 15, 1967, predating *Humanae Vitae* by nearly a year. If, after getting *The Church and the Second Sex* off to the press, Mary Daly turned to her long-burning project on how Vatican II could actually be realized, only to see that it was futile, that would be a weighty additional torc on the tension involved in writing it.

My own hunch is that, for all the relevance and heft of the numerous seismic events in this period, events which mark the Church's membership and character to this day, the most significant event for the specific moment of this doomed manuscript was the death of Daly's mother, on December 15, 1967. I once heard Mary Daly speak at the Quaker Meeting House on New York City's Rutherford Place in, I think, 1992. She was exasperated and understandably wary, being in the middle of the dispute about not admitting male students to her classes that led to her retirement. But when asked about her mother, her entire demeanor brightened and she told stories of her mother that I found startling, warm, and wonderful. I now realize she was at that time in the process of writing these stories into *Outercourse:* how her mother's faith was a foundation to her but her version of raising a daughter in it was not the usual one at that time; how their landlady washing plates under running water in a tiny apartment moved her mother to keenly remember her Irish grandmother; how her mother told her to be about her own work, leaving her free to explore the life of the mind, instead of being allotted the daughterly tasks of that time – and of mine, a generation later – grooming women for the twinned purposes of marriage and drudgery.

I suspect that losing her mother enabled Mary Daly to lose the Church. She had, perhaps, only remained positioned within it this long because she was born into it, and it was her mother who had provided that birth. This is not to pander to the Catholic maternal piety of the day, which encouraged the faithful to cleave to the Church itself ("Mother Church"), by suggesting that the death of a real mother necessarily ushered in a new relationship to the ecclesial mother. Rather, it is to heed Daly's reflections in her memoir about the contents of *CEB?* and to observe that what she says of its theory of the Church is perhaps true of the Church in her own life: that it had been the "frame" by which she had been "framed" (negatively).[23] However, the original framing (positively) of her ecclesial belonging was given to her by her beloved mother, and so, for all its faults, she was perhaps not free to disown the Church during her mother's lifetime. Something in her mother's death may have allowed her

---

[23] Daly, *Outercourse*, 102.

to keep her mother's love but desist from being framed by the Church.

How would this have worked? Was it that Daly did not leave the Church during her mother's lifetime out of a sense of not wanting to hurt her mother, to whom faith mattered so much, for whom it was a life-giving frame? Or was it instead perhaps feeling that she had to hold together the concerns of the Church and her own emerging radical critique of it for her mother's sake despite the acute tension, because her mother had been so supportive of her pursuing her theological education, and so to leave the Church as a result of it would be a betrayal of that support and the sacrifices involved in it? I speculate, based on my own experiences, that rather than either of these, it was probably that a space opened up, unexpectedly, following her parent's death; a space which Mary Daly could step into and inhabit.[24] In such a space, attachments that were predicated on other, deeper, attachments are enabled to yield. Taking these considerations into account, the unfinished status of the manuscript seems less intriguing and more inevitable.

Having come to the end of the intrigues suggested within the text, a further one arises from how Daly treated it: Why was this manuscript kept and archived? Her memoir gives the impression that she herself came to reject its contents. In which case, why did she not choose to destroy the manuscript? Did Daly want it to be read

---

[24] Daly describes the space after her mother's death as a "11:12" space. Not only was this the time her mother died, but it is also a phenomenon repeated throughout her life, wherein the space is found not to be totally full, or where a sequence can extend beyond the bounds of the known clock. Ibid., 104–106.

again one day, as we are doing now? This final intrigue is amplified by the Lorde affair mentioned in the editor's introduction to this volume. It was only after Lorde's death that her papers revealed Daly had in fact written back to her, and Daly herself disclosed this only after Lorde's death.[25] Some have thought this a deliberate strategy on Daly's part, to give Lorde unhindered voice.[26] It is not fanciful then to query whether the notes for the second half of this book are lurking somewhere, respect for some as yet unrevealed factor having kept them so. At the same time, as noted above, this manuscript bespeaks a splitting that means I, for one, would be very surprised indeed if the remaining three chapters had ever met their ink.

The impact of Daly's work cannot be underestimated, although it is probably fair to say this is felt much more within the theological realm than the philosophical.[27] *Catholicism: End or Beginning?* deserves its place in the story of this remarkable oeuvre. Yes, it is dated as a piece of theological argumentation, tackling ontology and ecclesiology in a way few authors find interesting or generative nowadays. It does not have the feminism many

---

[25] Alexis De Veaux, *Warrior Poet: A Biography of Audre Lorde* (New York: W. W. Norton, 2004).

[26] As Laura S. Levitt put it: "It allowed especially a few generations of feminist scholars with race and class privilege to hear Lorde's call, a call addressed specifically to you but really, as you seem to have known, a much larger call directed to all of us through you." "A Letter to Mary Daly." *Journal of Feminist Studies in Religion* 28(2) (2012): 112.

[27] See Elizabeth Hedrick, "The Early Career of Mary Daly: A Retrospective," *Feminist Studies* 39(2) (2013): 457–483. Hedrick's main point is that the foundational historical references for European witchcraft were discredited before she used them.

would assume should be there. And it is, obviously, incomplete as a new ecumenical thesis for Christian faith as a phenomenon, or Catholic ecclesiology as an expression of it. And yet one also sees in this manuscript a store of new material of interest for "Daly Studies": signature developments in her writing technique, especially the reconceptualization of nouns by capitalization;[28] the structure of her later thoughts, how the outside–inside in this manuscript pre-mimics the "background–foreground" of her later philosophical framework; and the intimation of her future concerns, not least the problem of being part of a Church whose very doctrine prohibits one's work.

But the manuscript is of interest not only to "Daly Studies." Theologically, it could receive future study as an extended meditation on baptism, on the core themes of death and re-birth as well as on the *realpolitik* of ecumenism (i.e., one baptism, regardless of denominational affiliation). Moreover, Daly's framing of the question of beginning or ending echoes the perennial one posed by the Deuteronomist ("Do you choose life or death?"),[29] and gives a particular way of tying that to a whole ecclesial body. Furthermore, Daly's promised consideration of Christ's role, not as "reformation" (the expected topic) but "revolution," in the seventh chapter, even as it never materialized, is a potential prompt to future Christic imaginations.

However, for theology, this manuscript is probably mostly of historical interest, being an example of a

---

[28] Undoing language to display its patriarchal complicity and become emancipated from it.

[29] Deuteronomy 30:19.

particular form of argumentation and a particular set of concerns. As such, and perhaps of most importance, it is a reminder of the perils of speculative theology: it may be satisfyingly "pure" as a form of logical reasoning, and the (patriarchal) establishment may have long favored it as superior, but it can be damagingly dismissive of the realities and nuances involved in the practical and contextual. In *Catholicism: End or Beginning?*, we see this vis-à-vis ecumenism. And in Daly's work that follows, we see it with regard to race, gender essentialism, imperialism, and transphobia.

To me, this manuscript is of most interest as an artifact that bears witness to the process of splitting, intellectually and religiously. As such, let it be an encouragement to anyone else in such a position, because tense and fraught as it is, look at the creativity to which it gave way.

4

Abstraction, Mysticism, and Revolution: From *Catholicism: End or Beginning?* to *Beyond God the Father* and *Pure Lust*

~

Jennifer Rycenga

Yes-saying by the Female Self and her Sisters involves intense work – playful cerebration. The Amazon Voyager can be anti-academic. Only at her greatest peril can she be anti-intellectual.

– Mary Daly, *Gyn/Ecology: The Metaethics of Radical Feminism*, xiii

Mary Daly loved the life of the mind. She traced her attraction to philosophy from her earliest metaphysical yearnings, to philosophy classes at the College of Saint Rose, in Albany, into her years of double-doctoral studies in Fribourg – one in philosophy, the other in theology. She describes her journey as a struggle for "intellectual autonomy."[1]

What the rediscovery of *Catholicism: End or Beginning?* reveals is how the struggle for intellectual autonomy was indeed genuine, and that the ultimate result of that contest was, at least momentarily, in doubt. We now know that Daly was destined to emerge victorious, becoming

---

[1] Mary Daly, *Outercourse: The Be-Dazzling Voyage* (San Francisco: HarperSanFrancisco, 1992), 69. When Daly attended the College of Saint Rose, it was an all-women's college. It became co-educational in 1969.

one of the foremost feminist thinkers of the Second Wave. Her strongest work – the trilogy of *Beyond God the Father* (1973), *Gyn/Ecology* (1978), and *Pure Lust* (1984) – prismatically and energetically balances philosophic exactitude, mystical urgings, revolutionary transformation, and ethical anger. *CEB?* provides a clear genealogy for Daly's philosophic rigor *and* mystical intuitionism. But only the merest whisps of revolution and righteous anger appear there. All four dimensions – philosophy, mysticism, transformation, and righteous anger – are integral to the biophilic energy of *Beyond God the Father* and her later works.

The rhetorical question in the title of her manuscript might hang in the air, if only we didn't know exactly how it all turned out. In her autobiographical *Outercourse* (1992), Daly dates her work on *CEB?* as 1969–1970, with the decisive break in her thinking marked by the spring 1971 publication of the article, "After the Death of God the Father."[2] As she states, *CEB?* "was the beginning of the end of my concern over the fate of catholicism [*sic*]."[3] Daly would soon declare herself to be post-Christian, puncturing the inflated mythos propping up the Father God/God Father.[4] She rejected *CEB?*, dubbing it (suggestively and legally) an abortion.[5]

---

[2] Ibid., 102, 134. Mary Daly, "After the Death of God the Father: Women's Liberation and the Transformation of Christian Consciousness," *Commonweal* 94 (1971): 7–11.

[3] Daly, *Outercourse*, 102.

[4] Mary Daly, *Beyond God the Father: Toward a Philosophy of Women's Liberation* (Boston: Beacon Press, 1985), 19; Daly, *Outercourse*, 152; Mary Daly, *Websters' First New Intergalactic Wickedary of the English Language* (Boston: Beacon Press, 1987), 203.

[5] Daly, *Outercourse*, 102.

The keys to Daly's ontological intuitionism and cease-less movement are present in *CEB?*, but not yet fully alive. While she chafes against theological constraints and lit-eralisms, she postpones social change to "perhaps [some] future culture" (4.9). Here, just before the launch of her spiral voyaging, Daly's thought can't escape the linear box in which she finds herself. She had not yet attained the autonomy that she desired. Daly later recognized that she was being "framed by that frame" of Catholicism.[6]

So what happened in that short interval between 1970 and 1972 that resulted in Daly's own clear voice? The short answer? Women. She participated directly in the revolutionary movement of women's liberation – in the streets, but especially in the classroom and in thought. The fecundity of the Women's Liberation Movement swept her into its tidal rhythms.[7] The community of women who were asking questions, rejecting patriarchy, and learning from each other provided Daly with abun-dantly sparking parallels to what she had been seeking in the pages of theologians and philosophers: universal-ism, telos, and a creative tension between immanence and transcendence. But now it was urgent, alive, and achingly real.

Daly always remained a resolutely ontological thinker. Her touchstone spiritual experiences adopted the lan-guage of *"be-ing"/"Be-ing"* from her childhood encounter with a clover blossom that declared, "I am," to the hedge at her graduate school that announced, "Continued

---

[6] Ibid.
[7] Daly, *Pure Lust: Elemental Feminist Philosophy* (Boston: Beacon Press, 2001), 175–176.

existence."[8] Therefore, it is hardly surprising that she was drawn to ontological thinkers. In *CEB?* she defends the ontological against those theologians of hope who sought to thoroughly de-Hellenize Christian tradition (2.6). These arguments are brought over into *Beyond God the Father*, but there she stresses dynamism and creative unpredictability – an *open-ended spiraling cosmology* – until she concludes that "all authentic human hope is ontological."[9]

I liken *CEB?* to what art historians observe using X-ray studies of paintings: the underlying architecture is present, but sketchy (even cartoonish), lacking color. The authors in this volume are in the enviable position of being among the first to analyze Daly's sketches in relation to Daly's biography and body of work. This essay outlines the aforementioned strands of Daly's mature work – philosophy, mysticism, revolutionary transformation, and righteous anger – and traces their presence (from strong to shadowy) in *CEB?* to their newfound presence/Presence, re-emergence, and transformation in *Beyond God the Father* and *Pure Lust*.

Mysticism, Thought, and Action: Beyond Dichotomies

In strong contradistinction to her fully feminist works, *CEB?* builds its intellectual arguments on the work of male philosophers, theologians, and scholars of religion.

---

[8] Daly, *Outercourse*, 23, 26–27 (clover blossom), 51–53 (the hedge on the campus of St. Mary's College enunciating: "Continued existence").

[9] Daly, *Beyond God the Father*, 28.

Despite Daly's consistent engagement with Simone de Beauvoir in her earlier book, *The Church and the Second Sex*, de Beauvoir is not even mentioned in *CEB?* But the male thinkers with whom she grapples here are vital for understanding her intellectual roots and the development of her intellectual autonomy. Conspicuous among them are Thomas Aquinas, Paul Tillich, Jacques Maritain, Teilhard de Chardin, and Mircea Eliade. In particular, her affection for Aquinas's thought remained with her throughout her journey for intellectual autonomy. She unabashedly acknowledged that upon being introduced to Thomas Aquinas, he "became my teacher. ... I learned to use my mind in an intensively systematic way" and gained "a habit of thinking philosophically in a rigorously logical manner."[10] While she would come to recognize and deplore his patriarchal limitations, she never lost her admiration for or gratitude toward him.[11]

Her break from these male thinkers is far from total. Each one of those mentioned above is referenced at least glancingly in her mature work. But her level of critique for all of them can be effectively discerned in the pages of *CEB?*

My overall reading of Daly is that she invites us to experience mystical intuition but thoroughly leavens any call to ecstasy with righteous ethical anger. It is a commonplace of Western mysticism that the person vouchsafed direct contact with the sacred should go back into

---

[10] Daly, *Outercourse*, 51.

[11] I experienced this directly when I brought a small selection of books to Mary Daly when she was in a medical facility during her decline. One was a volume of Aquinas's *Summa Theologica* [*Theologiae*]. She so appreciated this book that she welled up with tears and took it right out of my hands to spend time poring over it.

the world and share this vision, no matter the risks. The lives and deaths of Socrates and Jesus are paradigmatic in this regard. Daly, with her concept of "boundary living"[12] between the deepest experiences of our own be-ing and the boring/bore-ing institutions and assumptions of the patriarchal world eschews the graded stages inherent in the Western paradigm.[13] It is as if the return to Plato's cave becomes, instead of a forced reimprisonment, a conscious ethical awareness of *who is being kept away from having similar experiences*. The ecstasy of the Intuition of Being is always simultaneous with perceiving/decrying/ridiculing the unholy impositions and fetters created by patriarchy. Daly herself would have howled if she knew of Richard of St. Victor's metaphor that the mystic's experience was like an orgasm, and service to the world likened to raising the child of one's ecstasy.[14]

Instead of bifurcating the world and the ultimate, Daly decided to focus on the dynamic "intuition of being" in the writings of Jacques Maritain. The concept resonated deeply with her own quest and led her to write one of her dissertations on Maritain.[15] His philosophic influence on

---

[12] Jennifer Rycenga and Linda Barufaldi (eds.), *The Mary Daly Reader* (New York: New York University Press, 2017), 128–129.

[13] Daly, *Beyond God the Father*, 40–43.

[14] Bernard McGinn, "The Language of Love in Christian and Jewish Mysticism," in *Mysticism and Language*, ed Stephen Katz (New York: Oxford University Press, 1992), 213–214; Gervais Dumeige, *Richard de Saint-Victor et l'idée chrétienne de l'amour* (Paris: Presses universitaires de France, 1952), 171–175. I can especially hear Mary's cackling at the idea that the mystical goal is "the busy household in which the mother cares for her children despite distractions and difficulties" (McGinn, "Language of Love," 214).

[15] Mary Daly, *Natural Knowledge of God in the Philosophy of Jacques Maritain: A Critical Study* (Rome: Catholic Book Agency, 1966).

Daly never wanes, and can be easily discerned across *CEB?* to *Beyond God the Father.*

But despite these strong roots and honest debt to Maritain, Daly's authentic voice comes when she experiences be-ing/Be-ing not in a static abstraction like "god," but as manifestations of the sacred through the active movement and history-altering cognition of women's collective self-definition. This living, active, unpredictable fount of the "Intuition of Being" would mean that though she could use the philosophic categories she had gained from Paul Tillich, Teilhard de Chardin, and Mircea Eliade, they would ultimately be found faulty in their fealty to the stag-nation of "tidy time" and desire for final resolutions or repetitions.

Another way to express what happened to Daly between *CEB?* and *Beyond God the Father* was to see that she had actual mystical experiences in the Women's Liberation Movement. Similar to her "teacher" Aquinas, this absorption in the moment/movement led to Daly's renouncing her previous works as those of a fore-sister, but, unlike Thomas, it resulted in the dynamism of near-constant creativity rather than silence afterwards.[16] There

---

[16] Mary Daly referred to most of her works prior to *Beyond God the Father* as the product of a "reformist foresister" (*Gyn/Ecology: The Metaethics of Radical Feminism* [Boston: Beacon Press, 1990], xi). In an even more condemnatory vein, she dubbed *Catholicism: End or Beginning?* as "an abortive effort" (*Outercourse*, 102). Aquinas, in 1273, had a powerful mystical experience that led to his permanently suspending work on the *Summa Theologiae*; he reported to his secretary that "all that I have written seems like straw to me." He died just four months later. Brian Davie, *The Thought of Thomas* Aquinas (New York: Oxford University, 1993), 9 and Frederick Copleston, *Aquinas* (Baltimore, MD: Penguin Books, 1955), 10.

would be no waiting for an "afterlife" but instead Daly would proclaim that "The Journey is itself participation in Paradise."[17] Women's specificity, and outrage over the perpetual injustice towards women's ontological status and very real human lives is what drove Mary Daly to break with the mentors whose echoes suffuse *CEB?*

Maritain and the "Intuition of Being" in *Catholicism: End or Beginning?*

Jacques Maritain (1882–1973) was one of Daly's most significant intellectual influences. While he was one of the leading Neo-Thomists of the twentieth century, Maritain also championed an existentialist universalism in his concept of the "Intuition of Being." Daly had a personal investment in understanding Maritain's Intuition of Being, since she had had similar experiences in her "Elemental" encounters with clover blossoms, hedges, and in dreams.[18]

Maritain was a catalyst and participant in the eclectic spiritual searching of both post–world war periods; from his earliest adult years he and his wife Raïssa affirmed mystical experiences of their own, and his metaphysics created space for an intuitive, experiential affirmation of the sacred. The post–World War II period saw a heyday of popular and scholarly writing on forms of mystical experience across religions: Aldous Huxley's *Perennial Philosophy* (1945) and Walter T. Stace's *Mysticism and*

---

[17] *Gyn/Ecology*, 6. This is also where she refers to patriarchal paradise as "stagnation (in a stag-nation)."

[18] *Outercourse*, 47–50 ("The Dream of Green").

Philosophy (1960) provide two convenient book-ends presaging the explosion of interest in non-Western traditions.[19] Maritain himself became engaged in the culture wars over the politics of comparative mysticism. He came to the defense of Stace, when, in 1957, an acerbic Catholic chaplain at Princeton (where Maritain was teaching) accused Stace of being an atheist, Marxist, and liberal corrupter of the youth.[20]

Maritain is a primary focus in the manuscript's second chapter, "The Mystery of Being and The Catholic Substance." The opening pages of Maritain's essay, *Approaches to God* (*Approches de Dieu*, 1953), on the Intuition of Being, are quoted extensively by Daly. She dwells with Maritain's universalization of natural theology: "the existence involved in anything at all implies some absolute existence," whether we recognize it in "man, mountain or tree" – or even a clover blossom or hedge (2.2).[21] She notes Maritain's debt to Heidegger but emphasizes his invocation of the Aristotelian and Thomistic "analogy of being." She recognizes that Maritain's "Intuition of Being" is meant as "a bait or an enticement which compels us to rise to a higher level" (2.2). But her focus remains with the Intuition of Being itself, rather than on that ladder of abstraction to a transcendent deity.

---

[19] Aldous Huxley, *The Perennial Philosophy* (London: Chatto & Windus, 1946); W. T. Stace, *Mysticism and Philosophy* (Philadelphia: J. P. Lippincott, 1960).

[20] G. W. Elderkin (George Wicker), "The Roman Catholic Controversy on the Campus of Princeton University," *Life* (October 7, 1957).

[21] Jacques Maritain, *Approaches to God*, trans. Peter O'Reilly (London: George Allen & Unwin, 1955), 3–4.

When she was writing *CEB?*, Daly was working out her own philosophic conundrums, as well as trying to don her increasingly public role as a rising radical catholic theologian (and an anomalous Catholic woman theologian, as she recognized in and after *The Church and the Second Sex*). So it would be understandable to hypothesize that she commented on Maritain hoping it would provide some Catholic cover for her. But her love of Maritain was more genuine than that. Significantly, Maritain never suffers the classic Daly feminist outrage that she visited on Tillich. The harshest thing she ever wrote about Maritain in no way impugns his philosophic integrity. In fact, she seems to consider the "Intuition of Being" analogous to her own philosophic directions in *Beyond God the Father*: "Although he was hardly a feminist or a social revolutionary, Maritain had an exceedingly fine sensitivity to the power of this intuition [of being] which, if it were carried through to social consciousness, would challenge the world."[22] She could see how a thinker's categories genuinely go beyond that individual person's

---

[22] Daly, *Beyond God the Father*, 203–204n.28. While describing it as a work from a fore-sister, Daly characterizes her Maritain dissertation as "a passionate treatise on the intellectual life" from "an ardent Thomist scholar" (*Outercourse*, 74). In a sideways thank-you, Daly resuscitates Maritain and her own doctoral thesis, without critique, in a well-concealed footnote in *Outercourse*: "The intuition [of Being] and its shocking abruptness are discussed in many of the works of Jacques Maritain ... For a thorough analysis of this 'shocking' intuition and its implications, see Mary F. Daly, *Natural Knowledge of God in the Philosophy of Jacques Maritain: A Critical Study.*" *Outercourse*, 440n.22. This is exceptional: written in 1992 with no shade thrown on Maritain for his gender. It is a moment that speaks volumes through its very silences.

limitations (in this case, Maritain's relative lack of socio-political engagement).[23]

Eliade and Tillich in the "Intuition of Being" in *Catholicism: End or Beginning?*

It makes excellent sense that Daly moves directly from her exposition of Maritain's "Intuition of Being" to Mircea Eliade's Religious Studies neologism, "hierophany." A hierophany is any manifestation of the sacred in the world. Anything – object, being, feeling, sensation – can be the occasion for a hierophany. Daly zeroes in on Eliade's hierophany being accessible through the religious value given to a stone. Here is the full quote from Eliade's famed *The Sacred and the Profane:*

> The hierophany of a stone is pre-eminently an onto-phany; above all, the stone *is*, it always remains itself, it does not change – and it *strikes* man by what it possesses of irreducibility and absoluteness and, in so doing, reveals to him by analogy the irreducibility and absoluteness of being. Perceived by virtue of religious experience, the specific mode of existence of the stone reveals to man the nature of an *absolute existence*, beyond time, invulnerable to becoming.[24]

---

[23] She articulates this explicitly when she was rebuffed by Peter Berger after attempting to thank him for his insights in *The Sacred Canopy*. She writes that she realized "one could write a lucid book such as *The Sacred Canopy* (which I still consider an important work, that is, useful to spring off from), while refusing to acknowledge its logical implications. Berger's abstract theory was split off from insight into the realities that I experienced every day of my life." Daly, *Outercourse*, 135.

[24] Mircea Eliade, *The Sacred and the Profane* (New York: Harper & Row, 1961), 155–156.

It is as important to examine what she does and doesn't include from Eliade (2.2). Her concern is the Intuition of Being, which she had experienced with her clover blossom announcing "I am," and which Maritain elaborated as "existence involved in anything ... implies some absolute existence." Just as she had eschewed Maritain's insistence to move beyond natural theology, she excludes in her quote the contention by Eliade that the ontophany he has named goes "beyond time, invulnerable to becoming." She had sensed correctly where this would lead – and it was nowhere she wanted to go. Unlike Maritain, Eliade's theoretical framework is subject to Daly's labrys in *Beyond God the Father* and *Gyn/Ecology* precisely because of this deep commitment to stasis, to that which is "invulnerable to becoming."[25] When Daly experienced a historically situated, highly specific hierophany in the Women's Liberation Movement that was all about becoming, Eliade's ontological limitations were revealed as openly patriarchal. When Eliade attempts to make a special case for Christianity having been a "qualitative leap" in the nature of hierophanies, Daly dismisses him with a "whatever" shrug of contempt in *Beyond God the Father*: "not my concern."[26] That shrug had been anticipated in how she selectively excerpted from *The Sacred and the Profane* in the manuscript.

Paul Tillich is the third theorist that Daly includes in her exposition of the Intuition of Being in *CEB?* She acknowledges that she is "indebted to Tillich's theological synthesis" and cites his controversial contention that

---

[25] Daly, *Beyond God the Father*, 159–160; Daly, *Gyn/Ecology* 44–45.
[26] Daly, *Beyond God the Father*, 35.

Christianity would still have meaning even if the historical Jesus had not lived (4.9). But the great uneasiness that Daly felt with Christology pushes her even further than Tillich did in this regard, casting the "well-spring of Tillich's thought" as "the affirmation of being" (2.2). This is not necessarily a far stretch for someone whose most famous work is *The Courage to Be*. But where Daly is headed, philosophically, is obvious: the Intuition of Being is valorized above any ladder of ascent to Christianity, or the specifics of the person of Jesus Christ. She is especially scandalized by what she names correctly as "Christolatry," condemning those theologians who would maintain Christian exclusivity to such a degree that they would say:

> that one cannot have religious experience unless there is some explicit faith in Christ. It reflects precisely that aspect of Christianity which the radical young, in their search for authenticity and for communion with the depth of reality, feel compelled to reject. (4.1)

Daly's ultimate rejection of Christian exclusivity in favor of authenticity was nigh.

Defining Definitive Breaks: Teilhard de Chardin

There was one more theorist to whom she clung in *CEB?*: Pierre Teilhard de Chardin. Calling him a "poet-prophet-scientist-theologian" harkens to her own desire to unite poetic and philosophic forms of thought, but she went further than that in her praise.[27] Just as Tillich had

---

[27] She vowed to write in a rigorous but "philosophically poetic" manner. See Daly, *Outercourse*, 49.

postulated the absence of the historical Jesus, Daly notes that Teilhard de Chardin was ready to abandon the concept of original sin because of its "life-defeating implications." When she reveals that Teilhard embraced "the possibility of believing at the same time and wholly in God and in the world," he would seem to be so in step with the biophilic direction in which she was moving, that the break from him seems surprising (4.6).

Beyond God the Father, though, discloses a chasm between Daly and Teilhard, which furnishes a strong example of her methodology as a feminist thinker. In his drive towards the unity of the Omega Point, or Omega-Christ, Daly detects a cascade of fatal errors. What she had previously thought to be an embrace of the world as sacred turned out to be a flattening of possibility, a reduction of diversity to a unity: "His Omega Point is a static, spatial image, and in using it he spatializes time. He *visualizes* the Omega as an *apex* of conic time, as a point, as the *closing bulb* on the tree of life, as the *North Pole*."[28] Daly had, by then, an Intuition of Being that involved time, history, and community intrinsically. She was not going to surrender that for an Omega point, especially not one culminating in an Alpha male Christ. And, indeed, the masculinist language, and Teilhard's own ambivalence towards full personhood for women, forms another component in Daly's dismissal of him.[29] These failings in his thinking had also led to a horrid misstep, wherein Teilhard offhandedly endorses "the modern totalitarian regimes [which], whatever their initial defects, are neither heresies nor biological regressions:

---

[28] Daly, *Beyond God the Father*, 192.   [29] Ibid., 190–191.

they are in line with the essential trend of 'cosmic' movement."[30] The cat has clawed its way through the bag of Teilhard's seeming optimism and future orientation – that future will be achieved by repression and force. And so her clinching argument, nearly understated in *Beyond God the Father*, "Teilhard tends to split off and reify being [as (in his own words but with Daly's emphasis)] a *pre-existing Being*."

The question remains – why does she spend so much time, and such valuable space in the concluding pages of *Beyond God the Father*, on Teilhard de Chardin? I believe that it is for the same reason that she had spent so much time on him in *CEB?* – because he held that level of importance to radical Catholics in the 1960s and 1970s, by virtue of being both a scientist and a Jesuit priest. Furthermore, he ran afoul of the Vatican censors, who forbade him from publishing his philosophic works. After he died in 1955, posthumous publications emerged and gained in popularity; the magisterium issued a warning against his writings in 1962, citing "ambiguities and indeed even serious errors."[31] So Teilhard wore the mantle of visionary, prophet, persecuted truth-bearer,

---

[30] Pierre Teilhard de Chardin, "The Grand Option" (1939). www .organism.earth/library/document/grand-option. No translator given. Originally published in *Cahiers du monde nouveau* 1 (1945): 247–263.

[31] "Monitum on the Writings of Fr. Pierre Teilhard de Chardin, SJ," Congregation for the Doctrine of the Faith. Original warning of 1962 reaffirmed in 1981. www.ewtn.com/catholicism/library/ monitum-on-the-writings-of-fr-teilhard-de-chardin-sj-2144. The Congregation for the Doctrine of the Faith is the organization formerly known as "the Inquisition," and still referred to as "the Holy Office." It recently underwent another name change – to the "Dicastery for the Doctrine of the Faith." But it will always be the Inquisition to me!

and modern thinker (his scientific reputation being unassailable) to his acolytes. Daly could see through that by the time of *Beyond God the Father*, but not yet in *CEB?*

The Catholic theorists who made the deepest impression on Daly – Aquinas, Maritain, and Teilhard – share a character trait of methodological clarity. Each of them came by this methodological precision honestly, through their professional facility with precise forms of rigorous thinking, such as paleontology (Teilhard), Aristotelianism (Aquinas), and medieval Thomistic logic (Maritain). Each of these thinkers moderates their precise denotative expertise with an experience and/or comprehension of ontological reality. This balance between discursive and intuitive reason is exactly what Daly knew as her Quest:

> I wanted a clear defense of intellectual rigor/vigor. This insistence on having it *all* – intuition *and* arduous reasoning that is rooted in intuition – was of deep importance to me. I loved both modes of knowing, which I recognized as essential to each other.[32]

In *CEB?*, Daly made the mistake of thinking she could weave together the abstractions of these thinkers into something that might point the way to a livable future, especially for women. But it was destined to fail, because of what Daly would come to see as the philosophic limitations of any reified being. It is with this that we can now turn to the two largest shifts between *CEB?* and her mature thought: "Realizing Reason," which "is both discovering and participating in the unfolding, the Self-creation, of reason" and "Be-ing."[33]

---

[32] Daly, *Outercourse*, 74.   [33] Daly, *Pure Lust*, 162.

Daly Reverses the Direction of Ill Ontologies

Before she reached the Intuition of Being in the crucial second chapter on "The Mystery of Being" in *CEB?*, Drs. Daly[34] asked her readers to go beyond any question of the specifics of Catholicism in order to engage in "the rediscovery of being." This involved the need to experience "wonder about the secret mystery of being. The question which is implied is sometimes put this way: Why are there beings and not simply non-being?" (2.2).

Daly traces this question from Schelling to Heidegger, whom she quotes approvingly (as she does Eliade and Teilhard) without even a glancing reference to the innate and historically specific authoritarianism in the thought of these men:

> Heidegger expressed it this way: "Why are there beings at all and not non-being? This is obviously the first of all questions, though not in the sense of a chronological order of questions." Indeed, for Heidegger, authentic thought by its nature tends to being. In man's thought, "being" lights up, coming forth from its hiddenness. He is of course not speaking of "a being" but of the being that makes beings to be. For him, authentic thought is concerned with the unveiling of being. (2.2)[35]

She then moves into the material on Jacques Maritain and the Intuition of Being that was later transformed into

---

[34] Mary Daly earned multiple doctoral degrees and always took pride in being addressed as "Doctor" (and sometimes playfully as "Doctors").

[35] Daly does not provide the source of the Schelling quote (*Philosophical Investigations into the Essence of Human Freedom*, 1809), but she gives Heidegger's (*Introduction to Metaphysics*, trans. R. Manheim [New Haven, CT: Yale University Press, 1958], 1).

"Be-ing" in *Beyond God the Father*. While she discusses a great deal of ontology in *Beyond God the Father*, the full weight of this (allegedly) foundational question would wait until Daly's own philosophic *Summa, Pure Lust*, for its full transformation.

For a series of complex reasons, *Pure Lust* rarely gets the attention, or garners the controversy, of *Beyond God the Father* and *Gyn/Ecology*. This is lamentable, because *Pure Lust* contains Daly's mature ontology in its fullest expression.[36] The process of writing *Pure Lust* involved "recapturing the ontological/philosophical emphasis" of *Beyond God the Father*.[37] The subtitles of the two books show this explicitly; we go from *Toward a Philosophy of Women's Liberation* to *Elemental Feminist Philosophy*.

Daly's affection for Maritain's Intuition of Being remains untarnished. She continues to insist that "intellectually extensive and abstract" thought can be in active dialectic with intuitive experience and thought. So while Maritain's contribution is secure, Tillich is no longer spared at all; nowhere is he shielded philosophically in *Pure Lust*.[38] Daly acknowledges that his thought has "vast

---

[36] I am deeply indebted to, and in agreement with, Laurel Schneider, in her article, "The Courage to See and to Sin: Mary Daly's Elemental Transformation of Paul Tillich's Ontology," in *Feminist Interpretations of Mary Daly*, ed. Sarah Lucia Hoagland and Marilyn Frye (University Park: Penn State University Press, 2000), 55–75.

[37] Daly, *Outercourse*, 274.

[38] I added the parentheses describing Daly's critique of Tillich here as philosophical, because she had already amplified Hannah Tillich's evidence of Paul Tillich's sexist sado-masochism in *Gyn/Ecology*, 94–95. I surmise that Daly knew that even though she had connected Tillich's personal sexual practice to philosophy, that the strength of that connection would be easily challenged/dismissed as too personal and unprovable (even though the evidence increasingly supports Hannah

scope and rigor," but his limitations make it such that Tillich serves only as a "springboard" for feminist analysis.[39] In order to function as that springboard, though, his ontological limitations have to be made clear. Even in *Beyond God the Father*, Daly critiqued Tillich's ontology for its abstraction of the sacred outside of historical specificity as "a super-reified Something."[40] But it took her until *Pure Lust* to fully articulate the problem embedded in the language of abstraction that had made philosophy so attractive to her as a young student, scholar, and professor, right through the writing of *CEB?*

She begins by distinguishing her project from the received tradition by virtue of the inherent dynamism of Be-ing, "In the classic philosophical tradition, *first philosophy* means ontology, the 'philosophy of being.' In the Elemental transition, *first philosophy* Names the philosophy of be-ing." She then unfolds what and how to think energetically and vigorously about this dynamism:

> Since this first philosophy is about Elemental be-ing, it is radically metaphysical, concerned with ontological potency, knowledge, passion, virtue, creation, transformation. Given this complexity, our thinking must be not only imaginatively intense and concrete, but also intellectually extensive and abstract.[41]

Tillich's telling). Thus, I feel that Daly revisited Tillich here in *Pure Lust*; significantly, she doesn't even feel the need to return to his sexual cruelties in this later book. For much more on the implications of Tillich's sexual proclivities, see Tracy Fessenden, "'Woman' and the 'Primitive' in Paul Tillich's Life and Thought: Some Implications for the Study of Religion," *Journal of Feminist Studies in Religion* 14(2) (1998): 45–76.

39 Daly, *Pure Lust*, 29n.   40 Daly, *Beyond God the Father*, 20–21, 36.
41 Daly, *Pure Lust*, 28.

Daly here realizes that it is not abstraction per se that creates reification. The fault in Tillich's ontology is in his ontological assumptions themselves.

What follows is a thinly disguised reminiscence of Daly's own acceptance of the limitations of a reified ontology, echoing her writing in *CEB?*:

> One of the positive things that can happen when biophilic women read such words is the eliciting of a memory of an intuition of be-ing. ... when reading the question "Why is there something; why not nothing?" a Wonderlusty woman might imagine that the question thus posed corresponds to her own ontological experience, to her Lust for Be-ing. She might imagine that the ontological question thus posed expresses an attitude identical with her own Wonder and gratitude that things *are*. Caught up in this Wonder, she might fail to notice anything suspect about the second half of Tillich's question: "why not nothing?" Musing women would do well to ask ourSelves whether this question would arise spontaneously in biophilic consciousness.[42]

It is Mary Daly herself, (or, more properly, her foresister), the author of *CEB?* who supposed that the male philosophers were posing the correct question. It is true that the pursuit of philosophy did open her sense of wonder/Wonder. Even in *Beyond God the Father* she still employs the language of "nothingness" and "non-being." But after she had developed the category of *biophilia* she realizes that even the willingness to imagine non-being was indicative of "necrophilia."[43] The ability to imagine non-being happens because "Thought that starts with the noun, *being*, cannot go behind it . . . Such thought is stuck, fixated, fixed and thus does not actively participate in Powers of Be-ing."[44]

Consider two of these descriptors in particular: fixated and fixed. An ontology that is obsessed with one ultimate, with something that can be defined as an object, has built-in limitations. And this is where, for Daly, the patriarchal assumptions in the Western tradition reinforce onto-logical limitations – like pinning a butterfly in a display case, even liberal patriarchal thinkers (of whom Tillich is a prime example) prefer to deal with objects that have been "fixed" in place, including (and Daly would say primordially) women.

Revolutionary Political Ontophanies

Chapter 1 of *Beyond God the Father* opens with two epi-grams. The first is Robin Morgan's "lust" for a "women's revolution" and the second Alfred North Whitehead's admonition to critique the assumptions that are so deep in the psyche of an age that they have gone unnoted.[45] In comparing *Beyond God the Father* with *CEB?*, both quotes mark a definitive break from her earlier perspec-tives. The passionate, precise poetry of the Women's Liberation Movement, and Morgan's focus on the women's liberation movement, goes much further than the general comments about women's awakening in the earlier manuscript. Whitehead might seem to mesh with Daly's philosophic movement towards an open ontology.

---

[44] Daly, *Pure Lust*, 29–30.   [45] Daly, *Beyond God the Father*, 1.

But this particular quote concerns a historical process. Between *CEB?* and *Beyond God the Father*, Daly made the turn into understanding history and time itself as dynamic and philosophically significant.

During the late 1960s, she attended anti-war meetings, but, like many white women at that time, found the overall atmosphere to be alienating. She then became involved with the National Organization for Women (NOW) in Boston and Worcester, as well as organizing women's studies in theology in the Boston area in the same period when the ideas for *CEB?* were percolating: 1969–1970.[46] While she never becomes a regular street activist, the Women's Liberation Movement changed her. In her 1985 "Original Reintroduction" to *Beyond God the Father*, Mary Daly proclaims that her "deep experiential knowledge of Elemental potency/potential in women ... made possible the writing of *Beyond God the Father*, and ... sustained my own journey."[47]

CEB? gives us the perspective from which to philosophically corroborate her assertion. In the extended quote below from *Beyond God the Father*, one can see how Daly had surveyed her philosophic ground, but without a motivating philosophic subject:

> What I am proposing is that the emergence of the communal vocational self-awareness of women is a *creative political ontophany*. It is a manifestation of the sacred (*hierophany*) precisely because it is an experience of participation in being, and therefore a manifestation of being (*ontophany*). ... the potential for *ontological* hierophany that is already beginning to be realized in the

---

[46] Daly, *Outercourse* 102–104. [47] Daly, *Beyond God the Father*, xi.

> participatory vocational self-consciousness of women does involve a leap, bridging the apparent gap between being and history. ... In the very process of becoming actual persons, of confronting the non-being of our situation, women are bearers of history.[48]

Eliade, Tillich, Maritain, even Teilhard, can be detected here, but they have been transformed in ways they never anticipated. Ontology and ethical outrage (the other side of hope, for it is because of disappointment, frustration, and anger that hope becomes necessary) are unified to close the false dichotomy of "being and history." This constitutes a leap beyond her earlier sources. The mystical Intuition of Being (now *Be-ing*) fuels a process of collective and individual change, an unending spiral unfolding revolution that is "creative."

Mystical bliss in the Western tradition, as iconicized in Bernini's *Ecstasy of Saint Teresa*, is an extended orgasmic moment of intimacy, blissfully outside of time and history. Daly instead takes the idea of a "heirophany," replaces its hierarchic etymology with the philosophically more open-ended "ontophany," then adds the words "creative" and "political" – neither of which would occur naturally in Christian theological understandings of mysticism. Daly's "ontophany" does not stand still, nor does it remain isolated or intimate. It expands because it is creative. It extends, for both the individual and the communal, because it is political. The Women's Liberation Movement of that time had interconnected the personal and communal in the famous slogan, "the personal is the

---

[48] Ibid., 34–35.

political."[49] Daly here has woven together individual and community, mysticism and creativity, ontology and politics.

It is within the phrase "confronting the non-being of our situation" that righteous anger emerges. The fact of oppression, of women being forcibly kept for centuries from the fulness of their own lives, means that patriarchy is actively tyrannizing and crushing be-ing/Be-ing. In a key footnote in *Pure Lust*, Daly (with Emily Culpepper's assistance) enunciates how oppression is always oppression of *something*, not *nothing*. In Culpepper's words, "oppressive conditions are a shock, a weight, a drain, precisely because they are a shock to something, ... That something is the sense of integrity of Self."[50] Daly's consistent rage against patriarchy comes from exactly this: the routes to self-actualization are actively and intentionally being blocked, channelized, crushed underfoot.

This sort of anger is missing from the pages of *CEB?* because it took the ontological insight of Be-ing/God the Verb for Daly to shift her vision from liberal reformist Catholicism to a fully panentheistic embrace of what the clover blossom and the hedge had told her: "I am" and "Continued existence." Thus, the question, "Why is there something; why not nothing?" became a staggering error rather than an intriguing abstraction that could ground metaphysics.

---

[49] Carol Hanisch, "Consciousness Raising: The Personal is the Political," in *Notes from the Second Year: Women's Liberation*, ed. Shulamith Firestone and Anne Koedt (New York: Radical Feminism, 1970).
[50] Daly, *Pure Lust*, 105n.

Consider the tepid tone of the few passages in *CEB?* that reference women in particular: "women are engaged actively in the struggle to liberate themselves from this mystique of the passive virtues"; "it can hardly be acceptable to the increasing number of liberated and self-actualizing women to be presented with an image of themselves as tempters responsible for the moral breakdown of the male"; and the vague hope that in "another, perhaps future culture, the hierophany might happen most strikingly through a woman" (4.7, 3.3, 4.9). One would never get the idea from these tame complaints that anything ontological was at stake. Once Daly realized that women had been sent to the stake for daring to Realize Reason, everything changed.

CEB? demonstrates that the mysticism embedded in Maritain's Intuition of Being is not containable within stultifying systems of faith. Though imbued with the same tame tone, the problem is well-stated here:

> Conceptions of faith which reduce it to a stagnant will-act of assent to a body of propositions handed down by authority, conceptions of faith that reduce personal autonomy or that breed intolerance toward others who do not adhere to the same belief-system – these all lead to indifference and even resistance to social and political reform, since they hinder the possibility for profound personal insight and for original thought and action (1.3).

Daly knew what a revolution could do – abstractly. But when she was directly enmeshed in the actual revolutionary feminist movement/moment, she was able to take the leap and the fall/Fall into Be-ing, declaring "*this* movement *is* movement. Realization of this is already the beginning of a qualitative leap in be-ing. . . . the final cause that *is movement* is in our imaginative-cerebral-emotional-active-creative be-ing."[51] This ecstatic philosophic utterance is unimaginable in the pages of *CEB?*

The Objectivity and Subjectivity of Revolutionary Diversity and Movement

"The revolution is magnificent. All else is bilge." Thus wrote the Polish-German revolutionary Rosa Luxemburg (1871–1919) from the midst of the 1905 Russian Revolution.[52] "Bilge" refers to stagnant, dirty, polluted, and dangerous water that collects (and endangers) the movement of a boat. I will take the liberty of translating this into Daly's language: "The women's revolution is biophilic. All else is necrophilic."

Luxemburg's passionate engagement in revolution first came to my attention via the philosophic–biographical account of her life by the twentieth-century Marxist–Humanist and feminist philosopher Raya Dunayevskaya (1910–1987). While a longer comparison of Dunayevskaya and Daly is not germane to this essay, it is intriguing to find in Dunayevskaya another woman philosopher, at the same moment in time, albeit coming from very different philosophic presuppositions, running parallel to Daly in key ways.

---

[51] Daly, *Beyond God the Father*, 190.
[52] Raya Dunayevskaya, *Rosa Luxemburg, Women's Liberation, and Marx's Philosophy of Revolution*, 2nd ed. (Urbana: University of Illinois Press, 1991), 7. Adrienne Rich wrote an introduction to this edition.

In her first book, *Marxism and Freedom*, Dunayevskaya made two statements that generated controversy in the contemporaneous Left. First, she claimed that the Montgomery Bus Boycotts were of equal importance in illuminating "the road to a new society" as the Hungarian uprising against the USSR. The Eurocentric and white biases of the Left made such a claim seem preposterous – until it obviously wasn't.[53] The second statement made a profound philosophic claim about the source of revolutionary change, but one that deliberately decentered the genius of the philosopher: "There is nothing in thought – not even in the thought of a genius – that has not previously been in the activity of the common man."[54] To this, Herbert Marcuse wrote "bluntly and impolitely" (his own words) to Dunayevskaya, accusing her of being "romantic" and "undialectic" while emboldening anti-intellectualism.[55] What Dunayevskaya was getting at, though, was the interpenetration of intellect with material human life, particularly in the movements of masses of people when they are collectively and individually reaching for a new, creative world.[56]

[53] Raya Dunayevskaya, *Marxism and Freedom ... from 1776 to Today*, 5th ed. (Atlantic Highlands, NJ: Humanities Press, 1982), 23, 19.

[54] Ibid., 28.

[55] Letter from Herbert Marcuse to Raya Dunayevskaya, January 8, 1955, in *The Dunayevskaya–Marcuse–Fromm Correspondence, 1954–1978: Dialogues on Hegel, Marx, and Critical Theory*, ed. Kevin Anderson and Russell Rockwell (Lanham, MD: Lexington Books , 2012), 4–5.

[56] Dunayevskaya was drawing from Hegel when he claims that while many (especially intuitional philosophers) had taken the comment that "there is nothing in thought which has not been in sense and experience," that the reverse was equally true, that "there is nothing in sense and experience that has not been in the intellect." See Friedrich Hegel's *Encyclopedia of the Philosophical Sciences in Basic Outline, Part I:*

Dunayevskaya made continuous philosophic commentary upon the Women's Liberation Movement of the 1960s and 1970s while it was happening. Two specific observations she made are relevant to Daly's transformation. First, Dunayevskaya notes how revolution creates new people, or what she terms "original characters": "A birthtime of history manifests itself not only in great social changes but in original characters, and Luxemburg was an original."[57] This is used by Dunayevskaya to describe Luxemburg's renewed creativity following a parting from her romantic partner, fellow revolutionary Leo Jogiches. A break was needed, Dunayevskaya theorizes, because Luxemburg's "further self-development was reaching for new heights ... in a rare fusion of the political, the personal, and, yes, the organizational."[58] The parallel I see is that Daly, too, had to effect a total break from catholicism and those male thinkers on whom she had previously relied. It was the revolutionary movement of women that rendered Daly an original character, self-defined and ceaselessly self-developing.

Even more suggestively *and* precisely, consider Dunayevskaya's open ontology of revolution from within the Women's Liberation Movement. She wrote that, "We are, at one and the same time, confronted with two seemingly opposite facts – that the individuality of each woman liberationist is a microcosm of the whole, and yet that the movement is not a sum of so many individuals but *masses in motion.*[59] Daly always perceived the importance of her own

---

Science of Logic, trans. Klaus Brinkmann and Daniel O. Dahlstrom (Cambridge: Cambridge University Press, 2010), Section 1, ¶8.

[57] Dunayevskaya, *Rosa Luxemburg*, 92. [58] Ibid.

[59] Ibid., 83; emphasis Dunayevskaya's.

individuality, and the power of the "participatory vocational self-consciousness of women" who "[i]n the very process of becoming actual persons ... are bearers of history."[60] Likewise, she understood that the women's revolution, as she named it in *Beyond God the Father*, was not merely the sum of individuals, but a collective awakening that augured much that could not be fully foreseen.

However, Daly's system ultimately foundered on the shoals of her own resistance to deeply confronting racism and imperialism, and on her sharp, often bitter hostility toward transgender people. While outlining Daly's short-comings on race, imperialism, and transgender peoples is well beyond the scope of this essay, her attempt to address the critiques raised by Audre Lorde, Elly Bulkin, and others after *Gyn/Ecology* resulted in an inadequate attempt to describe what she termed "Dreadful and Daring Diversity" (her capitalization).[61] But Daly left a hint, which forms a fine parallel to what Dunayevskaya said of the revolutionary dimensions of the One and the Many in the substance of material earthly existence. Daly quotes Rachel Carson on tidal/Tidal reality, "The tides present a striking paradox ... the force that sets them in motion is cosmic, lying wholly outside the earth ... but the nature of the tide at any particular place is a local matter, with astonishing differences occurring within a very short geo-graphic distance."[62] In other words, there is a way to ontologize diversity without erasing the lived experience of any group or individual.

[60] Daly, *Beyond God the Father*, 34–35. [61] Daly, *Pure Lust*, 176.
[62] Quoted ibid., 175, from Rachel Carson, *The Sea Around Us* (New York: New American Library, 1961), 144.

Part of the excitement at the rediscovery of *CEB?* consists precisely in how it reveals that Daly's mature work was inspired (in a way that *CEB?*, however thoughtful and deep it may be, is not) by the actual lives, ideas, and corporal existence of women. Daly's concept of women's "liberation consists in refusing to be 'the Other' and asserting instead "I am" – without making another "the Other."[63] That assertion of "I am" – learned from a clover blossom – is why, in marked distinction to *CEB?*, her later works positively bubble with biophilia. Her tone is confident, attractive through its enthusiasm, and alive to the present moment. Yet these works are also intellectually rigorous; she makes demands on her reader and, as this essay's epigram suggests, encourages cerebration.

Daly was a cogent participant and witness at the Greatest Awakening of them all – half the human race! This reveals why *CEB?* cannot answer its own titular question. We can discern that she was prepared to follow a well-trodden Catholic pathway toward individual enlightenment, until she found herself in the midst of a social movement that was unsettling, larger, and ultimately far more compelling. The question of the future of the Catholic Church devolved into nonsense once Daly had lived within a collective revolutionary subjectivity. Her mystical insight was a historically motivated apprehension of ontological reality via a social movement. This is what makes Daly an original character, and why she *had* to write after her mystical experience (unlike Aquinas).

Daly became an original character when she experienced sparking from other women, when the possibilities

---

[63] Daly, *Beyond God the Father*, 34.

within life itself, and the artificial choking of that freedom, became obvious because it was embodied. Her spiraling cosmology, in its specificity, emerges when she knows that the process of ontological "unfolding ... is an event in which women participate as we participate in our own revolution."[64]

I agree with Laurel Schneider that "the radical aspect of Daly's work lies not in her rejection of the western epistemological and theological traditions but in her creative and critical use of these traditions to begin building a systematic project."[65] *CEB?* shows us the cluster of ideas Daly took from christianity: speculative rigor, mysticism, Intuition of Being. But these influences alone cannot reveal her as an outraged/outrageous mystic. What she gained from Aquinas and Maritain was of lasting value; she never abandoned the methodological and ontological insights she gained in her encounters with them. Daly had an ability to hold near opposites in creative tension, like Aquinas's rigor and Maritain's intuition, which echoed her desire to be both philosopher and poet. But the superstructure to which Aquinas and Maritain gave their fealty – the Catholic Church – could not uphold the third dimension that Daly brought to the table, namely the self-developing transformation of living people, including herSelf.

In the pages of her final work, *Amazon Grace*, she playfully recapitulates the story of her intellectual life, "On the face of it, linking Jacques Maritain and Susan B. Anthony might seem a bit odd. The result of this linkage might appear to be an Odd Couple. So? We live

---

[64] Ibid., 40.   [65] Schneider, "The Courage to See and to Sin," 56.

in an odd world."[66] The reason Susan B. Anthony and
Jacques Maritain can be linked, though, is not limited to
Daly's idiosyncrasies (though massively tinctured with
them). It is because of the ultimate creative political
ontophany:

> All Wild creatures and Other realities participate in Be-
> ing, by which I mean "Ultimate/Intimate Reality, the
> constantly Unfolding Verb of Verbs which is intransitive,
> having no object that limits its dynamism."[67] The Terrific
> Shock of encountering and Realizing Be-ing . . . is simple
> and direct. It is absolutely surprising and joyous. It is Self-
> transformative and changes Everything. It is unforget-
> table. It opens pathways that go on and on. It makes one
> Realize how Lucky she is. The Prayer that comes to mind
> is "Thank you! Thank you!"[68]

---

[66] Mary Daly, *Amazon Grace: Re-Calling the Courage to Sin Big* (New York: Palgrave Macmillan, 2006), 46. Also in Rycenga and Barufaldi, *The Mary Daly Reader*, 363.

[67] See *"Be-ing,"* in Mary Daly, *Websters' First New Intergalactic Wickedary of the English Language* (Boston: Beacon Press, 1987).

[68] Daly, *Amazon Grace*, 45; *The Mary Daly Reader*, 362.

5

Catholicism: End or Beginning?
An Open-Ended Journey Toward
a Theology of Difference

~

Zahra Moballegh

Out of the Historical Context: My Story with Daly

It was around 2002, and I was not yet twenty years old.
As a student of philosophy, I was eagerly attending
courses, listening to lectures with my entire being, flying
throughout the card catalogs and shelves in the central
library, and reading any book whose title I found
appealing. The study of philosophy became the most
central and important thing in my life. "I soared with
it ... I found it all exhilarating."[1] I had a small notebook
in which I made a list of any woman philosopher whose
name was mentioned in a book or article. I even suggested
to a famous newspaper to write a weekly column about
the lives and ideas of these women, but they didn't find it
interesting. Although I had never experienced a woman
professor teaching a philosophy course, I could imagine
myself, and my other female classmates, as future philosophers. I encouraged all the women around me to read

---

[1] Mary Daly, *Outercourse: The Be-Dazzling Voyage* (San Francisco:
HarperSanFrancisco, 1992), 59.

more philosophy as I led study groups in classical philosophy and literature.

Once, in a course on early Greek thought, the professor explained the idea of metempsychosis attributed to Pythagoras. Paraphrasing an uncertain quote from a Pythagorean, the professor said, "If a human being dies without having been good enough in life, their soul will pass into the body of a sheep. If the sheep, in turn, fails to be a good sheep, the soul will then transfer into a frog." Turning to the class, the professor asked, "And what if it is not good enough as a frog?' The class began laughing and everyone ventured a guess. "It will become a beetle, an earthworm, or a stone!" The professor sneeringly replied, "It will become a woman! Being a woman is the divine punishment of three times failing from humanity." I was frozen. Disheartened and demoralized, I turned back and looked at my classmates. Everyone – including all the women – were still laughing. I stared at those women whom I had encouraged to become philosophers. They too were laughing. I stood up, and in a trembling voice said, "It's so abhorrent!" and left the class. I expected other students to leave the class with me. But nothing changed inside that room.

Some days earlier, I had had a dispute with a famous professor of Qur'anic studies. When it came to theological explanations for the phenomenon of prophecy, the professor insisted that one of the necessary conditions of prophecy is masculinity. After I clearly explained my arguments about the prophecy of Maryam (Mary), according to the text of the Qur'an, the professor harshly responded, "Who are you, a girl, to challenge me and the long history of Muslim authorities in understanding the Qur'an?"

To be sure, this was not the first time that women were insulted in a philosophy class. I had been insulted at the university many times because I am a woman. Women are used to such domineering men and are regularly humiliated by patriarchal teachings and misogynist views. We have had to bear the male-centered atmosphere of the academy on the grounds that all these views were ultimately advocated by the authority of religious dogmatism. Despite these experiences being commonplace, these early moments in my career aroused something deep within me. Namely, that there was a profound lack of religious criticism within feminist philosophy. As a young philosophy student, I didn't have a defendable alternative to argue against these phallocentric ideologies that marginalize women from many kinds of subjectivity. Socio-political clichés of equality did not suffice in my philosophy classes. I needed a more profound epistemological foundation to critically engage those patriarchal professors and that masculine hegemony. Those events confronted me with my own theoretical weakness and charged me with uncovering the roots of religious misogyny, intolerance, and suppression.

After leaving the class, I went to the central library to search the catalogues for feminist theological writings. I could find only very few rough and inept sources. The next day, I went to the newly established library at the Academy of Arts. It was very close to the campus; its architecture was a combination of Persian ancient gardens and friendly modern spaces, with a welcoming colonnade of brickwork. It was a paradise for me, and it became my second home after a while. For months, I explored that library and delved into the BDs (books on philosophy),

BLs (books on religions, mythology, and rationalism), and HQs (works on the family, marriage, women, and, more broadly, gender and sexuality studies). I read whatever was in the shelves on feminist epistemologies, ethics, and revolutionary theological works. But it wasn't until the next year, when I started reading a second-hand book entitled, *Beyond God the Father*, that I felt I had finally found a bright path. The book was not that easy for me at that time. It was unlike anything I had ever read before. I could feel Mary Daly calling out to me, telling me that I needed to have the "courage to see and to be in the face of the nameless anxieties that surface when a woman begins to see through the masks of sexist society and to confront the horrifying fact of her own alienation from her authentic self."[2]

At that time, no one in Iran knew of Mary Daly. There was no work on feminist theology and philosophy of religion in Persian. Wikipedia and philosophical online encyclopedias were relatively recent and included very few entries – with no entry on, or even mentioning, Daly. Worse, and more painful still, was that the terms "feminism" and "feminist" had clearly derogatory denotations in the academy, even among intellectuals. If anyone talked about such approaches, they would be immediately anathematized.

With so many questions, I tried to find a way to contact the author. There was very little information on the slow dial-up internet of the early 2000s. I sent an email to a blog where an interview with Daly was published.

---

[2] Mary Daly, *Beyond God the Father: Towards a Philosophy of Women's Liberation* (Boston: Beacon Press, 1973), 4.

No reply reached me. I was alone with a second-hand copy of *Beyond God the Father* as my only hope to find my way.

My mother had taught me that every author lives within her work. I read the book again. This time, I tried to hear Daly's voice through her written words. Not only was her use of process philosophy and existentialism for developing a theology of "Be-ing" deeply inspiring, but the integrated epistemology of emotion–reason she weaved in the warp and woof of her ontology captivated me. It sparked the idea for my Master's thesis. The Mary Daly who was speaking to me through the text took my hand to begin a journey. Or perhaps an exodus.

Nearly two decades later, many things have changed within me, among the women in Iran, and in the world. The Daly in me has matured. I have gone beyond those feminist criticisms, including Daly's, which simplify the structures of suppression to those of gender, race, and different kinds of social categorizations. In all of my classes, I include texts by women philosophers, specifically parts of Daly's *Beyond God the Father*. Although this issue was several years ago used as an excuse to prevent me from teaching in the philosophy department, today there is a growing demand for courses and workshops on feminist thought in the academy. When I ask the students how they imagine the Divine – whether they practice any religion or are atheists – increasingly, more students have feminine perceptions of the deity. *Beyond God the Father* is now translated into Farsi and became a best-seller when it was published. Every year, more theses on feminist philosophies and theology are submitted in Iranian universities. A few women have even been tenured in philosophy departments. We have come out of travails and suppressions. Against all the denunciations and disparagements, we haven't succumbed to the male imperium at the academy, let alone in the complicated society of Iran. The larger structure is almost intact, there, in the world outside. Inside us, however, those written words of Daly "became flesh and tabernacle among us."[3] The journey we have started with Daly still "does continue because the Verb continues – from whom, in whom, and with whom all true movements move."[4]

I share all of this not only to tell my personal story of encountering Mary Daly's work, but also to emphasize how our different contexts shape our interpretations of texts. *Beyond God the Father* was the only piece written by Daly that could be read in Iran in the early 2000s, with no specific information about the author's social context, and no epistemic background to be contextually interpreted. Nonetheless, it was read, and it left a profound influence on its limited, yet eager, Iranian readers. In line with many other theologians, Daly endeavored to remove the personified, static images of God. In a similar way, her multiple readers would also contribute to a theological turn by removing the God–author image, withholding from assigning a fixed, ultimate message to the author. Coincidentally, during the years when Daly was writing her first works, Roland Barthes introduced his idea of the death of the author (1967), explaining that the multiple parts and meanings of any writing are to be focused within the mind of the reader. Although I was inspired by Barthes's insight, I don't believe that "a text's unity lies

---

[3] John 1:1–18.   [4] Daly, *Beyond God the Father*, xxix.

not in its origin but in its destination."[5] I don't believe that one can read Daly's text (or any text) completely detached from its authoritative origin. Rather, I prefer to approach Daly's works in a way that the reader can recover and resurrect the voice of a dead author through the unique process of a reading shaped by her own context.

The recently discovered manuscript by Mary Daly, *Catholicism: End or Beginning?*, is inevitably going to be read and evaluated in different contexts, through different lenses, and from different perspectives. The significance of Meg Stapleton Smith's work in this volume is not to be reduced only to publishing a new, unfinished book by Daly – which should be regarded as a landmark in Daly Studies and in the contemporary theology of peace. More to this point is the inclusiveness of this volume that embraces different critical readings of an unfinished intellectual work. Stapleton Smith has brought manifold readings of this text before its readers. This "aborted manuscript" is interpreted through the lens of Daly's close friend, Mary E. Hunt, who believes that "the easiest way to misread Mary Daly is to read her out of context." At the same time, it can be understood as an open-ended journey from the point of view of someone who has not experienced the historical context in which Daly wrote. Those unfamiliar with the social context of 1970s America – or who are not white, Christian Americans, or who hold neither feminist concerns nor religious affiliations – will inevitably approach this manuscript from

---

[5] Roland Barthes, "The Death of the Author," in *Image, Music, Text*, trans. Stephen Heath (London: Fontana, 1977), 148.

distinct perspectives. This multiplicity of interpretations underscores both the depth of Stapleton Smith's undertaking and the narrative richness of Daly's text.

Daly's manuscript demonstrates an inclusive quality that invites diverse narratives and interpretations. *CEB?* speaks not only to Catholics and Christians but also reaches out to adherents of other faiths – and even expresses a profound concern for atheists. Some, including contributors to this volume, may view the absence of explicit feminist critique as a regression in Daly's thought. I will argue, however, that this absence can be understood as part of a broader, more universal approach to faith – one that Daly herself explicitly advocates.

In approaching *CEB?* as a comprehensive critical engagement with faith, I will decontextualize the manuscript from its original historical and cultural setting in order to read it through my contemporary Middle Eastern, Islamic, and womanist lenses. This dual process of decontextualizing and recontextualizing occurs inevitably for two interconnected reasons. First, I was not among Daly's intended audience when she was writing this text; her primary readers were American Catholics grappling with a profound crisis of religious consciousness. Second, I have neither direct experience of that crisis nor access to the cultural and social circumstances that compelled Daly to respond to it with such urgency. My engagement with the text, therefore, is fundamentally different from that of Mary Hunt, whose lived experience closely parallels Daly's context, or Lisa Cahill, whose historically grounded insights and documentary knowledge enable her to challenge and enrich the manuscript with factual depth. Each of these approaches enters into dialogue with the text through distinct questions and interpretive frameworks, revealing a plurality of meanings. These meanings are not shaped solely by the reader's background or standpoint but emerge from what Hans-Georg Gadamer calls a "fusion of horizons" (*Horizontverschmelzung*), a dynamic interplay between the historical horizon of the author and the present horizon of the reader.[6] Thus, every interpretation of CEB? presented in this volume represents a rebirth of the text – an emergence of new meaning within a new interpretive horizon.

In what follows, I try to see this manuscript within the frame of the bigger picture of philosophy of religion and feminist theology today. In so doing, I challenge the text with these questions: What does this manuscript bring to contemporary debates in the philosophy of religion and feminist theology? Where can we map this manuscript within the landscape of contemporary feminist theology and the philosophy of religion? Does the manuscript offer anything valuable to these fields today?

Approaching the manuscript through these questions, I then argue that this is where Daly gets close to the idea that *theology is anthropology*. In turn, I suggest that she abandoned Catholicism (and all organized religions) because they restrict the infinite process of dialectical faith. In *CEB?*, Daly paves the way for her version of process theology that is, at the same time, an implicit announcement of the end of Catholicism.

In the third part of the chapter, I analyze Daly's conservatism in *CEB?* I concentrate on her methodology to

---

[6] Hans G. Gadamer, *Truth and Method*, 2nd ed., trans. Joel Weinsheimer and Donald Marshall (New York: Continuum 2003), 306–307.

place some of the progressive aspects of the text in the foreground. In *CEB?*, unlike in her other works, Daly writes through doubt. The resolute tone in Daly's other works transforms into a flexible, relativist style of speech in *CEB?*, and her method of argumentation involves more empathy toward what she is critiquing. Within all four extant chapters, despite her critical insights, she leaves a place to see positive (and sometimes invisible) aspects of Catholicism, Protestantism, and different readings of faith. She lets every view be seen and every voice be heard. In so doing, she develops what I will call a "logic of doubt" that can be seen as an epistemic value alongside her empathetic conservatism.

The incompleteness of the text can be seen as resonant with the very doubts that enhance its interpretive richness. Daly intentionally leaves space for the reader to participate in completing the picture. It is therefore more fitting to regard this manuscript as an open-ended journey – one that Daly initiates and into which she invites us to walk alongside her. I will explain that according to the centrality of the doubt (both as a method and a concept), *CEB?* can be regarded as a turning point in initiating a "method of doubt and dialogue" within the realm of theology and philosophy of religion in a universal perspective. The stance of crawling in the between, in opposition to the traditional logic of certainty distinguishes *CEB?* from many famous works in the field of theology.

By way of conclusion, I briefly explain how Daly has outlined a framework of a theory of difference. She gives the concept both a structural role and a foundational place in the development of a theology of difference. While she merely plants the initial seeds of this theology, her innovative approach emerges as one of the manuscript's most significant contributions. It is an important voice that deserves greater attention in contemporary discourses within theology and the philosophy of religion.

Daly's Conservative Valediction to Christianity in *Catholicism End or Beginning?*

A predictable interpretation of *CEB?* would be the inference that at this stage of her life, Daly was still a Catholic who had hope for reform within the main structures of the Church. *CEB?* can be classified among the works of the "early Daly," when she believed in the potential of Christianity to bring about social reforms in the Church and in the world. Thus, the duality in the title of the manuscript (*End or Beginning?*) can be understood in terms of the second possibility for Catholicism – that Daly writes to show a new beginning or a re-birth for Catholicism. More importantly, according to this interpretation, some may conclude that the reason Daly stopped working on this draft was that in the midst of writing *CEB?* she lost her faith in the possibility of any effective reform within the structures of the Christian faith. So, she abandoned a book that was not revolutionary enough to challenge the corrupt, androcentric nature of the Catholic Church. As Lisa Cahill explains in her analysis, during the writing of *CEB?*, Daly probably "was convinced that the hope inspired and the reforms promised by the [Second Vatican] Council were destined to a dead end."[7]

---

[7] See Lisa Cahill, "Reformist Catholicism: The Road Not Taken for Mary Daly," in this volume.

Such an understanding is likely the most justifiable reading of this unfinished manuscript. Through a different reading of *CEB?*, however, I try to explain how Daly can be seen as a post-Christian theologian within the pages of the existing draft. Contrary to her optimistic view of Christianity in an interview in 1968, probably right before she set about writing *CEB?*, the Daly of *CEB?* doesn't find any glimmer of hope for reform within the limiting structures of any institutional religion. In the interview, she talked about the possibility of recovering "liberating elements" in the Christian faith:

> Now hopefully we can still discover within Christianity the seeds of liberation. You can find within Christianity the message of the dignity of the human person. It's there. At the same time you can find the regressive element. I think the important thing is to try with what insight we have at this particular point to distinguish the regressive elements in Christian doctrine from the liberating elements.[8]

But it seems that Daly changed her mind when she decided to begin a new book project about the end of Catholicism. Indeed, she began a project intending to go beyond any religion which has an institutional nature. So, she started implicitly to show not only the death of Catholicism but the death of every ideology that categorizes people according to their degrees of belief or knowledge in a certain collection of propositions. In *CEB?*, Daly set forth to develop what can be named a "theology of difference," which addresses all people, including

---

[8] "Mary Daly and the Second Sex," *U.S. Catholic* 34(5) (1968): 21–24.

atheists and radical opponents of religion. In *CEB?*, by critiquing the fundamental concepts of Christianity, Mary Daly surpassed the reductive theological approaches of Catholicism/Christianity. Simultaneously, through developing her existential explanation of faith, she went on to theorize difference as a central concept in her new theological approach. The "difference" Daly had in mind is radical enough to initiate a philosophy for theological difference.

The question we confront in *CEB?* is whether the manuscript affirms the core structures of the Christian faith – particularly those of the Catholic Church – or whether it serves as a declaration of the death of Catholicism, and perhaps of Christianity as a whole. As Daly writes, "Has Catholicism reached its end, or is there hope for a genuine new beginning?" (Introduction). We can seek Daly's view on this question both at the level of her terminology in this text and within the discourse she is forming through her systematic and dynamic discussion of the basic concepts of Christianity. I will try to dislodge Daly's implied abandonment of Christianity by reconstructing her existential–humanist account of faith. Through this reconstruction, the signs of a theology of difference will be exposed as well. In the meantime, by analyzing the hidden dialectic between Daly's direct audience and the horizon she extends, I will engage the question of why Daly writes her anti-Christian position with doubt and equivocality.

To start with the terminology that Daly employs regarding Catholicism, I want to concentrate on the two sets of opposite vocabulary that logically provide an implication of Daly's concern for the deep crisis or tension within Catholicism. On the one hand, Daly talks about the possibility of a reform in the existing structures of the Catholic Church, using a positive language of birth and beginning. The set of concepts such as re-birth, new beginning, re-discovery, resurgence, heritage, going forward, hope, creative dialectic, integration, union, and maturity altogether constitute an impression of a reform in what has been there for centuries. These concepts in the Introduction and Chapter 4 may lead the reader to expect a hopeful reformist Catholic author behind the text of *CEB?* However, on the other hand, Daly applies a more impressive collection of concepts to describe the situation and fate of Catholicism which contrasts with that expectation. Deterioration, surrender, self-destruction, descent, death, demise, loss, dissolving into meaninglessness, impossibility, and end are all used with more frequency in the text. Together, these form the image of an author who has lost hope in the possibility of any reform. This latter set of vocabulary is not only statistically more frequent but also carries greater emotional weight. From this, one might infer that the author's departure from Catholicism is marked by a sense of ambivalence or regret.

More objectively, this abandonment can be recovered in Daly's text by reconstructing a discourse of faith that is in contrast with the different readings of Christianity. Daly doesn't simply discard some concepts or structures of the secularized Catholic Church. As a philosopher, she fundamentally denies the way of conceiving reality within the limited framework of Christianity. Her hero-philosopher in this denial is Nietzsche for announcing the death of God, which is, in Daly's view, a "symbolic affirmation of the impending demise of an entire world view – of a static otherworldly vision of reality" (1.3). In abandoning this whole worldview, all of its constituents should be rejected. And this is what Daly endeavors to do in this manuscript. *CEB?* is Daly's attempt to criticize the most essential concepts and the main structures of Christianity as an institutional religion. She rejects the historical and biblical content of the main concepts that constitute the whole identity of her contemporary Catholicism and Christianity. At the same time, an existential discourse of faith gradually comes into being that leads to a theology of difference and peace.

Daly traces the root of the contemporary crisis back to a concept that has been lost in the history of Christianity. She concentrates on the concept of "faith" as the heart of any possible religion in the future. For Daly, faith is found neither in ecclesiastical doctrines nor in biblical revelation. Rather, faith is premised upon anti-formalism because faith doesn't have a propositional nature. Inspired by Tillich, Daly maintains that the core of faith is the unceasing dialectical nature of existential doubt. Instead of being an act of admitting certain propositions, faith is an ever-lasting process of doubting. Importantly, the dynamic concepts of faith and doubt don't have a personalized God or a static doctrinal concept as its distinguished object.

In *CEB?*, Daly investigates the challenging post-biblical texts to find the possible seeds of an authentic notion of faith. The traces of an existential understanding of faith can be found in a few passages of the New Testament that refer to agape. This existential idea of agape, as a "spontaneous and creative" process of love toward God, however, was not enough to convey "the Christians [*sic*] attitude toward God" (1.1).

Daly reviews different approaches to the idea of faith in the works of both canonical religious figures and contemporary Christian thinkers. In all of these approaches, Daly finds something problematic. Most of the traditional approaches ultimately empower authoritarian views that destroy subjectivity and autonomy. In such accounts, even in the "most cohesive and original synthesis" of Thomas Aquinas, the grains of authoritarianism ultimately replace the authentic, internal awareness with "dogmatic literalism or verbal fundamentalism" (1.1). These approaches restrict the idea of faith within the narrow walls of static concepts. Without permitting any kind of relativity and diversity, they contaminate the sacred territory of faith. Modern secularized revisionists, for example, don't consider the inevitability of some kind of doubt for making an inner dialectic within the process of faith to push it forward. Other theologians offer visions of faith that imply ideological and historical dogmatism, intolerance, or resistance against social reforms. Even the theology of hope doesn't satisfy Daly since it can't adopt an ontological language for discovering the most fundamental basis of faith, that is, the immediate existential encounter with (non)being.[9]

Above all, Daly believes that many approaches to the idea of faith in the history of Christianity are essentially exclusive. I contend that this is the main point of divergence for Daly to dissociate her way from Catholicism and Christianity. Daly's arguments against Christian exclusiveness reveal her moral and universal concerns in

---

[9] This critical review of the history of Christian faith can be found mainly in the first chapter of *CEB.*

understanding the nature of religion. She criticizes Christian exclusiveness on different, hierarchical levels. Different forms of exclusiveness have penetrated throughout the whole body of Christian doctrines, like sexual exclusiveness (4.10), epistemic exclusiveness (1.1), and (what Daly calls) Christolatry (4.1). All of these forms of exclusivism involve a moral contradiction within Christianity. While solidarity and love are the ethical principles of the Christian faith, the essential exclusive nature of dogma brings about hostility, injustice, and discrimination that generally yield institutionalized immorality.

More important for Daly is Christianity's exclusivism in relation to the world. Daly reprehends the self-centered point of view of the Christians in the West, as well as the theological accounts of faith by Christian theologians that "exclude the possibility of faith or of revelation for those who have not received the Biblical message" (1.2). This latter criticism implies a presupposition about the nature of religion. Daly condemns how the idea of faith has been employed/understood in the Christian tradition because it has reduced the concept of faith to being synonymous with Christianity. Even more, Daly rejects the suggestion that "we need more religion and less Christianity," since it involves a kind of persistence on a purely biblical (in contrast to institutional) version of Christianity (2.6). In all, what she seeks in her theological approach cannot be recovered in Christianity. Thus, Daly excludes Christianity (both as a biblical and an institutional religion) from the circle of authentic faith due to its "narrowness of vision and lack of openness to a more universal form of religious experience" (2.6).

Similarly, the discourse of faith in *CEB?* can't endure the Christian explanations for God. It is not only that Daly's articulation of God in this manuscript is impersonal, but that there is no divine realm other than human intersubjectivity and the common existential experiences by human beings. Daly's discussion of God is more than vague and inconsistent within *CEB?* It seems that in some cases she cannot easily get rid of the historical image of a personal, anthropomorphic god, especially when she uses Christian terminology to speak about a deity (Chapter 4, *passim*). Nevertheless, reconstructing her radically different alternative for the Divine is not difficult.

Daly challenges the historical theological idea that God is somewhere and is something outside the world of human beings (3.6). In this manuscript, she rejects any kind of a personal understanding of a supreme deity. Instead, Daly substitutes the idea of God with a theoretical, intersubjective ground for her existential, humanist faith discourse. According to this discourse, faith is born from an inner experience of non-being. Every human has an experience of what can be called the anxiety of being. This anxiety has no finite, nor determined object. It is only a deep, ontological concern about not being there anymore. Every being is there because they have overcome the threat of non-being. This ontological intuition of the threat of *being not* is the ground of faith.

Daly completes this argument by implicitly dealing with the problem of intersubjectivity. I reconstruct Daly's argument in the following way: If this ontological intuition is an inner, personal experience, then what guarantees that such intuitions have objectivity and result in a universal theological system? To provide a basis for the objectivity of ontological anxiety, Daly needs to establish a common ground which underlies all these intuitions. This ground guarantees the unity of all these experiences in a comprehensive intersubjective reality. This reality, according to Daly, is not beyond human beings – it is not somewhere or something that transcends the inter-related community of human beings. It is the very realm of being in which every particular being is now maintaining her being against the continuous threat of nothingness. So, Daly's alternative for the concept of God in traditional religion is an intersubjective commonality which is being/ becoming constituted through the participation of being in every moment.[10] This participatory reality cannot be static. Reality as such is presently being constituted in every moment that finite beings are struggling against non-being. So, any theology that is based on this ground is a process and humanist theology.

To continue reconstructing Daly's argument, I contend that this same explanation serves as the basis for the possibility of developing a universal theology. If the ontological intuition and the anxiety of being is merely personal and subjective, it wouldn't bring about a universal process theology. In line with her discourse of faith, Daly doesn't seek the universal in a transcendental, separate realm. She discovers universality within the common inner experiences of human beings. Daly writes, "The experiences of man's threatened existence and of the anxieties that accompany finitude and the threat of non-being

---

[10] This is why Daly prefers Jaspers's term "the Encompassing" to other similar terms. One can infer this preference by Daly through her emphasis and through using this more than other terms. See *CEB?* 2.6.

is universal. By contrast, belief in 'the divine promise' or in the Resurrection of Jesus is by no means as universal" (2.6). So, the divine ground that makes Daly's universal theology possible is an intersubjective reality that is constantly being made through a common, participatory human ontological activity. There is no need or free space for entering some *deus ex machina* to guarantee the objectivity of religious belief or the universality of theology – indeed, such *deus* is against universalism for Daly. The very ontological fact that every being that exists participates in the power of being is enough for Daly to constitute a universal theological system. Hence, it can be said that *CEB?* is the dawn of the idea of *theology is anthropology* in Daly's thought. And in Daly's work, this idea is notably presented in a more advanced way than in the Feuerbachian version, which was primarily a critical idea.[11] Daly, indeed, presents this idea through the creation of a systematic, humanist theology that principally is godless.

One may then ask what is theological in this ontological account?[12] This question, in fact, paraphrases the question regarding the meaning of theology for Daly. As I see it, for Daly, the main problem that gives birth to any theology is the problem of the dialectic relation between

[11] Ludwig Feuerbach, *The Essence of Christianity*, trans. George Eliot (Buffalo, NY: Prometheus Books, 1989), 270.

[12] In a broad sense, every ontology involves a kind of theology within itself. In the traditional understanding, ontology is a philosophical explanation for a fundamental unity among everything that is. Such foundation has usually been regarded as something ideal, abstract, or divine that transcends the concrete situation of the plural, distinct things in the world.

the finite and the infinite. To answer this question in her distinct way, Daly redefines the infinite as the universal power of being. In this new sense, the locus of infinity is within the participatory process among concrete, finite beings. Instead of a transcendent realm for an infinite, supreme Being, the infinity is being formed in the inter-subjective commonality of the finites. Hence, what Daly is creating is an authentic, humanist theology. And this theology is thoroughly based on a concrete, immanent ground. Daly incisively spreads the transcendent within the concrete lives of finite beings. She writes, "Transcendence is not realizable through flight from the concrete present. Quite the opposite; it is attainable only by a transforming confrontation with the concrete situation" (1.9). The theology constituted on this concrete ground, contrary to most versions of theism, cannot be static since its source of infinity is an endless process of fulfilling the meaning of becoming more authentically human (2.8). Neither the meaning of faith nor the image of the divine – nor the content of revelation – can be destined and determined a priority (2.7). Everything in this theology is interactive and in process.

To conclude, I want to emphasize that between Daly's theological system and that of Christianity, almost no crucial concept, nor the main structures, are the same. Indeed, they are two radically different worldviews. Following the destruction of the whole worldview of Christianity announced by Nietzsche, Daly constructs a new discourse of faith that has nothing in common with what was "destructed." Therefore, I claim that the theology constructed in *CEB?* is an obviously non-Christian discourse of faith. And this manuscript is a tacit portrayal of a post-Christian theologian. The project of integrating the "Catholic substance" and the "Protestant principle" has logically failed. Even Daly anticipated this end at the outset of *CEB?* when she writes, "It may be that we can no longer imagine ourselves to have the sweeping vision of the great theological systematizes of the past" (Introduction).

Daly's account of faith in *CEB?* can be regarded as a kind of *conservative* valediction to Christianity. As I read this manuscript, out of the historical context in which it was written, I can observe Daly's departure from Christianity toward a thoroughly new discourse on faith. When I, a reader outside of Daly's historical context, reconstruct the new discourse she is constructing in this text, I find her indicating implicitly her post-Christian position.

Conservatism, Empathy, and the Logic of Doubt in *Catholicism: End or Beginning?*

Now, if we accept the foregoing interpretation of *CEB?*, ineludible questions will be raised. Why does Daly not explain her post-Christian position unequivocally? Why are there many sentences in this manuscript that lead the reader to regard Daly as a reformist, yet Christian, in this text? As Siobhán Garrigan puts it, "For all its claims to be on the side of the radicals, *Catholicism: End or Beginning?* is offering a rewording of standard Catholic teaching."[13] How should Daly's post-Christian theology be

---

[13] Siobhán Garrigan, "Feminist Intrigues at the Limits of Schizoid Theology," in this volume.

understood in line with her positive views toward Christianity in some parts of the manuscript? (4.1). While the faith discourse Daly constructs in this text is obviously non-Christian, how is it that the same text indicates her loyalty to Christianity? Should we conclude that the manuscript is inconsistent, and that Daly presented conflicting ideas within a short, unfinished manuscript?

To explain my answer to this question, let us focus on these lines of *CEB?* in which Daly clearly represents herself as a Christian. Daly writes, "*[W]e* must break out of the bonds of *our* exclusiveness, and [...] *we* must become able to speak a language that can be meaningful to those who are not attuned to 'the biblical message'" (2.6; emphasis mine). In this passage, Daly writes from the point of view of a Christian and a Catholic who seeks integrity and inclusiveness. She uses the pronouns "we" and "us" to refer to her point of standing: she is on the side of Christianity. Thus, her direct audiences are Christians who feel a crisis between their traditional faith and the contemporary situation. In *CEB?*, Daly both regards herself a Christian and speaks primarily to Christians. If one wants to find pre-textual signs within *CEB?* to show that the Daly of this manuscript still believes in Christianity, locating the direct audience of the text and these "we" pronouns are the best indications.

But this is not the whole story. In the sentence quoted above, the "Christian author" speaks with an admonitory tone to say that they should not be closed off toward non-Christians. She critiques the excluding point of view of Christians and Christianity. Here, Daly is inviting us to expand our point of view from the limited Christian one into a universal perspective. In other words, the Christian author spreads in front of her audience an infinite horizon that encompasses the Christian point of view as well as non-Christian and even anti-Christian points of view. Daly asks her direct audience to get out of their limited perspective and look at this broader horizon. Indeed, she withdraws her own narrow point of view in order to construct a limitless horizon in front of her direct audience. This horizon includes a more expanded potential of possible, future readers. Therefore, the direct, restricted audience of this text develops into a boundless spectrum of readers.

This conversion from a Catholic viewpoint into a universal horizon flows through the whole manuscript. The above quotation is only one example of this constant dialectic in the text. Throughout *CEB?*, Daly establishes a dialectic between Catholicism (and Christianity) and her universal discourse of faith. This dialectic uncovers the exclusive essence of the institutionalized religion and the universal perspective of the dynamic *theology of difference* that she is constructing. One can observe this dialectic in different levels within the text: a dialectic between Daly's direct audience and her potential diverse readers, between the exclusiveness of Christianity and the universalism of the new discourse of faith, and between Daly's first point of view and the perspective she prescribes.

I contend that Daly intentionally puts herself on the side of Christians to give this dialectic the form of an invitation. Daly's direct audience in the manuscript are Christians – but this is not due to the fact that Daly regards herself a Christian. Rather, it is because those Christians who feel a crisis in their faith are the ones whom Daly believes ought to change and develop their point of view. Daly presupposes that radical change is only possible when exclusive and restrictive theological viewpoints develop into broader perspectives. Only if these closed views become more open can real change happen. The revolution Daly hopes for becomes possible when the authoritarian views start to change. The structures of power can transform when those who have benefited from these structures understand the benefits of universalism and altruism.

Daly invites Christians to look at other possibilities, to be open toward other faith traditions, and to have tolerance for other cultures. The strategy she applies to this invitation is empathy. Daly can feel empathy toward her previous fellow Catholics because she had the same experiences of anxiety and fear in confronting the crisis of faith. This is why she admires those who have abandoned the church but are still able to retain some kind of connection with their previous environment. Such people, she believes, "have a high tolerance of ambiguity and a high valuation of honesty" (1.8). Though Daly doesn't use the term empathy, she applies it as a textual method to take the hands of her audience and lead them toward a broader perspective. To borrow words from the pioneer of theorizing empathy, Edith Stein, through empathizing we can experience the others and become "we."[14] In most cases, Daly stands on the side of those whose perspective she wants to change. She speaks in

---

[14] See Edith Stein, *On the Problem of Empathy*, trans. Waltraut Stein (The Hague: Martinus Nijhoff, 1964), 17.

their vernacular in order to invite them to speak in a more comprehensive language.

This phenomenon could be understood as Daly's conservatism, or her lack of enough courage to announce that she has desisted from Christianity. When we consider her point of view in this text, however, we can comprehend this conservatism in terms of an empathetic invitation. Throughout this manuscript, Daly does not always stand with Christianity. She also becomes "we" with the outsiders, "the others," and those who are outside the cliché divisions within Christianity. She becomes "we" with all people, with different ideas and approaches. Indeed, the authentic "we" that she unites with is the inclusive circle of diverse cultures, lifestyles, and beliefs that encompasses dualities and divisions. Her conservative position can thus be understood as a methodological choice for conducting an inclusive dialogue. The author of *CEB?* constitutes integrity through empathizing with her diverse readers. The "we" she unites with glides smoothly from Catholics to all the people of world, with all of their diversities and complexities. The paragraph below is a good example of how the author's identity is flowing through the text. Daly writes:

> There is no clear guarantee, of course, that *we* will achieve synthesis and not simply further disintegration. *We* can be sure, however, that the preservation of an ancient monolithic institution – or the creation of a new one – is no guarantee against disintegration. On the contrary, *our* hope for higher integrity is rooted in *our* capacity for institutional and theological diversity. *We* need religious diversity – not based on "dogmas" but upon a variety of concerns, interests, and life-styles, and cutting across the

institutions. "Catholic" and "Protestant" divisions which are almost meaningless. *We* need this because this is how *we* are in fact: complex, alienated, incomplete. (1.9; emphases mine)

Another aspect of Daly's conservatism in this manuscript is how her writing is often infused with doubt. Daly not only explains that the core of faith is doubt, but she also applies the method of doubting for the constant movement toward a more profound understanding of what she looks for. This method is not the same as the Hegelian dialectic that there should be an antithesis in front of any thesis to reach a synthesis. The method of doubt requires confronting the dilemmas from very different points of views. What Daly is offering is closer to feminist standpoint epistemologies. In *CEB?*, we constantly see this repeating method: Daly presents an idea by a thinker, studies different aspects of that idea, discusses its positive and weak points, and, finally, through critiquing that idea, she goes into a deeper position. She even criticizes Tillich and his theological synthesis, as well the theology of hope to which she is indebted (Introduction). *CEB?* doesn't firmly remain in any position as the final account.

A text that doesn't reach a final destination may seem to offer nothing other than a constant nomadic theological state. However, Daly's ontology necessitates incompleteness for her epistemology. According to Daly's ontology, every finite being is participating in an infinite, indefinite community of beings. The authenticity of human beings comes from this awareness that there is no ultimate point of affirmation or clarity in this infinite community. This participation is not based on a clear and distinct idea or concept. Such clarity and distinctness are the features of a dualist, traditional epistemology in which the subject is separated from, and dominant upon, the object. In the dualistic, absolute view of traditional epistemology, the subject can grasp the object, making it a possession of "himself" through the light of reason. By way of contrast, in Daly's epistemology, there is no separation between the consciousness and what it is aware of. All finite conscious beings are making the intersubjective infinite consciousness. It is being constituted every moment through the unceasing participatory act of *be-ing*, struggling against non-being.

Daly's epistemology is primarily based on the inner intuitions of the anxiety of not-being. This intuition doesn't have a clear object. It is an emotion that provokes our deepest levels of consciousness. So, the language for explaining this intuition is poetic, mythical, and mingled with ambiguity. Despite all of her criticisms against the sacralizing ways of interpreting the myths, Daly doesn't agree with demythologization theology because she believes in the epistemological significance of myth. She discusses that the myth "is the language of a reality that is not empirical but existential" (3.2). Hence comes the preference for the Dionysian way of approaching reality; a way that "exalts ecstasy, freedom, and feeling" (3.6). In this epistemology, the cliché dualities become meaningless, since it depicts an embracing integrity of the subject and the object, of the intellect and the emotions, of the reality and the consciousness (3.3).

Throughout *CEB?* Daly firmly holds to this method of doubt. Not only does she declare that the core of faith is the endless doubt, but also practically adheres to this as a core logic of her thought. This prevents her from speaking through clichés, dogmas, and resolution. She doesn't even confirm the decision of Camus's hero who finally admits nihilism, because it involves a kind of terminating confirmation. Daly invites us to ask ourselves in every situation "whether a stubborn affirmation of the absurd, and a rejection of the experience which makes possible a sincere leap of faith, will lead any closer to authentic humanization than will the opposite form of rigidity" (3.4).

I think a significant accomplishment of *CEB?* is developing the logic of doubt that has been interwoven within the whole text. This is not a common logic in theological discourse. Most traditional theological writings employ a language of absoluteness and resolution, guiding their readers along what is presented as the straight and certain path. Some modern revolutionary works in theology apply a passionate, intense, objective style to convince their readers of transformation. Daly, too, usually speaks with enthusiasm and resolution in her later works. This incomplete manuscript, however, is a different work. It proceeds with doubt. Its language represents its author's hidden fear and trembling in the writing of every line. There is no clear formulation for any argument or claim nor a distinct definition for any concept. Everything remains in ambiguity. The author doesn't stick to any firm view. She negotiates with the diverse sides of every view. Instead of making a way through different ideas, she crawls in the between of ideas to participate in the making of the encompassing horizon of humanity.

This logic of doubt and the language of ambiguity present in the manuscript can be regarded as a real revolution in the theological discourse. Daly initiates the method of doubt into her theological discussion as an epistemic virtue. The doubt has epistemic value since it pushes us forward to see other possibilities, to be open to other views, and to be brave to abandon our previous positions. Maybe this doubt required Daly to give space to her readers to complete her writing, so she left the work unfinished. I know that such interpretation of the incompleteness of the manuscript is more praising than justifiable. But I see it in harmony with Daly's unique method in this special writing. Thus, if *CEB?* has something new to offer contemporary philosophy of religion and theology, that innovation is the very logic of doubt and the method of crawling in the between. The novelty of this logic has the potential for developing a new methodology for theological conversations in the future.

The First Seeds of a Theology of Difference

As I have described, Daly extends her explanation of faith on the basis of an unconditioned universalism. In her view, an authentic account of faith should be constituted on a common experience that every human being can share in. She constantly refers to the atheists, the revolutionary young generation, the radicals, Marxists, the outsiders, non-religious thinkers, non-Christians, and other cultures to include their perspectives in her explanation of faith. She profoundly believes that authentic faith is a process that demands dialogue with others.

The idea of communication is one of the central aspects in the formation of Daly's version of faith. For her, communication should have no boundaries. Even the language of faith should be as universal as possible – it is not to be restricted to any particular revelation of ideology. This is why she prefers the Hellenistic, ontological language of existential anxiety. Daly even emphasizes that the metaphysical language of faith "should be understandable to non-philosophers because all do in fact experience the anxiety of non-being" (1.6).

Such an inclusive approach to faith, I believe, necessarily requires renouncing any form of religion that has an organized, determined, and doctrinal structure – including Christianity. Organized religions necessarily encourage self-centered views, privileging their worldview as the only righteous one. This monopolizing essence of organized religions fosters insider–outsider divisions and results in antagonism. Whereas in Daly's mind faith means a constantly unfolding love, the nature of institutional religions contradicts the generous love which entails an absolute openness to everyone.

The network of concepts such as love, communication, and openness, alongside the logic of doubt, I believe, can be regarded as the first seeds in the making of a theology of difference. Daly could synthesize these concepts in a harmonized account of a humanist theology. The very fact that she does not talk about equality and justice in terms of the established meanings for these terms indicates that she thinks through a deep understanding of "difference" instead of "justice." For me, this means that Daly doesn't romanticize *difference* in terms of the restricted categories of sex and gender. Contrary to the analysis of Nancy Frankenberry based on other works by Daly, in *CEB?* the idea of difference has a constitutional function that forms the main structure of Daly's theology.

In *CEB?*, Daly applies "difference" as a cornerstone that makes her humanist theology possible. This foundation also renders her theology political. This is not romanticizing difference or misusing it as a decoration for some kind of postmodern thought. Here, difference is being theorized as the foundation of a concrete, anthropological theology. *CEB?* seems to be one of the first instances wherein difference is being theorized for constituting a theological discourse.

Daly does not accomplish her explanation of the idea of openness to others. Her discussions remain simple and unpolished in most cases. She doesn't articulate her concepts and ideas to reach enough philosophical maturity. She doesn't deal with the related, effective problem of hidden structures of power that challenge the possibility of absolute openness and inclusiveness. No attention to the moral problems of openness and alterity is seen in *CEB?* The text is blind to the various possible forms of dominance, suppression, and discrimination that a privileged existential theology may produce. It doesn't give any explanation about the criterion for objectivity in her recommended version of Dionysian awareness. In short, many challenging aspects of a possible theology of difference are not included in *CEB?*

Another frustrating shortcoming in this work that makes the discussion of difference inarticulate is Daly's confined sources and studies, or in Lisa Cahill's words, the lack of "profundity." At the time that Daly was writing *CEB?*, important works by thinkers including Emmanuel Levinas and Jacques Derrida were published. Their works could have provided Daly with an inspiring, abundant theoretical context to advance her insights regarding diversity and otherness. It seems that she had read restrictively from postmodern critical writings on the ideas of difference, dialogue, otherness, ethics of alterity, deconstructionism, and phonocentrism – all of which could enrich Daly's discussions and give her critical lenses through which she could revise her views. Even her reference to Heidegger doesn't go beyond a superficial use of his idea of "angst." Imagine how more effective and contemplative would have been her work if she had been acquainted with concepts such as *Einfühlung* (empathy), in Edith Stein, and *Sorge* (care) and *Erschlossenheit* (disclosure) in Heidegger.

I think if Daly had studied these and other related works, she could have successfully presented a landmark work on theology of difference within *CEB?* Despite a full articulation, Daly's account of inclusiveness, openness, and community throughout this text gets close to the formation of a theology of difference. As mentioned, Daly allows no boundary for the inclusive feature of ontological faith. *CEB?* doesn't seem to be a seminal book that makes a remarkable change in theology and philosophy of religion. Yet, it can usher into theorizing "difference" in more complicated, flowing ways that shed light on those aspects of difference for theology that have remained hidden so far.

I believe that Daly not only initiated a philosophical approach to feminist theology in *Beyond God the Father*, but also inaugurated a theology of difference that heads toward a theology of peace in *CEB?* Though seeds of this approach to theology have remained underground, as this manuscript is now uncovered and published, those seeds have the potential to sprout and open up a new discourse in the contemporary philosophy of religion.

An Afterword

René Descartes emphasized clarity and distinctness as the most fundamental epistemic values. In contemporary epistemological debates, however, courage and honesty have also emerged as vital – internal, moral virtues that are now recognized as central to the pursuit of knowledge. The unfinished manuscript of Mary Daly, the mother/sister of feminist philosophical theology, however, doesn't correspond to the epistemic rules of the "father of modernity." The nomad nature of this manuscript, with its perplexity, ambiguity, and conservatism, may, at first glance, irritate today's readers. And for good reason. But there may be some other story behind this aborted text.

Half a century after CEB? was written, I can empathetically grasp some of the reasons that may have prevented Daly from speaking openly and directly. I don't mean to compare my situation with that of Daly. Our contexts have basic differences. But I can understand that a thinker may bear self-imposed censorship in order to convey her voice instead of being completely suffocated. When the only way to convey a message is through a veil of ambiguity, conservatism – contrary to contemporary epistemic values – takes on the weight of an ontological virtue. At times, speaking or writing from within fear and doubt is itself an expression of ontological courage – one that carries greater epistemic value than silence or conformity to the pre-established frameworks of academic trends or prevailing social norms. I truly love this honest confession by the Islamicist feminist, Aysha Hidayatullah, about the epistemic fears and uncertainties that we, sometimes hypocritically, conceal behind our resolute tones. She speaks for Daly, for me, and many of us when she says, "Academic books, in order to be published, must be read in a tone of assertiveness that may, or perhaps even must, obscure the vulnerability and tentativeness of the transformations entailed in the act of writing."[15]

If we are to be participants in the power of being, in Daly's term, we should know that we all are fragile, incomplete, and sometimes wandering in the between. We should accept that our ways of participation are inevitably different. Our ways are conditioned by our different contexts and situations. But the will to make a change puts us in the way of contributing to the unceasing process of *be-ing*. Through writing, either clearly or beneath the veils of fear, we can join the universal power of *be-ing* there.

---

[15] Aysha A. Hidayatullah, "Claims to the Sacred," *Journal of Feminist Studies in Religion* 32(2) (2016): 135. https://doi.org/10.2979/jfemistudreli.32.2.22.

6

A More Dalyan Christianity

~

Xochitl Alvizo

Introduction

In her unfinished manuscript, *Catholicism: End or Beginning?*, Mary Daly reveals what she most values in Christianity, outlines the essential elements of how the church understands its nature and its practice, and provides us with an ecclesiology apt for both the struggling church of her time and of ours. To do this, she draws on two key elements throughout her text, the "Catholic substance" and the "Protestant principle." These she identifies as the main resources required for Christianity to have a new beginning. The Catholic substance is made up of "the sacraments, the creeds, liturgical ceremonies, and dogmas," which are the "heritage" of Christianity (2.0). The Protestant principle is "an attitude which is self-critical, and which recognizes the relativity of all objectification of faith." Moreover, the symbols and structures of the faith, such as those making up the Catholic substance, "are finite and not ultimate" (Introduction). For Daly, the Catholic substance and the Protestant principle are radical elements of Christianity that must be centralized anew; bringing them into focus is not for the purposes of determining a new sweeping vision for the church but to affirm that the resources for its future are contained therein. At the same time, however, this is precisely where the problem exists – when elements of the Catholic substance are *fixed*, void of the Protestant principle, and made into idols resulting in a movement toward extreme traditionalism, or what she calls "demonic sacramentalism" (Introduction). Effectively, instead of the Catholic substance communicating the encounter of the early community's experience with Jesus, church hierarchy distorts and fossilizes it in a way that encourages people's disinvestment in their direct connection with the divine and calls them instead to trust the authority of the hierarchy to define faith for them. This disallows the practice of "authentic faith" for the people of the church.[1]

There is a crisis of faith within the "contemporary Christian consciousness" of both Protestants and Catholics (presumably those in the US, specifically) that is at the heart of Daly's concern. The crisis of faith is brought about by the tensions and transitions of the time and by a distortion created by the hierarchy of the church regarding the nature of faith. The distortion is a result of the failure to keep a balance between the Catholic substance and the Protestant principle, which is to say: a balance between (1) "the incarnation and the concretization of [the] spiritual presence, that is, the whole body of objectifications [of faith], including symbols and structures" and (2) "an attitude which is self-critical, and which

[1] I use quotation marks here only to indicate that "authentic faith" is Daly's expression and is a central concern of hers throughout the manuscript. Subsequently, I will no longer use the quotations marks but still use the phrase as Daly uses it.

recognizes the relativity of all objectification of faith" (Introduction). The relationship between these two and the substructures that distort them make up the overarching framework of Daly's uncompleted manuscript. She argues that while the Protestant principle and the Catholic substance are alienated one from the other, they are in fact the appropriate lens through which the crisis of faith must be understood (Introduction). She builds the case that the Protestant principle and the Catholic substance are "two complementary aspects of integral Christian faith," and essential for all Christians (Introduction). These two aspects of faith must always be kept in an ongoing dialectic, in productive tension, and in balance.

The dramatic tensions, current polarizations, cultural transitions, and crises of faith that Daly writes about are all concerns that resonate with the issues that plague the church today – whether Protestant or Catholic: A legacy of sexual abuse – child sexual abuse in particular – along with its systematic cover-up, has come to light in the Catholic Church as well as the Mennonite, Southern Baptist, and evangelical churches today; the refusal to affirm the full human dignity and inclusion of LGBTQ+ persons; the liberal/conservative polarization across the many Christian denominations in the US; systemic anti-black racism; and the denial of the full human dignity and bodily autonomy of women and queer persons reflected in policies being brought to state legislatures all across the country and justified on religious grounds.[2] As Daly puts

---

[2] I here acknowledge that Mary Daly's own work has been used to buttress transphobia and transmisogyny, and caused great harm to trans

it, "the same problem of tyranny over the spirit, of over-institutionalization, can be seen in Geneva as well as in Rome" (Introduction). Pointing to the imbalance between the Catholic substance and Protestant principle, according to Daly, the former is used as "a block to intellectuality and freedom of the spirit" and the latter as "idolatrous not only in relation to the Bible, but also in relation to its own structures" (Introduction). She argues, in short, that the Catholic substance needs to be relativized and the Protestant principle needs to do more than just relativize (1.1) – they must complement one another and be kept always in tension. The reintegration of the Catholic substance and Protestant principle helps bring about a more authentic faith that responds to the crises of the contemporary Christian consciousness. She maintains that this synthesis is central to constituting authentic faith in contrast to a faith divested of religious experience and genuine participation and would lead to a life-fostering process that is the real activity of *living out* the faith.

With the publication of *Beyond God the Father* in 1973, Mary Daly publicly declared Christianity to be irredeemably patriarchal and oppressive to women, and brothers, "if there are any here."[3] At the time of writing this

persons and the larger queer community. I do not contest this fact, even while I also draw from the constructive and liberative aspects of Daly's work. There are ways in which Daly's own writing and logic can be used to correct the faults within her work; I aim to do this in a future piece.

[3] She came to this conclusion after being a viewing witness at Vatican II, where the hoped-for reforms regarding women's ordination and participation in the church were not fulfilled. See the Autobiographical Preface in the 1975 edition of *The Church and the Second Sex* (pp. 9–11). In her "Exodus Community" sermon, as the first woman invited to speak from the pulpit of Harvard Memorial Chapel, she does allow room for

manuscript, however, Daly still claimed her religious tradition and considered it to be a *living* faith. In this essay, I argue that in taking Daly's challenges seriously, those who still call themselves, ourselves, Christian can move toward the authentic faith for which she was calling. A faith that in reintegrating the Catholic substance and Protestant principle also brings the reintegration of two other essential aspects of being church – death and conscious awareness: death of "symbols [that] no longer speak to our age" and conscious awareness that the divine is deep within the human self and that connection with the transcendent is immanently available (1.1). Daly writes to invite Christians back into an evolutionary process that keeps faith *moving* toward "ever greater" self-awareness and understanding such that "the assimilation of the reflective and self-critical Protestant principle into the Catholic consciousness" may bring a new quality to what Christians have inherited (Introduction).

I contend that the whole of Daly's manuscript is in response to the fact that she sees that the Catholic substance is losing its meaningfulness. As she notes, "The Catholic substance appears to many to be dying. The symbols which are the language of faith fail to speak to many, particularly to the young" (2.0). Thus, the Catholic substance, which she defines as the "the sacraments, the creeds, liturgical ceremonies, and dogmas," is reaching

men to take part in the sisterhood as she invites all who are present, "Sisters – and brothers, if there are any here ... let us affirm our faith in ourselves and our will to transcendence by rising and walking out together from the land of our fathers into an unknown place." See "The Women's Movement: An Exodus Community," *Religious Education* (Sept./Oct. 1972): 332–333.

"more and more to blind eyes and deaf ears" (2.0). Effectively, the Catholic substance has lost its meaningfulness for people within the church and especially for those on the boundary of it, such as the "radical young" about whom she is most concerned in the 1970s (2.6). This is a result of the church hierarchy intentionally advancing a distorted understanding of faith and of *church as the people of faith* not having adequate resources to navigate their existential crises – instead internalizing the biases perpetuated by the Catholic Church, particularly that the divine is mediated by the "Church Fathers (4.10)." Daly understands Christianity to be bigger than Christianity, that is, as alive and transforming beyond the ways institutions end up *fixing* its substance to just *one* instance of the experience of and with transcendence. Daly's call, which she begins in this manuscript, but leaves for us to complete, is to not lose sight of how authentic faith can indeed be restored and that the church has within it the resources it needs.

In what follows, I draw out the three themes that dominate Daly's unfinished manuscript – faith, the mystery of being, and consciousness-raising – in order to explore an ecclesiology that takes seriously not only the relativity of Christianity, but the fact that Christianity has been employed to diminish people's sense of being and inhibit their direct sense of access to the divine. I explore an ecclesiology that uses these themes as a lens and framework to reimagine the nature and practice of church that maintains an open (experimental) posture and builds upon the contributions of the radically Catholic feminist that Mary Daly was at the time of her writing. I imagine the direction she might have taken if she had not so keenly reasoned herself out of the tradition in the process of writing this manuscript.

Faith

The *nature* of faith is the first issue Daly tackles in her manuscript. According to Daly, people understand faith to be compulsory and externally imparted upon them because the Catholic Church promotes it as a set of propositions to be accepted. "True faith" is reduced to "uncritical assent to propositions *proposed by ecclesiastical authority* for acceptance by believers" (1.0). Daly identifies this as the core of the problem of the distortion of faith – faith as passive submission and as externally imparted. She argues that this understanding of faith results from "the fact that the Catholic Church has come increasingly to experience itself as *a severely threatened institution*," and so its fixed formulae is one way in which it seeks a semblance of security, exerting its authority over people by separating them into oppositional categories of heretics and believers. This is, of course, false security and must be abandoned "if the Catholic substance is to be *reborn*" (1.0; emphasis mine throughout).

To explain what faith *is*, Daly draws from both St. Paul and Thomas Aquinas, first to illustrate the inseparability of faith and love, and then to underscore the futility of attempting to divide them. Faith, while distinct from love, *involves* love, and has the character of being reciprocal – unable to exist outside of the response and inner commitment of the believer. Offering a genealogy of how faith has been variably understood by the Catholic Church, she delineates the way that Aquinas's sophisticated thinking led to a distortion of faith that set up a perfect storm for the "surrender of personal autonomy" and the creation of authoritarian structures in which one is subject to the laws of another (1.1). Aquinas brought faith and charity into a unified framework, linking the unseen (faith as belief) with the visible (the act of will expressed through charity). Over time, however, this synthesis "deteriorat[ed]" into what could be described as a mere "will to believe" (1.1). This distortion of faith, and misunderstanding of Aquinas, becomes a critical problem in that it ultimately infantilizes religious experience by only requiring assent to propositions, and nullifies the need for "profound and authentic inner commitment" (1.1). The distortion set up an "other-directed" situation in which "dogmatic literalism or verbal fundamentalism," in the form of assent, "becomes the believer's surrogate for deep religious awareness" (1.1). So instead of direct "reliance upon the promises of God," as is the case with Abraham, Jesus, and Paul, the "assertion of dogmas" becomes the substitute for faith and results in giving great power to "the institutional church, with its hierarchy of priests and preachers," that in turn set a worldview in which "the universe and human society [are] seen as essentially hierarchical" (1.1). All this, Daly argues, prepared the ground, "whether intentionally or not," for authoritarian structures (1.1).

For Daly, authentic faith requires one to seek "deep religious awareness" with one's full self. Faith does not objectify its "object" but *participates* in it – it is neither passive nor willing to outsource its faith experience to a hierarchical authority. And key to the human experience is the existential quest for transcendence, which is also an essential aspect of faith. At stake is people's conscious, critical, participation in their *authentic faith*, which, at its core, always maintains a commitment to the dignity and autonomy of the human. Whether the church, Protestant or Catholic, can assist in this quest in light of its distortions is Daly's underlying question. The deep quest for transcendence requires eliminating the prejudice "that the deity is outside [of humans]," which Daly insists has become an "almost [systemic] blindness" (3.6). The "loss of the sense of God's immanence," then, "paves the way for shallow moral judgements and . . . hinders insight into the complexities of one's situation" (3.6). Humans are therefore left without "inner resources to resist," turning to external authorities in ways that diminish their own sense of self and of authentic faith (3.6). The goal is to "uproot the sources of alienation within," achieve "a new awareness of the self, of the other, and of the environment," and tap into the divine immanence *within* (3.6). This produces a faith that is experienced as a "driving force rather than as a doctrine" – a driving force that initiates "the passionate innovating and changing of the world toward the Kingdom of God" (1.10).[4] Striking about her treatment of faith is the strong and clear thread of a positive anthropology. Her central concern regarding the distortion of faith within both traditions is how it diminishes and damages the personal integrity of those who adhere to these distortions. This, for Daly, is

---

[4] I will note that this is one of the only places that Daly writes in direct reference to the Kingdom of God or some measure of gospel language. In her manuscript, the gospel, as part of the Catholic substance, is a given – she does not lay out a description or summary of it. Her greater concern is that the gospel, the good news, is being stifled and distorted by the hierarchy of the church.

"inherently unacceptable" (1.2). Her esteem for human potential was high and she does not want the "possibility for profound personal insight and for original thought and action" hindered in people of faith (1.3). Authentic faith, as she understood it, does not require surrender to a hierarchy or to an external authority, but involves one's full personhood. It is a commitment that *moves* the holder; thus, it rejects a worldview that is static or holds an "otherworldly vision of reality" (1.3). Participation and dynamism, as key aspects of faith, are also central to her understanding of transcendence. When Daly references transcendence as part of religious, existential, human experience, she is not pointing to something beyond or outside of the material and concrete, but toward a depth of being within it. A depth of being connects one to ultimate intimate reality, a reality that is very present but not always very perceptible when one's full and active engagement is inhibited or discouraged. Both transcendence and authentic faith are meant to *move* people and transform their present reality, which she believes humans are fully capable of doing.

The problem of faith that Daly identifies is effectively ecclesiological – it is about the theology upon which the church is built and how the church as the body of Christ embodies (or not) a divine way of being in the world that may be judged as "madness" in as much as it resists the alienation and "the standards of repressive and manipulative Western culture" (3.7). Today, just as in the early 1970s, when Daly is writing, people are not inclined to embrace an understanding of faith as assent, judging it a static interpretation of the past that does not take into account the living dynamics of personality, context, and changing environments. This for Daly was part of the reason that the Catholic Church, and Christianity writ large, was losing credibility with younger generations (1.1). "[T]hings and acts" are being given inordinate value to the point of idolatry and thereby lose their value as symbols capable of "pointing beyond themselves" (1.6). Faith demands the courage to "transcend the subtle forms of idolatry to which we are inclined" and that the church hierarchy has promoted (1.6).

The heart of the crisis of faith Daly diagnoses is found at the intersection of the idols the church has made, the diminished self to which humans resort in order to uncritically assent to belief-systems that replace authentic faith, and the authoritarianism of the church's hierarchy and the caste system it creates among people of faith. In contrast, authentic faith is consciously engaged in and moves one into a deeper sense of connectedness with the divine, with that which is infinite and the ground of all being. A renewed ecclesiology that takes seriously Daly's contributions, will be marked by the commitment to nurture authentic faith by affirming people's direct access to the divine and their right to full participation, reflecting an anthropology in which the full human dignity of the person is recognized and their capacity for active, conscious, and critical engagement is promoted.

The distortion of faith that the church creates within the people of faith and the consequent alienation it fosters from both themselves and the divine is thus Daly's first concern in the manuscript. For Daly, what is key is that the divine is the ultimately sacred – the ground of all being. The church, as an institution, is supposed to facilitate connection with the divine and, more importantly, *participation* in it. Instead, it often functions in direct opposition to this purpose, effectively and actively shutting down access to the divine. Addressing this problem and revealing the substructures that support it, Daly identifies two key losses: The loss of the meaning of symbols and the loss of the depth of the mystery of being. The power of religious symbols goes hand in hand with awareness of the mystery of being – when you lose one, the other is also incomplete. Attending to both losses is how Daly begins to point toward the remedy needed for the regeneration of faith and leads us to the second main theme of the manuscript – the mystery of being.

Mystery of Being

In this section, I delineate the interrelated threads that constitute the substructures undergirding the existential crisis facing the church and Christianity at large: the loss of the meaning of symbols and the loss of the mystery of being, with the resultant existential anxiety and alienation it produces. Of greatest significance in this section of Daly's manuscript is the point that the rediscovery of the mystery of being, which she asserts is requisite for the rebirth of the Catholic substance, involves ultimate existential questions (2.3). Her invitation to the Christian-identified reader is toward deep existential participation.

Existential Anxiety, Alienation, and Non-Being

A priori for Daly is the ground or mystery of being, which "implies some absolute existence, free from nothingness and death" behind all existence about which it is

important to wonder and contemplate (2.2). To wonder
about the mystery of being is both an intellectual and
profoundly emotional experience – it is authentic thought
in a quest for a deeper level of awareness. Writing still as a
Catholic theologian, Daly understands the Christian message to be part of the mystery of being. She is concerned
with the alienation from God that people experience
because of the deeply embedded prejudice that "the deity
is outside [humanity]" (3.6). Worth quoting in full, she
beautifully explains that the existence of this prejudice:

> suggests that there is something deeply distorted in the
> Christian heritage. Moreover, it testifies to the profound
> alienation of modern man, who is like someone sitting on
> top of a volcano. It is as if conscious reason, unnaturally
> separated from the unconscious, were balanced precar-
> iously on the hardened surface of the latter, rather than
> receiving life from it. (3.6)

Daly situates this alienation as part of the current context
of "technocracy" wherein "there is the pseudo-participation" in most aspects of life substituting for "genuine
participation in the depth of being and for authentic
human encounter," which she argues "amounts to isolation in a most deadly sense" (3.7). Of value for her,
however, is that in the experience of this isolation and
meaninglessness there is also the potential for new
awareness:

> [T]he lonely crowd around us. The experience of living
> with the surface of our minds, imaginations, and senses is
> common. The experience of nothingness, of boredom,
> pervades our atmosphere. *Yet* when this becomes acute
> enough the question of being may be born again and our

fall upward toward the plenitude of reality may receive new impetus. (3.7; emphasis mine)

Notice her hopeful *yet* for the possible "fall upward." While people may be tempted to avoid the anxiety or threat of non-being by "settling for a shrunken form of self-affirmation, a stunted form of existence," Daly has the high expectation that humans can nonetheless face that non-being, even in its difficulty, and receive new impetus (1.6). To face it is to take it into consciousness and reach "to fuller existence in self-transcending activity" (1.6). Unfortunately, the common response of shrinking one's own being is facilitated by the institution of the church through "con-crete forms of church life" that are escape mechanisms intended to ward off uncertainty (1.6). Church, instead of offering the tools for depth of engagement with ultimate reality, becomes a panacea that stifles active engagement and participation. The myth of the Fall, for example, is a key example she turns to as evidence that while religion recognizes this experience of anxiety and tries to capture it through myth, it erroneously makes the existential questions raised into the answer instead of being willing to dwell and wrestle with the anxiety. The myth of the Fall from paradise, appropriately an expression of humanity's aware-ness of its alienation, existential estrangement, is interpreted with an overall negative evaluation of humans in which women are "tempters responsible for the moral break-down" of men (3.3). The myth of the Fall, instead of being understood as an expression of human existential questions, as rigid adherence to a particular interpretation. is normed, becomes a simplified answer that effectively stifles further depth and inquiry.

A multiplicity of things gives rise to existential anxiety: guilt, falling short as a moral agent, the inescapability of death, and, of course, the experience of meaninglessness – "the absence of clear-cut ultimate answers" (2.7). Existential anxiety is part of "the universal human condition of being finite and aware of this finitude," but how one copes with this anxiety is what matters (2.7). Daly admits that the *courage to be* in the face of existential anxiety is difficult and complex (2.7). Unlike other kinds of courage, such as the Greek military virtue which has an object of fear to be overcome, existential courage has no "definite" object, only a deep anxiety that arises when facing the abyss of non-being (2.7). For Daly, taking into consciousness "the non-being in ourselves, in others, and in the world," and awareness of the divine as always present and immanent, allows for a revolution of self and world. Existential courage is necessary to access this awareness and change.[5] Thus, the *courage to be* cannot co-exist with a diminished sense of self (2.7).

Returning to the myth of "the Fall," then, Daly shifts the focus from a downward loss to "a fall upward" (3.7). She explains that what is captured as a loss in the myth, also represents "a dream for the future" and is therefore not an end or a definitive explanation, but encouragement to begin anew, "a source of growth toward integration and yet further integration" (3.7). The myth, reengaged *as* myth, with all the power of meaning that that entails, can again become a tool that "propels us onward and

---

[5] Daly is explicit that the idea of existential courage is "an idea developed at length and with powerful persuasiveness by one of this century's great systematic theologians, Paul Tillich" (2.7).

upward" as people of faith. The potential for this new "Fall" is a renewed awareness of one's alienation and "a desire for *a voyage deeper into inner space*" (3.7; emphasis mine). This voyage into "inner space" is an interruption to the "normality" that keeps people looking outward to an external authority and unconsciously engaging in the technocracy of the time. An underlying premise is that there is something troubling about what has become "normality," requiring people *not* to take a deep inner voyage. In fact, Daly argues that "in our civilization every effort is made to prevent people from making it" (3.5). The contraindication to this normality is a kind of mysticism that helps heal our "appalling state of alienation" (3.5).

Mysticism, the transitioning toward conscious awareness, toward communion with the mystery of being, and toward participation with the divine, begins with recognition of the loss, the split from the very source and ground of being – the true "Fall." Daly specifies that this communion, with its requisite existential courage, has two sides, "individualization and participation" (2.7). The *courage to be* necessitates affirmation of "oneself as a self *and* as a part," emphasizing that "in the face of the threat of absorption into a larger whole or into a process" one must "affirm oneself as a self, as an individual" within that whole (2.7; emphases mine). While the *courage to be* is interrelated to "the courage of individualization," it is also "equally important *to participate consciously and actively in the universe*," and recognize oneself as a part of that larger whole that is the ground of being (2.7; emphasis mine). The ecclesiological significance of these two sides of the *courage to be*, of self-affirmation and of participation as part of the whole, are central for building upon Daly's contributions.

Together conscious awareness and the courage to be constitute an active process through which one comes to understand "God" as "the ground and power of being" and not as "a divine person" or "supreme being" (2.9). Through this revelatory process, one is "grasped by the power of being-itself" in a way that includes the participating self within that mystery (2.9). This active process involves a turning inward, a (re)turning that acknowledges the divine as immanent *and* within oneself and is thus both grounded and transcendent. This is where the message of Christianity may regain its significance, in becoming aware "of the mystery of the self as well as of the mystery of the community," which *is* about becoming aware of the mystery of being – self and community and the mystery of being opens the possibility and sustains awareness of the *powerful symbolic meaning* of that which makes up the Catholic substance (2.6).[6] Connection with the mystery of being both relativizes symbols as symbols and returns the power of their meaningfulness. Daly asserts that religious symbols sans the mystery of being, their meaningfulness, lead to the present predicament of being thought of "univocally and even literally," stripped of their "profoundly analogous power" and no longer pointing beyond themselves to something greater, more ultimate (2.5).

The world of myth and symbols is necessary to human existence, to trying to capture human connection and communion with ultimate reality – the mysticism of being. Conscious awareness and the *courage to* be liberate

---

[6] Here Daly specifies the cross and the resurrection as key examples.

the church, the people of faith, from the Catholic hierarchy and its monopoly on the sacred: "unless we achieve this inner freedom we remain in a state of childish literalism, blindly accepting or rejecting 'doctrines' of which we have no real understanding" (2.5).

Daly insists on "a present disclosure" of and access to a "God before us" *now*, a divine reality somehow manifest to us *now* (2.6). Neither an anthropomorphic image of "the divine promiser" nor a stagnant "image of the supreme being" is appropriate. Thus, she turns toward an understanding of God as "the ground of being," the "experience of something ultimate in value and meaning" (2.6). She wants to move people beyond the small and limited constructs of religion into which Christianity has settled. Fixed constructs stifle conceptualizations of God that enable the church to be open to a new future. This is a shift away from the framework of faith as "belief-systems and will acts," and the "subject–object scheme" that reduces divine reality to a "thing" (1.5). Daly's invitation is instead to a conscious-active awareness that engenders faith as "a movement toward that which is totally other and yet intimately present" (1.5). So, if commitment to affirm people's direct access to the divine is the first mark of a more Dalyan ecclesiology, the dual need of individuation and of participation as two sides of the *courage to be* is the second.

This active, living, and engaged movement reflected in the two marks of a more Dalyan ecclesiology begins to point us toward the ecclesiological implications that the three intersecting threads of Daly's interventions presently bring to the church: the nature of faith, the mystery of being, and, to follow, consciousness-raising.

Consciousness-Raising

Throughout her manuscript, Daly writes extensively about people's need for consciousness – for depth of awareness and engagement with oneself, the world, and God. This need for depth intersects directly with the need for authentic faith and the church's regeneration: "In order to find genuine inwardness, to find ourselves, and to find the deep source of the Catholic substance and of the Protestant principle, *we have to fight off the false consciousness imposed upon us by our culture*" (3.0; emphasis mine). The loss of consciousness is connected to the alienation she sees as particularly acute in "technological society." To reconnect with one's "inner space" is therefore to resist "technocracy" and counter the "normalcy" it creates. False consciousness and the loss of awareness that plague the faithful and inhibit access to the "deep source," plays into the infantile faith the church hierarchy sets forth.

Consciousness-raising is a means to the necessary "myth-breaking" that helps people understand myth *as* myth (3.3). Daly draws on existentialist philosopher Karl Jaspers to capture the significance of myth, stating, "our life would be wretched and lacking in expressiveness if the language of myth were no longer valid." This is because mythical thoughts "bring us closer to the imageless transcendence which no myth can fully express" (3.2). Understanding myth as myth allows for and encourages "constant theological effort" and "regeneration" (3.3). Daly affirms that along with aesthetics, beauty, and story, mythical thought is "the language of a reality that is not empirical but existential" (3.2). Humanity is not satisfied by objectivity alone. Myths are expressions of a problem. However, taking the myth of the Fall as an example, the myth is mistakenly interpreted by the Church Fathers as "a pseudo-historical 'explanation' which in fact explains nothing" (3.1). Part of the mistake is the unwillingness or inability to dwell in the questions and engage with myth "as an expression of the baffling mystery of human existence," which is a key part of religion (3.1). Daly acknowledges the fact that there are no easy answers, so we need to be able to stay in the ambiguity, especially as people of faith (3.2).

The ecclesial task then is to nurture "religious awareness" and depth of engagement in relation to the Catholic substance that is the symbolic expression of the communion we seek in response to the experience of alienation. In contrast to "lapsing into literalism or succumbing to cultural limitations of time and place," theology is sourced in "mythical thought and in on-going human experience" (3.3). This central truth "should operate to conserve that which is of value in tradition while at the same time criticizing and transforming that which is alienating and dehumanizing in the mythical content and in theological formulations of the past" (3.3). Ongoing human experience is a part of theology. This, then, brings us back to the absolute necessity of the Protestant principle which Daly insists must be kept in balance with the Catholic substance. "Authentic theology," as with authentic faith, calls one to maintain productive tension between "the heritage of the past and the insights of the present." She states, "[authentic faith] does not fail to recognize that the deep source of revelation manifests itself in the contemporary situation and demands openness to the radically new" (3.3).

As revelation manifests itself through culture and the "contemporary situation," and thus human experience, it calls for awareness of the "inner" – of the connection with the depth and ground of being that is possible and which counters the default alienation that is encouraged by society and institutional powers. Church as communities of the gathered can be spaces/places where one practices and supports each other in this connection with the inner in order to resist "the standards of repressive and manipulative Western culture" that define the sacred as outside of the self (3.6). In this way, church has the potential of being a counter force of practice and of struggle against the alienating practices of both the institutional church and the world.

The practice of bringing the Protestant principle to the Catholic substance, and maintaining a balance between the two, moves the church and the self towards regeneration. This requires, "first of all," the affirmation of the self "as a self" (2.8). People's willingness to practice existential courage and employ the Protestant principle through their "struggle for autonomy ... for authenticity and for fidelity to the rational principle within, even if this means painful clashes with external authorities, civil or ecclesiastical," is where Daly places her hope (2.8). She attempts to liberate people from the dogmatism of the Catholic church and toward valuing the Protestant principle: "courage demands that we be constantly ready to [criticize] established laws, doctrines, and practices and that we be ready for the *emergence of new forms*" (2.8; emphasis mine).

Still, the Protestant principle must be kept in balance with the Catholic substance because, "the courage to be also involves self-affirmation as *a part*" (2.8; emphasis mine). Even if, currently, "in a distorted fashion," there is still value in the Catholic substance in "the voice of tradition, the body of symbols, doctrines and structures we have inherited." Employing a balance between the courage to be a self and the courage to be a part means also a balance between the Catholic substance and the Protestant principle. She states, "The courage to be as a part demands that we continue to recognize whatever there is of value in the tradition which formed us and which formed the Christian community, *while participating in the process of developing that tradition*" (2.8; emphasis mine). Using the resources from within the tradition, Daly effectively relativizes the power of the church's hierarchy and clericalism, both of which are facilitated by the distortion of faith, and calls people first to regain their own sense of awareness and participation with the divine and second to regain their own right and power to shape the tradition and push back against the distortions and biases that would diminish and inhibit their self-actualization within the faith and the church. The practice of consciousness-raising fights off the false consciousness that keeps one in an infantile state of (non-) participation and recognizes the ongoing nature of theology as it takes in human experience and the contemporary situation. Consciousness-raising, which brings about depth of awareness and engagement with oneself, the world, and the divine (and therefore also to the ongoing development of theology), is the third mark of a more Dalyan ecclesiology.

Inner Space, Ecclesial Space, and the Regeneration of Symbols

Ecclesiologically, the significance of the work that Daly left unfinished is in the assertion that the life, vitality, and renewal of the church is dependent on the inner (mystic) life, depth of awareness, and participation of the self with the mystery and ground of all being. Individuals who make up the church, the body of the Christ, overcome their alienation, reconnecting and affirming themselves as selves and as part of the larger whole that is the tradition, in a conscious, open, and critically engaged way. This, however, requires taking a risk. Consciousness-raising is diametrically opposed to both what the institution of the church has set up for its members and how a technocratic society habituates its people. Both theologically and ideologically, institutions of church and society actively thwart the ways people seek to connect with their inner life and affirm themselves as both an individual and a part because of the demand for change that inevitably results from that communion – a communion that is aware of the depth of the mystery of being, is grounded in that inner connection, and will therefore no longer settle for symbols of the Catholic substance that have been stripped of their living power. This courageous effort, then, is a struggle that requires a community of support to genuinely engage in the kind of transcendent religious experience that ignites one's sense of wonder "about the secret mystery of being," brings "profound emotion," and *moves* people toward their self- and their communal actualization (2.2, 1.3).

At stake for those remaining within Christianity is the battle against alienation, with all the ramifications for how people in turn live out their lives as Christians and as church (3.5). The force of Daly's ecclesiological diagnosis is its call to reimagine the church's understanding of its relationship with God and, in as much as the divine is and can be captured by symbols, with its myth, creeds, and the whole of the Catholic substance. Theological reflections on the nature of God goes to the heart of the very nature of the church. Daly propounds an ontological reflection on God, not as a static form, which is the mistake she finds in the popular theological contemporaries of her time, but as a necessarily open-ended and even experimental reflection on the divine that avoids idolatry, which is, again repeated to stress the point, why she emphasizes the need for the Protestant principle. She explains, "Having learned from our calamitous idolatry, we may be ready for a new assimilation of the Protestant principle ... we may reach for a qualitatively new and more detached form of re-mythologizing" (3.7). She affirms that while the church may indeed "fall again," its falling becomes an opportunity to "fall upward," reaching not for perfection, as "this is in fact impossible," but so that *we are liberated to do [that] which is within our grasp*" (3.7; emphasis mine). Opposed to the Catholic Church's expectation of people's adherence to what it considers orthodox, Daly proposes a theology in which it is all right to fall, to fail, and to try again for the sake of communion, participation, and regeneration. Her ecclesiological call is to be willing to remain in the questions, calling the church into new possibilities and not rushing to resolutions or settling for easy answers that do not satisfy the human "drive to know what it is to be fully human" (4.2). Effectively, the condition of the world and of Christianity, with all its crises and failure to witness to the good news, is such that Daly judges it a fruitful time to renew its theological underpinnings.

So, while the early church's experience with Jesus, in whom the early followers witnessed "a certain transparency to the divine," and the movement sparked by the original revelatory encounter are at the root of church, people's *continued* openness to authentic religious experience, to genuinely personal encounter with transcendent reality, must *persist* in order to play its role in the ongoing interpretation of its myths and symbols (4.9). The alternative is the "codified and dogmatized forms" with which the church tries to capture the original religious experience (3.5). Despite these problems that Daly diagnoses, she nonetheless affirms the church's *raison d'être*, stating, "on some deep level, beneath that of conceptualizations and pictures, an *encounter with transcendent reality* has been transmitted down through Christian history – originally sparked by *the meeting of a small community* living over nineteen hundred years ago with the historical person, Jesus of Nazareth" (4.5; emphases mine). The hardened distortion of that genuinely transcendent religious experience with Jesus Christ that no longer communicates the essential unity between humanity and the divine begs for a renewed ecclesiology that will more faithfully represent the new possibility for human existence that the good news represents.

A More Dalyan Ecclesiology

Ecclesiologically, then, Daly points out that people need that place where they get to experience, connect with, imagine, practice, and participate in a new divine reality. Hers is a call to the church writ large to be and form many such places, spaces, and opportunities for that transforming encounter. That kind of encounter, which brings about the "regeneration and transformation of lives," is still very much possible. And while the process of transmitting the original revelatory experience with Christ has many forms, and "none of these forms were or could be adequate," they can nonetheless be genuine (4.5). This is an ecclesiology that is grounded in the recognition that the person of Jesus represented the New Being (Christ) and revealed transcendent reality. Understanding this may help explain the high valuation of humans that runs through Daly's manuscript – Jesus was human and capable of revealing God and we can do likewise if we are open and willing to engage with the depth and mystery of being. The affirmation that the church can continue to facilitate this, without having to fix itself to an idealized/idolized form is the value that Daly brings to the fore. It promotes many possible forms of church that attempt to manifest both the "original revelatory experience" and the embodied experience of it today in its full human spectrum. These genuine encounters happen differently and must not be stifled. The balance she calls for between the Catholic substance and the Protestant principle, the divine and the human aspects of the interpretation of symbols and myth, and the self as a self and as a part, are built-in correctives within the tradition. They each are the inherent radical elements that keep the church a *living* body with all the implications that come with being alive, which include death and regeneration.

Before leaving Christianity and deeming it irredeemably patriarchal, Daly affirmed the possibility of change and openness while nonetheless grounding the birth of the church in the original encounter with Jesus Christ.[7] Though distortions developed along the way, she believed

---

[7] See Mary Daly, *Beyond God the Father: Toward a Philosophy of Women's Liberation* (Boston: Beacon Press, 1985).

in the possibility of Christianity and the church's repair, at least while she was still writing the manuscript. The elements of the Catholic substance to which the church must bring the Protestant principle are a result of genuine encounter with transcendent reality (Jesus Christ as the New Being) but have been rigidified through time by the hierarchy of the tradition. The result is that the fossilized symbols are effectively confused for the encounter itself and become a substitute for genuine transcendent experience. However, bringing balance between the Catholic substance and the Protestant principle would represent a commitment to a reflective and critical process of being church that remains open and values *ongoing human experience*.

With this manuscript, Daly astutely takes the Catholic substance out of the hands of the hierarchy and in an almost cursory manner affirms that genuine religious experience is not limited to the confines of the Catholic Church or even to Christianity itself. Her manuscript is about getting to the underside, to the heart of the experience of a divine encounter, which opens a possible new way of being and relating. And, for Daly, theologizing on the boundary of Christianity as she writes, with one foot out the door, what matters most is "bringing about the regeneration and transformation of lives" – which is still very much possible today (4.5).

Daly points out that the experience of transformation, which is part of what she refers to when she speaks of transcendence, is about that which moves people toward *more*, beyond the problematic default of the world. Transcendence is that which rattles one to the core and moves the human to choose differently, to commit to a different possibility of life, both as a self and as a part. Daly writes that in light of the reality of "war, racism and other forms of discrimination, and poverty," the church, if it is to be a force of good news, must be radicalized and "raise its own level of consciousness" (4.6–4.7). What she makes clear throughout her manuscript is that the church and Christianity's radicalization happens as people reconnect to their own inner world, where the divine also dwells, and as they *participate* in that which is the ground of being. There are no sweeping or monolithic expressions of this Christian consciousness or its ensuing movement toward "the transformation of this world" (4.6–4.7). Faith, and the work it inspires, inherently involves courage and open-endedness, such that a "[person] of faith cannot have a clear idea at the outset of the theological, liturgical, or organizational forms which will most adequately incarnate [their] new plane of awareness" (1.9). Daly names the synthesis of the Protestant principle and the Catholic substance as the "theonomous synthesis" – the religious paradox that emerges when bringing together revelation and humanity, transcendence and immanence. The theonomous synthesis is like the process of creating art, wherein the artist cannot predict the outcome of bringing together their idea and the material. So too the Christian – the church cannot predict its form as it brings together the substance of faith and its own reflective and critical self with its ongoing human experience. Through the theonomous synthesis, the people participate in the form-creative process that makes manifest something divine, that reveals transcendent experience, and copes "with the problems immediately before us in the concrete present, through our tentative efforts at rebuilding" (1.9). Revelation is understood with acknowledgment that "Human consciousness is active in the revelatory process, experimenting with its insights, interacting with them, remolding them in the context of new problems and situations" (1.9). This is important because the assertion she advances is that "We never have revelation 'pure,' and to imagine that we do is the basic error of all fundamentalists and traditionalists" (1.9).

A more Dalyan ecclesiology, therefore, assumes the need for diverse forms of "incarnating revelation," of *being* church. Forms of church are not to be based on "dogmas," or a set prescription, "but upon a variety of concerns, interests, and life-styles, and cutting across the institutions 'Catholic' and 'Protestant' [–] divisions which are almost meaningless" (1.10). The necessary diversity of church forms is to reflect the reality of human existence, "complex, alienated, incomplete" (1.10). A more Dalyan ecclesiology recognizes that the structures of church always have the potential to both "incarnate and at the same time distort revelation," distort the good news. Thus, congregations based on such an ecclesiology maintain a self-reflexive posture and understand themselves as "always temporary and provisional" in all its structures and forms. And while there is no guarantee that the desired synthesis is achieved, "the preservation of an ancient monolithic institution – or the creation of a new one – is no guarantee against disintegration" either (1.10). My own research with emerging forms of church evidences this kind of ecclesial energy, where people both experience disaffection with the tradition and stay within it seeking to transform church beyond what they have inherited.[8] At times, such churches also lead people in new directions. Research with millennial Christians and emerging churches reveals multiple ways Christians are addressing the issues and concerns of the day and how church congregations are being impacted – from reorienting religious values toward more liberal expressions, to rehabilitating church polity, to moving toward more political activism as a congregation, disaffecting from church altogether toward a more humanistic pursuit of the divine, or also actively confronting their institutional leaders as with the Catholic Church and its sexual abuse crimes.[9]

I bring the insights of my research with emerging congregations with the radical feminist contributions of Mary Daly to begin moving toward an ecclesiology that encourages us (those who identify as Christian) to reimagine what it means to be church today and how best to practice it with our congregations or small communities of faith. In this chapter, I have identified three marks of a more Dalyan ecclesiology: first, commitment to affirm people's direct access to the divine and their right to full participation; second, recognition of the dual need of individuation and of participation as two sides of the *courage to be*; and third, commitment to consciousness-

---

[8] See Xochitl Alvizo, "A Feminist Analysis of the Emerging Church: Toward Radical Participation in the Organic, Relational, and Inclusive Body of Christ," PhD dissertation, Boston University, 2015.

[9] See Rachel C. Schneider, "The Emerging Church Movement: Possible Futures and Trajectories," and Daniel Rober, "Millennials, Secularization, and Catholic Sexual Abuse Crisis: A Generational Examination and Reflection," in *The Emerging Church, Millennials, and Religion*, vol. 2, *Curations and Durations*, ed. Terry Shoemaker, Rachel C. Schneider, and Xochitl Alvizo (Eugene, OR: Cascade Books, 2022), 203–233 and 110–125.

raising – to nurture the mystic life that is religious awareness and engagement with oneself, the world, and the
divine. I contend that these Dalyan marks are key contributions to what the church needs to help it more faithfully
embody and give witness to the good news before the
world, a world that is wrought with trauma of violence,
abuse, dehumanization, and exploitative systems of power.
Such an ecclesiology sets the theological foundations for
manifold manifestations of church, each giving varied witness to the good news of Jesus Christ in and for its particular context, to be a place/space where people get to
experience, connect with, imagine, practice, and participate
in a new divine reality. Further, such communities of faith
will also embody sensibilities that guard it from becoming a
"mummified bod[y]."[10] These I draw from and build on an
earlier piece I co-authored with Gerardo Martí:

- We are capable and autonomous selves with both individual and communal access to the divine and the mystery of being.
- We are enmeshed in systems of power and in continual
  need for systemic analyses of power dynamics, including both the role of institutional power differentials and
  the power differentials embedded in the social con-
  struction and employment of race and gender.
- We must prioritize the practice of reflexivity, insisting
  that self-reflexivity, engaged in as part of a community,

[10] In the introduction to the manuscript, Daly emphasizes the need for the
church to maintain its posture of incompleteness, as she writes, "There
would be no point, for example, in attempting to preserve elements of the
Catholic substance as mummified bodies. If some symbols no longer
speak to our age, then they should be allowed to die."

is imperative for theology and praxis and includes the recognition that one's inherited religious heritage is born of and formed by particular socio-political contexts, interests, and locations and requires ongoing critical reflection and interrogation.[11]

The church, as a body, must take seriously the fact that humans are themselves also bodies in need of ongoing physical, emotional, and psychic nurturance, healing, and regeneration. Church, in the form of congregations, community, represent possible loci for the awakening of latent potentiality, which is why the immanence of the divine and the affirmation of the divine within is critical so that said potentiality will not be limited by the powers that be who would like to hold onto and wield their power exclusively. The mystic life that Daly promotes is key to people's awakening and to bringing the religious experience to the ground – the good news to the concrete conditions of their reality. What is of greatest value is access to that which brings about regeneration and transformation of lives.

I suggest that these sensibilities help the church reflect an anthropology in which the full human dignity of persons is affirmed and their capacity for active, conscious, and critical engagement is promoted. They help nurture courage in light of existential anxiety as well as communion and psychic liveliness so that the church as the

---

[11] Xochitl Alvizo and Gerardo Martí, "Emerging Out of Patriarchy? The Emerging Church Movement from a Feminist Practical Theological Perspective," in *The Emerging Church, Millennials, and Religion*, vol. 1, *Prospects and Problems*, ed. Randall Reed and Michael Zbaraschuk (Eugene, OR: Cascade Books, 2018), 236–259.

people of faith are always willing to critically engage with the symbols and structures of the faith that are originally and continually born of communion with themselves, others, and the divine. Representing a renewed ecclesiology, these three marks and three sensibilities may shed light on physical, metaphorical, political, and psychic places/spaces that the church has yet to travel. Humans, like Jesus Christ, made of body and blood, make up the church, and such a church is inextricably bound up with the wounds that come with that existence. A renewed ecclesiology allows society and the church's deep entrenchment with the sins of sexism, misogyny, anti-black racism, clericalism, white supremacy, heterosexualism, and colonialism – as well as the additional harms caused when church takes dogmatic and fundamentalist form, to bear upon its embodied form and insist that these be allowed to shape our understanding of what it means to be Christian and what it means to be church today.[12] Daly's question of whether or not Catholicism, and really Christianity, is at its end or a new beginning is a question that remains before us today. Let us today take up her question and be willing to fall upward.

---

[12] The examples of these are many, but one need only think of any of the many small "Christian" movements that revolve around a male leader who is revered as prophet or guru and then is revealed to have used their leadership position to abuse and sexually exploit their followers.

APPENDIX

Catholicism: End or Beginning?
Mary Daly

Introduction

This book will analyze the problem of the crisis in the contemporary Catholic consciousness which is often called a crisis of faith. In a sense it would be more accurate to say that I will analyze the problem as it presents itself in the comtemporary Christian consciousness, since this should not and in fact cannot be understood in a parochial and limited context. However, the main focal point of interest will be the Catholic consciousness. One reason for this choice of focus is the following: At this point in history it appears to many that the attempt of Protestantism to become relevant to the modern world has failed. Indeed, one sociologist of religion has affirmed that Catholicism now stands as surrogate for Christianity as a whole and that the future of Christianity depends upon the success of Catholicism's efforts to confront modernity. He sees a terrible dilemma in the Catholic situation, for in the unavoidable effort to catch up with the contemporary consciousness the church may destroy its symbols' power to sustain religious awareness. Moreover:"Is it not precisely those established expressions of Catholic faith, unchanged and defensively clung to, which rendered Catholicism increasingly irrelevant to the advancing western world that preserved within its own ranks the interior intensity and authenticity of faith?" (1)
     This dilemma is sometimes expressed with more poignancy by conservatives than by enthusiastic young revolutionaries, since the former feel keenly the sense of loss that accompanies the breakdown of traditional structures. One archconservative Catholic philosopher expressed this sense of loss in moving terms: "It is the dying who suffer the cruelty of the new Church. Their faith is stolen from the and this robbery of the only gift that ultimately means anything to man is something we shall never forgive the heresiarchs in our midst" (2). More objective thinkers would be less inclined to blame the "heresiarchs" for what appears to be an inevitable stage in the evolution of human consciousness beyond the literalism of the past— an evolution which has been occasioned by the convergence of profound

A.1 The first typewritten page of Mary Daly's unfinished manuscript, *Catholicism: End or Beginning?*, discovered by Meg Stapleton Smith in the archives of Smith College, Northampton, Massachusetts.
Source: Smith College Special Collections.

A.2 Mary Daly, 1975, Woodstock Women's Center, New York.
Photo by Diana Davies (original in Smith College Special Collections). As a
photojournalist working in New York City at the height of the Women's
Liberation Movement, Diana Davies documented in the 1960s and 1970s many
of the Movement's most important players and events.

SELECT BIBLIOGRAPHY

Alvizo, Xochitl. "A Feminist Analysis of the Emerging Church: Toward Radical Participation in the Organic, Relational, and Inclusive Body of Christ." PhD dissertation. Boston University, 2015.

Alvizo, Xochitl and Gerardo Martí, "Emerging Out of Patriarchy? The Emerging Church Movement from a Feminist Practical Theological Perspective." In *The Emerging Church, Millennials, and Religion*, vol. 1, *Prospects and Problems*. Edited by Randall Reed and Michael Zbaraschuk, 236–259. Eugene, OR: Cascade Books, 2018.

Anderson, Kevin, and Russell Rockwell, eds. *The Dunayevskaya–Marcuse–Fromm Correspondence, 1954–1978: Dialogues on Hegel, Marx, and Critical Theory*. Lanham, MD: Lexington Books, 2012.

Anderson, Pamela Sue. *A Feminist Philosophy of Religion*. Oxford: Wiley-Blackwell, 1997.

Aquinas, Thomas. *Summa Theologiae: Latin/English Edition*. Edited by Laurence Shapcote, John Mortensen, and Enrique Alarcon. Lander, WY: Aquinas Institute of Sacred Doctrine, 2012.

Barth, Karl. *Kirchliche Dogmatik*. 13 vols. Zurich: Verlag der Evangelischen Buchhandlung, 1932–67.

Barthes, Roland. *Image, Music, Text*. Translated by Stephen Heath. London: Fontana, 1977.

Berrigan, Philip. "Blood, War, and Witness." In *American Catholic Exodus*. Edited by John O'Connor. Washington, DC: Corpus Books, 1968.

Bloch, Ernest. *Man on His Own*. Translated by E. B. Ashton. New York: Herder & Herder, 1970.

Boyd, Malcolm, ed. *The Underground Church*. New York: Sheed & Ward, 1968.

Brown, Robert McAfee. "The Church's Ecumenical Outreach." In *American Catholic Exodus*. Edited by John O'Connor. Washington, DC: Corpus Books, 1968.

Burrell, David. *Freedom and Creation in Three Traditions*. Notre Dame, IN: University of Notre Dame Press, 1993.

Camus, Albert. *The Myth of Sisyphus and Other Essays*. New York: Vintage Books, 1955.

Coblentz, Jessica and Brianne A. B. Jacobs, "Mary Daly's *The Church and the Second Sex* after Fifty Years of US Catholic Feminist Theology." *Theological Studies* 79(3) (2018): 543–565.

Copleston, Frederick. *Aquinas*. Baltimore, MD: Penguin Books, 1955.

Cox, Harvey. *The Secular City*. New York: Macmillan, 1965.

Culpepper, Emily Erwin. "Introduction to Special Section in Memory of Mary Daly." *Journal of Feminist Studies in Religion* 28(2) (2012): 89–90.

Daly, Mary "After the Death of God the Father: Women's Liberation and the Transformation of Christian Consciousness." *Commonweal* 94 (1971): 7–11.

  Amazon Grace: Re-Calling the Courage to Sin Big. New York: Palgrave Macmillan, 2006.

  Beyond God the Father: Toward a Philosophy of Women's Liberation, with an original reintroduction by the author. Boston: Beacon Press [1973], 1985.

  The Church and the Second Sex, with the Feminist Postchristian Introduction and New Archaic Afterwords by the Author. Boston: Beacon Press, [1968] 1985.

  "Glory to God the Verb." *Border Religions of Faith: An Anthology of Religion and Social Change*, 56–64. New York: Orbis Books, 1987.

  Gyn/Ecology: The Metaethics of Radical Feminism. Boston: Beacon Press [1978], 1990.

  Natural Knowledge of God in the Philosophy of Jacques Maritain: A Critical Study. Rome: Catholic Book Agency, 1966

Outercourse: The Be-Dazzling Voyage. San Francisco: HarperSanFrancisco, 1992.

The Problem of Speculative Theology. Washington, DC: Thomist Press, 1965.

Pure Lust: Elemental Feminist Philosophy. Boston: Beacon Press [1984], 2001.

"The Qualitative Leap Beyond Patriarchal Religion." *Quest: A Feminist Quarterly* 1(4) (1975).

Quintessence ... Realizing the Archaic Future: A Radical Elemental Feminist Manifesto. Boston: Beacon Press, 1998.

Websters' First New Intergalactic Wickedary of the English Language. Boston: Beacon Press, 1987.

"The Women's Movement: An Exodus Community." In *Women and Religion: A Feminist Sourcebook of Christian Thought.* Edited by Elizabeth Clark and Herbert Richardson, 265–271. New York: Harper & Row, 1977.

Davies, Brian. *The Thought of Thomas Aquinas.* New York: Oxford University Press, 1993.

Derrick, Christopher. *Trimming the Ark.* New York: P. J. Kenedy & Sons, 1967.

De Veaux, Alexis. *Warrior Poet: A Biography of Audre Lorde.* New York: W. W. Norton, 2004.

Dewart, Leslie. *The Future of Belief.* New York: Herder & Herder, 1966.

Dunayevskaya, Raya. *Marxism and Freedom ... from 1776 to Today,* 5th ed. Atlantic Highlands, NJ: Humanities Press, 1982.

Rosa Luxemburg, Women's Liberation, and Marx's Philosophy of Revolution, 2nd ed. Urbana: University of Illinois Press, 1991.

Eliade, Mircea. The Sacred and the Profane. New York: Harper & Row, 1961.

Feuerbach, Ludwig. *The Essence of Christianity.* Translated by George Eliot. Buffalo, NY: Prometheus Books, 1989.

Gadamer, Hans G. *Truth and Method,* 2nd ed. Translated by Joel Weinsheimer and Donald Marshall. New York: Continuum, 2003.

Garoudy, Roger. *From Anathema to Dialogue.* Translated by Luke O'Neill. New York: Herder & Herder, 1966.

Goldstein, Valerie. "The Human Situation: A Feminine View," *Journal of Religion* 40 (1960): 100–111.

Groppi, James. "The Church and Civil Rights." In *The Underground Church.* Edited by Malcolm Boyd. New York: Sheed & Ward, 1968.

Grumbach, Doris. "Never the Twain Shall Meet." *Commonweal* (February 1969): 616–618.

Hanisch, Carol. "Consciousness Raising: The Personal is the Political." In *Notes from the Second Year: Women's Liberation.* Edited by Shulamith Firestone and Anne Koedt. New York: Radical Feminism, 1970.

Hedrick, Elizabeth. "The Early Career of Mary Daly: A Retrospective." *Feminist Studies* 39(2) (2013): 457–483.

Heidegger, Martin. *Introduction to Metaphysics.* Translated by R. Manheim. New Haven, CT: Yale University Press, 1958.

Hidayatullah, Aysha A. "Claims to the Sacred." *Journal of Feminist Studies in Religion* 32(2) (2016): 134–138.

Hinsdale, Mary Ann. "Vatican II and Feminism: Recovered Memories and Refreshed Hopes." *Toronto Journal of Theology* 32 (2016): 251–258.

Hunt, Mary E. "Celebrating and Cerebrating Mary Daly." *Journal of Feminist Studies in Religion* 28 (2012).

"Religious Resources for Survival: Ecofeminism and Earth Community." In *Living Cosmology: Christian Responses to Journey of the Universe.* Edited by Mary Evelyn Tucker and John Grim. Maryknoll, NY: Orbis Books, 2016.

Huxley, Aldous. *The Perennial Philosophy.* London: Chatto & Windus, 1946).

Jantzen, Grace. *Becoming Divine: Towards a Feminist Philosophy of Religion.* Manchester: Manchester University Press, 1998.

Jaspers, Karl and Rudolf Bultmann. *Myth and Christianity.* New York: Noonday Press, 1958.

Jung, C. G. *Psychology and Religion*. New Haven, CT: Yale University Press, 1938.

Katherine, Amber L. "'A Too Early Morning': Audre Lorde's 'An Open Letter to Mary Daly' and Daly's Decision Not to Respond in Kind." In *Feminist Interpretations of Mary Daly*. Edited by Sarah Hoagland. University Park: Pennsylvania State University Press, 2000.

Keefe-Perry, L. B. C. "Theopoetics: Process and Perspective." In *Christianity and Literature* 58 (2009).

Kerr, Fergus "Why Still Read Aquinas?" In *Thinking Faith: The Online Journal of the British Jesuits* (2014).

Lacroix, Jean. *The Meaning of Modern Atheism*. Dublin: Gill & Son, 1965.

Laing, R. D. *The Politics of Experience*. New York: Ballantine Books, 1967.

Lorde, Audre. "An Open Letter to Mary Daly." In *Sister Outsider*. Trumansburg, NY: Crossing Press, 1984.

Madigan, Patricia. "Women During and After Vatican II." In *Catholicism Opening to the World and Other Confessions: Vatican II and Its Impact*. Edited by Vladimir Latinovic, Gerard Mannion, and Jason Welle. London: Palgrave Macmillan, 2018.

Mannion, Gerard. "Women and the Art of Magisterium: Reflections on Vatican II and the Postconciliar Church." In *Catholicism Opening to the World and Other Confessions: Vatican II and Its Impact*. Edited by Vladimir Latinovic, Gerard Mannion, and Jason Welle. London: Palgrave Macmillan, 2018.

Maritain, Jacques. *Approaches to God*. Translated by Peter O'Reilly. London: George Allen & Unwin, 1955.

McEnroy, Carmel. *Guests in Their Own House: The Women of Vatican II*. Eugene OR: Wipf and Stock, 2011.

McGinn, Bernard "The Language of Love in Christian and Jewish Mysticism." In *Mysticism and Language*. Edited by Stephen Katz. New York: Oxford University Press, 1992.

Metz, Johannes Baptist. *Faith in History and Society: Towards a Fundamental Practical Theology*. New York: Crossroad,

1977. *Theology of the World*. Translated by William Glen-Doepel. New York: Herder & Herder, 1969.

Moltmann, Jürgen. *Religion, Revolution, and the Future*. Translated by M. Douglas Meeks. New York: Charles Scribner's Sons, 1969.

Theology of Hope. Translated by James W. Leitch. New York: Harper & Row, 1967.

Way of Jesus Christ. London: SCM Press, 1990.

Nietzsche, Friedrich. *Beyond Good and Evil*. Translated with commentary by Walter Kaufmann. New York: Random House, 1966.

The Will to Power. Translated by A. M. Ludovici. In *The Complete Works of Friedrich Nietzsche*. Edited by Oscar Levy. New York: Macmillan, 1924.

Novak, Michael. *A Theology for Radical Politics*. New York: Herder & Herder, 1969.

Nygren, Anders. *Agape and Eros*. Translated by Philip S. Watson. Philadelphia: Westminster Press, 1953.

O'Dea, Thomas. *The Catholic Crisis*. Boston: Beacon Press, 1968.

Paul VI. *Decree on the Apostolate of the Laity*. 1965. Available at: www.vatican.va/archive/hist_councils/ii_vatican_council/documents/vat-ii_decree_19651118_apostolicam-actuositatem_en.html.

Pastoral Constitution on the Church in the Modern World. 1965. Available at: www.vatican.va/archive/hist_councils/ii_vatican_council/documents/vat-ii_cons_19651207_gaudium-et-spes_en.html.

Radford Ruether, Rosemary. "Theology by Sex." *New Republic* 169 (1973): 24–26.

Rahner, Karl. *Foundations of Christian Faith: An Introduction to the Idea of Christianity*. New York: Seabury Press, 1978.

Rober, Daniel. "Millennials, Secularization, and Catholic Sexual Abuse Crisis: A Generational Examination and Reflection." In *The Emerging Church, Millennials, and Religion*, vol. 2, *Curations and Durations*. Edited by Terry Shoemaker, Rachel C. Schneider, and Xochitl Alvizo. Eugene, OR: Cascade Books, 2022.

Robinson, John A. T. *Honest to God*. Philadelphia: Westminster Press, 1963.

Ross, Susan. *Extravagant Affections: A Feminist Sacramental Theology*. New York: Continuum, 1998.

Roszak, Theodore. *The Making of a Counter Culture*. New York: Doubleday and Co., 1969.

Rycenga, Jennifer and Linda Barufaldi, eds. *The Mary Daly Reader*. New York: New York University Press, 2017.

Schneider, Rachel C. "The Emerging Church Movement: Possible Futures and Trajectories." In *The Emerging Church, Millennials, and Religion*, vol. 2, *Curations and Durations*. Edited by Terry Shoemaker, Rachel C. Schneider, and Xochitl Alvizo. Eugene, OR: Cascade Books, 2022.

Schüssler Fiorenza, Elisabeth. *In Memory of Her: A Feminist Reconstruction of Christian Origin*. New York: Crossroad, 1983.

Jesus: Miriam's Child, Sophia's Prophet: Critical Issues in Feminist Christology. London: T&T Clark, 2015.

Smith, Wilfred Cantwell. *The Meaning and End of Religion*. New York: Macmillan, 1963.

Stein, Edith. *On the Problem of Empathy*. Translated by Waltraut Stein. The Hague: Martinus Nijhoff, 1964.

Teilhard de Chardin, Pierre. *The Future of Man*. Translated by Norman Denny. New York: Harper & Row, 1964.

Tillich, Paul. *Christianity and the Encounter of the World Religions*. New York: Columbia University Press, 1963.

The Courage to Be. New Haven, CT: Yale University Press, 1952.

Dynamics of Faith. New York: Harper & Row, 1957.

Systematic Theology, 3 vols. Chicago: University of Chicago Press, 1951–1963.

Tobin, Mary Luke. "Women in the Church Since Vatican II." *America* (November 1, 1986).

Toynbee, Arnold. *Christianity Among the Religions of the World*. New York: Charles Scribner's Sons, 1957.

Trible, Phyllis. *God and the Rhetoric of Sexuality*. Philadelphia: Fortress Press, 1978.

Turner, Denys. *God, Mystery & Mystification*. Notre Dame, IN: University of Notre Dame Press, 2019.

Vanchak, Edward. "More from St. Paul on a Female Priesthood." *National Catholic Reporter* (May 26, 1965).

Wagoner, Walter. "Thoughts for Protestants to be Static By." *Christian Century* (February 19, 1969): 249–251.

Weber, Max. *The Sociology of Religion*. Translated by Ephraim Fischoff. Boston: Beacon Press, 1963.

West, Traci C. "The Gift of Arguing with Mary Daly's White Feminism." *Journal of Feminist Studies in Religion* 28(2) (2012): 112–117.

Wilder, Amos. *Theopoetic: Theology and the Religious Imagination*. Philadelphia: Fortress Press, 1976.

Wilhelmsen, Frederick D. "Schism, Heresy, and a New Guard." In *American Catholic Exodus*. Edited by John O'Connor. Washington, DC: Corpus Books, 1968.

Zagano, Phyllis. "Women and the Church: Unfinished Business of Vatican II." *Horizons* 34 (2007).

Zuckerman, Phil. *Faith No More: Why People Reject Religion*. Oxford: Oxford University Press, 2012.

INDEX